NICHOLAS OF CUSA ON LEARNED IGNORANCE

NICHOLAS OF CUSA ON LEARNED IGNORANCE
A Translation and an Appraisal of De Docta Ignorantia

by

Jasper Hopkins

The Arthur J. Banning Press
Minneapolis

Library of Congress Catalog Card Number 80–82907
ISBN 0–938060–23-6

Printed in the United States of America

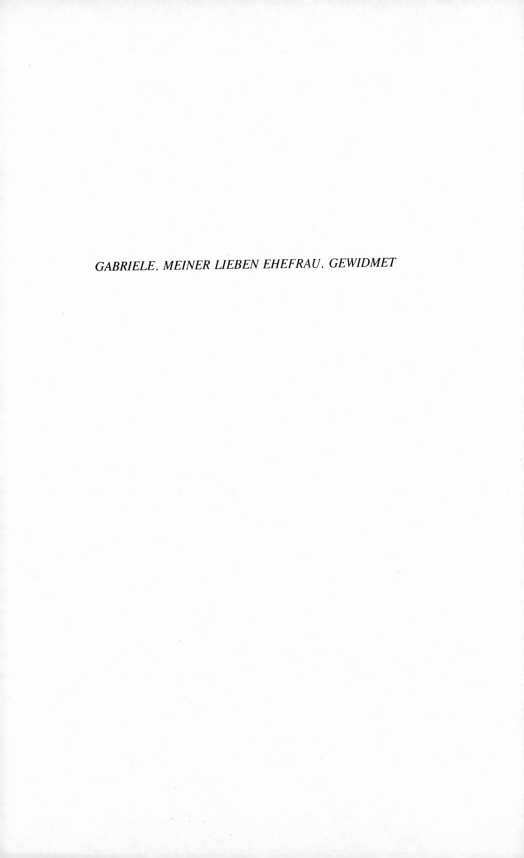

GABRIELE, MEINER LIEBEN EHEFRAU, GEWIDMET

PREFACE

Like any important philosophical work, *De Docta Ignorantia* cannot be understood by merely being read: it must be studied. For its main themes are so profoundly innovative that their author's exposition of them could not have anticipated, and therefore taken measures to prevent, all the serious misunderstandings which were likely to arise. Moreover, the themes are so extensively interlinked that a misunderstanding of any one of them will serve to obscure all the others as well. In such case, the mental effort required of the reader-who-interprets must approximate the effort expended by the author-who-instructs. No words are more self-condemning than are those of John Wenck, at the conclusion of whose critique of *De Docta Ignorantia* we read: "*Et sic est finis scriptis cursorie Heydelberg*": "And this is the end to what was written cursorily at Heidelberg."[1]

Nicholas has not made his reader's task easy. For in spite of his claim to have explained matters "as clearly as I could" and to have avoided "all roughness of style," many of his points escape even the diligent reader, since the explanation for them is either too condensed, or else too barbarously expressed, to be assuredly followed. And yet, from out of the vagueness, the ambiguity, the amphiboly, the enthymematic movement of thought, there emerges—for a reader patient enough to *solliciter doucement les textes*—an internally coherent pattern of reasoning. The present translation of this reasoning aims above all at accuracy.[2] To this end the rendering is literal, though with no deliberate sacrifice of literate English expression. Only a literal translation (but not word for word) permits the subtle twists and turns of Nicholas's arguments to shine forth.[3] The earlier, radically inaccurate rendering by Germain Heron (1954) distorts Nicholas's arguments—and thus belies history by making the author of *De Docta Ignorantia* appear as someone mindlessly unable to develop even the semblance of a systematic line of thought. For even when Nicholas's arguments are specious, as they often are, they are specious in an ingenious and programmatically coherent way.

My introduction to *De Docta Ignorantia* aims at being a critical interpretation rather than at being an appreciation or an *abrégé*. On behalf of those students who are unfamiliar with Nicholas's thought, I append the following extended footnote.[4] Such students may also want to consult *A Concise Intro-duction to the Philosophy of Nicholas of Cusa* (Minneapolis: University of Minnesota Press, 2nd edition 1980) before undertaking their study of *De Docta Ignorantia*. The bibliography published in the *Concise Introduction* is sup-plemented by the selection at the end of the present volume. A penetrating understanding of *De Docta Ignorantia* can only be acquired by reading it in conjunction with John Wenck's attack and Nicholas's clarifying response. These latter treatises have been translated and appraised by me in a companion volume entitled *Nicholas of Cusa's Debate with John Wenck* (Minneapolis: The Arthur J. Banning Press, 1981). This volume also contains my newly edited Latin text of Wenck's *De Ignota Litteratura*. And the introduction includes an important critique of Vincent Martin's "standard" interpretation of Nicholas's metaphysic.

I gratefully acknowledge the support of this project by the National Endow-ment for the Humanities and by the University of Minnesota. The former awarded a stipend under its Translations Program, and the latter granted an additional quarter's leave. I am also grateful to Richard Meiner, of Felix Meiner Verlag, for his encouragement of the entire project. I have profited from the advice of Rudolf Haubst, director of the Cusanus Institute, who together with Mechthild Zenz, received me cordially in Mainz. Fritz Kaiser, Oberbibliotheksrat at the Stadtbibliothek in Mainz, and Richard Laufner, director of the Stadtbibliothek in Trier, were also kind in their assistance. I express special appreciation to Jules and Gudrun Vuillemin, in whose home I enjoyed stimulating intellectual discussions at various times during my pro-longed stay in France. Finally, I am indebted to Robert Marshall of Sweetbriar College for his expertise in Italian and to Peter Petzling of my own university for his extensive knowledge of bibliography and his willingness to share his comprehension of *Geistesgeschichte*.

Jasper Hopkins
Philosophy Department
University of Minnesota

CONTENTS

Introduction   1
On Learned Ignorance
   (*De Docta Ignorantia*)
     Book I   49
     Book II   87
     Book III   125
Corrigenda   161
Abbreviations   162
Bibliography   163
Praenotanda   170
Notes   172
Index   205

INTRODUCTION

A mélange of intellectual tension and excitement pervaded the Universities of Heidelberg, Padua, and Cologne, where Nicholas of Cusa (1401–64) studied in the early fifteenth century. The ecclesiastical clash between the competitive claimants to the papacy—a rivalry adjudicated by the powerful Council of Constance (1414–18)—had badly divided the faculties of law by engendering the dispute over the Conciliar Movement. Moreover, the theological faculties had scarcely adjusted to the prolonged debate between Ockhamism and Thomism, nominalism and realism, when the very underpinnings of Scholasticism were weakened by the rise of Jean Gerson's version of the *devotio moderna* and by the renewed spirit of Eckhart's speculative mysticism. At Padua advances in the study of mathematics and of natural philosophy fostered the promulgation of new hypotheses about the scope of the universe and the movements of the heavens. And the influence of humanism opened new ways of looking at the past and, at the same time, expanded the horizon of literary learning. On every front, it seemed, the theoretical foundations had begun to shift, thus encouraging—indeed, demanding—the appearance of new conceptual syntheses.

Nicholas of Cusa's *DI* was one such synthesis.[1] In it can be found the influence of Eckhart, of the Hermetic tradition, of Pseudo-Dionysius,[2] and of Boethian mathematics, together with a newly devised cosmological framework and a newly conceived theology of redemption. In spite of much speciousness, this treatise of three books is a monumental achievement. Rich with suggestiveness, it prefigured, it its bold tendencies, certain dialectical features of later German philosophy. We cannot be sure about the length of time required to produce this magnum opus. We know from the dedicatory letter to Cardinal Julian Cesarini that the central notion of learned ignorance—i.e., of embracing the Incomprehensible incomprehensibly—came to Nicholas while he was at sea, en route from Constantinople to Venice (i.e., sometime between November 27, 1437 and February 8, 1438). And we know from the *explicit* of Book Three that the work was completed at Kues on February 12, 1440. Between these two temporal boundaries Nicholas organized, refined, and put into writing his fundamental conceptual scheme—which he confessed to have cost him great effort (*labor ingens*) and from whose main outlines he later never

1

fully veered. Given the political activities in which he was enmeshed—activities associated with the Council of Basel and the Council of Ferrara—it is likely that he wrote the treatise during intermittent intervals, not all of which found him in Kues. Yet, we must guard against supposing that the entire system was developed, even intermittently, within the timespan marked by the foregoing dates; for the letter to Cesarini implies that its author had long been brooding over how best to achieve such a synthesis—one which hitherto could not be formulated, given the absence of its organizing principle.

To be sure, *DI* is a highly organized work, whose third book, as Cassirer rightly points out,[3] is no mere incidental theological appendage but, instead, the essential culmination of the unified system. Book One deals with the *maximum absolutum* (God), Book Two with the *maximum contractum* (the universe), Book Three with the *maximum simul contractum et absolutum* (Christ). As God is a trinity of Oneness, Equality-of-Oneness, and the Union thereof, so the universe (and each thing in it) is a trinity of possibility, actuality, and the union thereof (which is motion), and so Christ, the hypostatic Union, is the medium between the Absolute Union and the maximum ecclesiastical union (viz., the church of the triumphant). God is in all things through the mediation of the universe, just as He is in all believers through the mediation of Christ. In all things God is, absolutely, that which they are, just as in all things the universe is, contractedly, that which each is, and just as Christ is the universal contracted being of each creature. Just as God ontologically precedes and unites contradictories, so the universe ontologically precedes and unites contraries, and the humanity of Christ ontologically precedes and enfolds all creatable things. In God center is circumference, just as God is the center and the circumference of the universe and just as Christ is the center and the circumference of the intellectual natures.

The fulcrum of Nicholas's system is the doctrine of *docta ignorantia*—the very doctrine reflected in the title of the work. But what exactly is this doctrine? And how is the title to be best construed? Paul Wilpert, in the opening note to his German translation of Book One, maintains that the title is more correctly translated as " *Die belehrte Unwissenheit*" than as "*Die gelehrte Unwissenheit*." By contrast, Erich Meuthen opts for the word "*gelehrt*" and for the title "*Das gelehrte Nicht-Wissen*."[4] Wilpert feels that the unknowing which Nicholas discusses is not so much an erudite or a wise unknowing (i.e., an unknowing which confers a kind of erudition or wisdom on the one who does not know) as it is simply a recognition-of-limitedness that has been achieved (i.e., an unknowing which has been learned, so that the one who has learned of his unknowing is now among the instructed, rather than remaining one of the unlearned). Wilpert is certainly right that in *DI* the emphasis is upon instruction in the way-of-ignorance and that the man of learned ignorance is not thought by

Nicholas to be a man of erudition. As is clear from the use of the verb *"doceo"* at I, 19 (55:5: "let us now become instructed in ignorance") and the verb *"instruo"* at III, 5 (210:1: "to instruct our ignorance by an example") Nicholas does mainly understand *"docta ignorantia"* as an ignorance which has been acquired and which distinguishes its possessor from those who are thus uninstructed.[5] Yet, it is equally clear from I, 1 (4:16–17: "the more he knows that he is unknowing, the more learned he will be")[6] that Nicholas also sometimes understands *"docta ignorantia"* as an ignorance which renders its possessor wise.[7] Indeed, in *Apologia* 2:9–10 Socrates is said to be wise precisely because he knows that he does not know. This kind of wisdom Nicholas would not call erudition (and in this respect Wilpert is also right); for it is available to the common man as well as to the highly schooled. Thus, Nicholas will later write his *Idiotae*,[8] in which he exalts the wisdom of the layman. But such a layman, with such a wisdom as Socrates's, might appropriately be called *gelehrt* (and in this respect Wilpert's statements are misleading). The best English translation will therefore be the traditional one: viz., "On Learned Ignorance," where "learned" is understood in the double sense distinguished orally by the different pronunciations *lūrnd* and *lūr´nid*—i.e., understood as both *belehrt* and *gelehrt*. For it is an ignorance which both distinguishes its possessor from the unlearned, or uninstructed, and elevates him to the place of the learn-ed, or wise.[9]

In the *Apologia* (21:13–14) Nicholas calls the recognition that God cannot be known as He is "the root of learned ignorance."[10] At 24:20–22 he reiterates this point in referring to learned ignorance as "a knowledge of the fact that [the symbolic likenesses to God] are altogether disproportional." But at 27:22–23 he speaks in a more general way; for now learned ignorance is said to be "the seeing that precision cannot be seen." In fact, *DI*, in its very first chapter, also contains this twofold exposition. Herein we are told that " the precise combinations in corporeal things and the congruent relating of known to unknown surpass human reason—to such an extent that Socrates seemed to himself to know nothing except that he did not know."[11] But we are also informed that "the infinite, qua infinite, is unknown; for it escapes all comparative relation." So the foundation and governing principle of Nicholas's system is this twofold recognition. In saying that nothing can be known by us precisely (and adding in *DP* 42:21–22 that only God's knowledge is perfect and precise), Nicholas does not mean that we therefore do not *know* anything. That is, he does not equate knowledge with precise knowledge and conclude that because we cannot have the latter we do not have the former. He does not voice unqualifiedly skeptical doubts about whether we know the objects in the world. We do know them, he believes, even though we do not know them in their quiddity or as they are in themselves. Just as we do not attain the precise truth about finite things, which are further specifiable *ad infinitum*, so we do not cognitively attain unto the Infinite God, who may be regarded as Truth itself.[12] Learned ignorance begins with this twofold awareness.

Nicholas must here be viewed as reacting against the theological doctrine of *analogia entis*—against all attempts to conceive of Divine Being other than symbolically, against all claims to have a positive-knowledge-of-God, whether derived from nature or from the "revelation" of Christ. What we know about God is that He is unknowable by us, both in this world and in the world to come.[13] Of course, on the basis of Christ's teachings and works, we ought, affirms Nicholas, to believe by faith that God is loving, merciful, just, powerful, etc. But if we are to conceive of this mercy, justice, etc., we will have to conceive of it analogously to our experiences in the human dimension. We will therefore infinitely misconceive it and, accordingly, not really be conceiving it but only something infinitely short of it. Our conception of God will therefore be, positively, only a shadowy befiguring of some possible—but, alas, all too finite—suprahuman being. Yet, at the beginning of *DI* I, 26, Nicholas ackowledges that such befigurings and imagings are indispensable aids to a believer's worshipping of God. Moreover, some of these imagings and symbolisms are more befitting than others,[14] when measured by the teachings of Christ, whose own life and works, faith and love, we are to emulate insofar as possible.[15]

And yet, learned ignorance is not altogether ignorance. For it instructs us that God must be Oneness, though a oneness which exceeds our conceptual capacity. And it teaches, likewise, that He must be trine, though this trinity too exceeds our comprehension. It teaches, furthermore, that in God oneness and trinity—indeed, all opposites—coincide, that God is Being itself, that the Word of God is "World-soul," as it were, that God is the center and the circumference of the universe, that He is present in each thing, that each thing is present in each other thing— and a host of other points, all presented in *DI* and all attesting that Nicholas, in descrying the limits of knowledge, is far from any thoroughgoing agnosticism.

In Nicholas's system there is an interconnection between our inability to comprehend God and our inability to know mundane things precisely. He expresses this interconnection most pithily in *De Possest* 38: "what is caused cannot know itself if its Cause remains unknown." In *DI* II, 2 the same point is stated in a slightly different fashion: "derived being is not understandable, because the Being from which [it derives] is not understandable—just as the adventitious being of an accident is not understandable if the substance to which it is adventitious is not understood."[16] If derived being is not understandable, still it is not hereby unqualifiedly unknowable. Rather, Nicholas means that we cannot understand how from all-enfolding Absolute Oneness there arose the contracted plurality that constitutes the universe—how if Absolute Oneness is eternal, indivisible, most perfect, and indistinct, then derivative being can in any respect be corruptible, divisible, imperfect, and distinct. In short, he is affirming that we cannot comprehend the creation qua creation and that a knowledge of God would have to precede a precise knowledge of any given thing.

I. *Maximum Absolutum*

Nicholas speaks of God as, indifferently, Absolute Maximality, the Absolute Maximum, the absolutely Maximum, the unqualifiedly Maximum.[17] By "the Maximum" he means "that than which there cannot be anything greater." It follows that the Maximum is also "all that which can be"; for if it were not, it could be something more than what it is. For the same reason, it is *actually* all that which can be. Moreover, it is greater than can be humanly conceived, since the human mind cannot conceive the totality of possibilities. Because the Maximum is absolutely and actually whatever can be, it is beyond all attribution of differentiated characteristics. Indeed, it is the *absolutely* Maximum in the sense that it is ultimately and undifferentiatedly everything which is. Hence, everything which it is, it is without opposition and is in such way that, in it, these things coincide and are indistinct and unitary. For this reason too the Maximum cannot be comprehended or conceived by us; for we cannot comprehend or conceive of that whose conception would require us to combine contradictory predicates. Moreover, the absolutely Maximum is so undifferentiated that even the absolutely Minimum coincides with it. (This point, says Nicholas, is clear from the following consideration: There cannot be anything lesser than the absolutely Maximum; for a lesser would have to be something which the Maximum would not be; but the Maximum is all that which can be. Now, the absolutely Minimum is also that than which there cannot be a lesser. Hence, the absolutely Minimum coincides with the absolutely Maximum.) Hence, the absolutely Maximum is infinite—given that not anything, not even the Minimum, is opposed to it or other than it, thus delimiting it.

There is no need to explain why the foregoing reasoning is specious. Of interest are several items other than the argument itself. First of all, we see that in commencing with his doctrine of God, Nicholas makes no attempt to prove God's existence. Rather, he here *premises* the existence of the Maximum and describes the Maximum as "what *is* (is actually) all that which can be." He will go on in I, 6 to advance some considerations in support of the proposition that the Maximum cannot fail to exist and that nothing at all would exist if the Maximum did not exist. But these considerations are not argued for in such way that they can seriously be regarded as attempts to undertake a proof.

Secondly, because of Nicholas's insubstantial reasoning on behalf of the doctrine that the absolutely Maximum and the absolutely Minimum coincide, this doctrine here appears to spring forth in too unmotivated a way. The underlying motivation may be better sensed from the intriguing and vivid illustration in *De Possest*, where the picture of a top spinning at infinite speed provides an elucidation for the claim that maximal motion and minimal motion are indistinguishable at infinity.[18] Of course, Nicholas denies that in the created world there actually is any infinite motion.[19] And, of course, it follows herefrom, as he also explicitly asserts, that in the created world there is not actually any absolute rest: everything in the universe is in motion, whether or not it appears to us to be.

Thirdly, Nicholas explicitly maintains in I, 4 not only that the Maximum is, coincidingly, all that which is conceived to be: he maintains as well that it is whatever is conceived not to be. If we set aside the philosophical problem about what it would mean to conceive something *to be* or to conceive it *not to be*—a difficulty familiar to students of St. Anselm's ontological argument—we will see that Nicholas is propounding the doctrine that in God even being and not-being coincide.[20] Since not-being (which is minimally being) is identical with maximally being, how can we—it is asked rhetorically in I, 6—rightly think that the Maximum is able not to exist?

Finally, in *DI* Nicholas nowhere says, in so many words, "*Deus est coincidentia oppositorum.*" In I, 4 he indicates that the absolutely Maximum is beyond all opposition, the word "opposites" being subsequently replaced by the word "contradictories"; and at the beginning of I, 22 God is said to be the Enfolding of all things, including contradictories. But only in the dedicatory letter does he first use the phrase "*ubi contradictoria coincidunt,*" when he speaks of the intellect's raising itself to "that Simplicity where contradictories coincide." It seems that God's being *beyond* contradictories is the same, for Nicholas, as His being the Simplicity where they *coincide*. For when in the *Apologia* he reiterates the phrase from the dedicatory letter (a phrase which John Wenck regarded as espousing a strategem),[21] he likewise affirms that God is beyond the coincidence of contradictories (e.g., is beyond the coincidence of oneness and plurality).[22] Although it sounds different to say that *in Deo contradictoria coincidunt* and to say that *Deus super coincidentiam contradictoriorum est*, Nicholas does not draw any distinction by means of these expressions but simply uses them interchangeably.

In I, 5 Nicholas introduces numerical considerations to establish that the Maximum is one; he will introduce different considerations in I, 7 to establish that the Maximum is three. No number can be an infinite number, we are told.[23] For if it were, it would be a maximum, and thus would be beyond all differentiation and thus would not even be number. And if number ceased, so too would all plurality, distinctness, and comparative relation, since these presuppose it. Although a number series may progress upwards without limit, it is only potentially unlimited, not "actually" so. That is, at whatever point we stop counting, we still will have counted only a finite set of integers, and that number at which we have stopped will itself be a finite number. But in descending the number scale, observes Nicholas, we must come to a source, or beginning, of number. For if there were no source of number, there could not be any number. For number is something generated. Moreover, that from which it is generated can only be oneness, which is a minimum because it is something than which there cannot be a lesser; hence, it must also be a maximum, because maximum and minimum coincide. But oneness cannot itself be a number, because number, which admits of comparative greatness, cannot be either a minimum or a maximum, which is beyond all comparative relation. (In the attempt to follow Nicholas's reasoning, we must bear in mind that he does not regard fractions as numbers but as relations between two numbers. Similarly, he has no notion of negative numbers. Nor does he consider either zero or unity to be a number.) If we read between the lines, it becomes tempting to detect in I, 5 a further reason for concluding that number has a beginning: viz., that if it did not, then there could not be numbering, since there would be no starting point in numbering. Hence, we could not know how many items were contained in a group of things. But surely if there are a number of, say, men (i.e., a plurality of men), then it must be *possible* to determine how many men there are—or so, at least, Nicholas would presumably contend.

All of the immediately foregoing serves to illustrate how the absolutely Maximum, because it coincides with the absolutely Minimum, is Absolute Oneness. God, who is the Absolute Maximum, is one both in the sense that there exists only one God and in the sense that there is no plurality in this one God's nature. In accordance with the illustration, we are now allowed to make the following inferences: (1)Anyone who would deny the existence of the one God must also deny the existence of the world, because in the absence of Oneness there can be no plurality. And (2) whoever would deny the oneness of the one God's nature must likewise deny His eternity; for only what precedes composition and otherness is eternal.

DI I, 6 is a curious chapter—one which gives rise to the controversy over whether or not Nicholas is intent upon proving the existence of an absolutely Maximum. I have already stated that he is not; and I, 6 is seen not to conflict with this statement. The title of the chapter, "The Maximum is Absolute Necessity," does not indicate that any proof of existence is being undertaken. Moreover, we must read this chapter in the light of the aim expressed at the end of chapter 5: "whoever would say that there are many gods would deny, most falsely, the existence not only of God but also of all the things of the universe— as will be shown in what follows." Even the opening section of I, 6 moves in the direction of showing that the Maximum so bounds all finite things that they cannot exist apart from it.

But in accordance with its heading, I, 6 also argues that the absolutely

Maximum, already premised as existing, is such that it exists necessarily. The reasoning here is thoroughly implausible and unrigorous. We are told that the Maximum is not able not to exist because not-being is not opposed to that which transcends all opposition. Similarly, we are presented with an exhaustive list of alternative possibilities, each of which is alleged to attest to the existence of the absolutely Maximum. Hence—we are supposed to conclude—it is not possible that the Maximum not exist; hence, the Maximum exists necessarily, as Absolute Necessity.

This chapter constitutes, perhaps, the nadir of the entire treatise of three books. For against the backdrop of the detailed debates conducted between Thomists, Scotists, and Ockhamists—debates packed with important logical, metaphysical, and terminological distinctions—Nicholas surely owed his own era a more elaborate and philosophically sophisticated presentation. His failure in this regard may say something about his philosophical intelligence. But, more likely, it reflects his penchant for another way of doing another kind of philosophy. Usually, his way of doing this other kind of philosophy—which we may call Neoplatonic, if we like—is not unintelligent. In the present case, however, his instincts and preferences have let him down. For he is all too content merely to sketch and to hint. Yet, we his contemporary readers are left with no idea of what he might have been hinting at when at the end of I, 6 he alludes, with no small measure of hyperbole, to "an infinity of similar considerations" which show clearly that the unqualifiedly Maximum is Absolute Necessity.

In line with the Christian tradition, Nicholas endeavors to work out a rationale for his belief that God is both one and trine—i.e., is triune. His strategy in I, 7 is to argue as follows: oneness is eternal, equality eternal, and union eternal; but since there can be only one eternal thing, it follows that oneness, equality, and union are a oneness which is trine or a trinity which is one. To this trine eternity Nicholas then likens the members of the Divine Trinity. He prefers this likeness to the traditional likeness—viz., of father, son, and spirit—which perhaps seems to him too creaturely a likeness to be befitting. Yet, he is willing to call Oneness *Father*, Equality of Oneness *Son*, and Union of both Oneness and Equality of Oneness *Holy Spirit*. He does not expect anyone to become a trinitarian on the basis of finding his arguments persuasive—any more than he expects anyone to become a monotheist on the basis of his previous points about the absolutely Maximum. He is not writing a *polemical* work, not confronting his readers with an *apologia* on behalf of Christianity. At this juncture he is simply trying to articulate philosophically the theological doctrines he holds by faith. If he can detect any rationale at all in these doctrines, if he can find some intellectual "picturing" of them, as it were, then his ignorance will, he believes, be to that extent more learn-ed. For the intellect, now having become more apprised of its limitations and incapabilities, will be less likely to mistake its symbolisms and images for anything other than a disproportional *similitude* of the underlying *reality*.

In assessing the nuances of Nicholas's philosophical approach, we really ought to do so—at least initially—from within the philosophical tradition in which he is writing. In I, 7 his method is akin to, say, Plato's in the second half of the *Parmenides* or to Proclus's in *The Theology of Plato*—except that whereas Plato is laughing up his sleeve at the monists by deliberately making use of fallacy, Nicholas has no comparable ulterior motives and no intentional use of sophistry. His conceptualizing is born from that Platonic and Neoplatonic matrix in which it is assumed to be perfectly intelligible to regard otherness and mutability and equality as *realia* and to draw conclusions such as "equality naturally precedes inequality" or "oneness is by nature prior to otherness." At the agora of Neoplatonic speculation, Nicholas's arguments in I, 7 would have gained some currency.

But not every chapter of *DI* proceeds in the Q.E.D. fashion of I, 7. Sometimes the language of *showing* has more to do with illustrating than with proving. [And sometimes even the very language of *proving* has more to do with affirming than with demonstrating (e.g., I, 17 (49:2))]. In I, 8 Nicholas claims to *show* that, apart from any occurrence of multiplicity, Oneness generates Equality of Oneness (i.e., that the Father begets the Son). He shows this, though, only in the reduced sense of illustrating it by the arithmetical proposition "$1 \times 1 \times 1 = 1$." In weighing his statements, we must be careful that we not automatically construe the verbs "*ostendere*" and "*probare*" as heralding a deductive proof, when all that Nicholas is promising us may perhaps be only such an illustration.

Not surprisingly, then, the most ingenious part of Book One—viz., chapters 12 through 21—utilizes both deductive and nondeductive inference. This fact can be clearly seen from the statement of method at the beginning of chapter 12: "We must first consider finite mathematical figures together with their characteristics and relations. Next, [we must] apply these relations, in a transformed way, to corresponding infinite mathematical figures. Thirdly, [we must] thereafter, in a still more highly transformed way, apply the relations of these infinite figures to the simple Infinite, which is altogether independent even of all figure." With regard to finite and infinite mathematical figures Nicholas advances deductive proofs. From the conclusions of the latter he infers, nondeductively, certain symbolic parallels in the case of Divine Infinity. For example, his method permits him to claim, in the title of I, 16, that "in a symbolic way the Maximum is to all things as a maximum line is to [all] lines." Pursuing his parallelism, he infers that the Maximum is the Essence of all essences and the Measure of all things.

In particular, he has contended that an infinite line is a straight line, a maximum triangle, a maximum circle, and a maximum sphere—in short, "is, actually, whatever is present in the potency of a finite line" (I, 13). The word "actually"is here misleading; and, indeed, it misled John Wenck, who pounced upon Nicholas as falsely teaching that there actually exists an infinite line.[24] In *Apologia* 32:9–11 Nicholas claims to have indicated sufficiently in *DI* that the actual existence of an infinite line is impossible. But he is not aware of how much trouble he causes for his readers when in I, 13 he begins by using the subjunctive ("if there were an infinite line") but soon switches to the indicative, thus obscuring the contrary-to-fact conditional nature of his claim: if there *were* an infinite line, it *would be*, actually, whatever is present in the potency of a finite line.

One infinite line cannot be longer or shorter than another; indeed, says Nicholas, these would be the same infinite line, since there could not be more than one infinite line. Now, since each "part" of the infinite line is likewise infinite, "one foot of an infinite line," so to speak, is convertible with the whole infinite line; and therefore in an infinite line one foot is not shorter than are two feet, which also are convertible with the whole (I, 16). In the infinite line, the part is the whole. Accordingly, an infinite line is indivisible; and in this regard it is unlike a finite line. But although a finite line is infinitely divisible, it is not divisible to the point that it is no longer a line. Hence, it is indivisible in its essence: "a line of one foot is not less a line than is a line of one cubit" (I, 17). It follows, we are told, that the infinite line is the essence of a finite line. But the essence is the measure of all the lines which participate in it, since not all of them participate equally in it. Hence, finite lines are measurable in relation to their degree of participation.

Nicholas transfers his considerations about the infinite line to apply in the case of God (I, 16): Just as the maximum line is the essence of all lines, so the Absolute Maximum is the Essence of all essences. Just as in the maximum line every line *is* the maximum line, so in the Absolute Maximum everything is the Absolute Maximum. Just as the maximum line is the measure of all lines, so the Absolute Maximum is the Measure of all things. Let us examine these three points, thus illustrated, one by one.

1. Nicholas calls God not only "the Essence of all essences,"[25] "the Form of [all] forms," "the Form of being," and "the Being of beings," but also, more simply, "the Essence of all things" (*essentia omnium*) and "the Being of things" (*rerum entitas*)[26]—the last two expressions coming from Thierry of Chartres. Perhaps all of these expressions seemed objectionable to Wenck, who in effect singles out the last two, seeing in them only signs of heresy.[27] In general, Wenck feels that Nicholas is in danger of losing the metaphysical distinction between Creator and creature—by teaching that God is all things[28] and that all things coincide with God.[29] And he sees both Nicholas and Eckhart

as committed, by their respective metaphysic, to a denial of the individual existence of things within their own genus.[30] Yet, none of Nicholas's statements either convey such meanings or entail propositions expressing them. When he says that God is the Being of [all] things and the Essence of all things, he is neither denying the respective finite essences of finite things nor confounding these essences with the Divine Essence. In *DI* he attributes to things their own essences. In II, 9 (146:2), for example, he uses the clause "since the essence of stone is distinct from the essence of man" in such way as, apparently, to be endorsing it. And in III, 12 (260:12–13) he speaks of each of the blessed—"having the truth-of-his-own-being preserved (*servata veritate sui proprii esse*)"—as existing in Christ Jesus as Christ. In the *Apologia* he explicitly repudiates Wenck's charge, insisting that things have their own respective form and being.[31]

"God is the Essence of all things" and "God is the Being of all things" are simply Nicholas's shorthand for "God is the Essence of all essences" and "God is the Being of all beings." And these latter expressions are intended to teach, not to exclude, the doctrine that finite things have their own being and their own essences. What they do not teach, but rather exclude, is the doctrine that finite things have underived and absolutely independent being—something reserved for God alone. But a thing's being can be totally derivative, in an ultimate sense, without thereby failing to be that thing's being. That is, its being can be totally dependent, in an ultimate sense, without its thereby failing to be its own, in some more immediate sense. So just as for God to be the Cause of all things does not ipso facto exclude the existence of secondary causes, so for Him to be the Essence of all things does not thereby exclude the existence of secondary essences. Indeed, God, is the Essence of all essences in the sense that if God were not what He is, these other things would not be what they are.[32] And He is the Being of all beings in the sense that if He did not exist, then no thing at all would exist.[33]

Though Nicholas's point is clear, it has sometimes been obscured by a failure of interpreters to grasp the meaning of two or three passages which, for one reason or another, they take to be key texts. For example, at the end of I, 17 there is the following passage: "We have now seen clearly how we can arrive at God through removing the participation of beings. For all beings participate in Being. Therefore, if from all beings participation is removed, there remains most simple Being itself, which is the Essence (*essentia*) of all things. And we see such Being only in most learned ignorance; for when I remove from my mind all the things which participate in Being, it seems that nothing remains. Hence, the great Dionysius says that our understanding of God draws near to nothing rather than to something." This passage does *not* teach that each thing in its being is God, that if we imaginatively strip away the attributes of some given finite being, we will arrive at simple Being itself, which is the proper

11

"core," as it were, of this thing.[34] Rather, Nicholas's point may be rephrased as follows:

> All beings participate in Being. To remove any being's participation in Being is to remove *that* being (i.e., to remove its existence). If participation is removed from all beings, then there remains only *Being*, i.e., Being itself, which was participated in. But Being itself is not a being, for it is not differentiated. Hence, it is not positively conceivable. But not-being is also not positively conceivable. Accordingly, in this respect, the case is similar with Being itself and with not-being. Since God is Being itself, Dionysius rightly says that our understanding of God is more like an understanding of nothing than of something.

Another example of a passage frequently misunderstood is II, 2 (101:1–3): "But since the creation was created through the being of the Maximum and since—in the Maximum—being, making, and creating are the same thing: creating seems to be not other than God's being all things." Some interpreters have supposed that Nicholas is here in some way identifying God and His creation. Nicholas is presented as teaching that "in creating, God somehow takes on privation—that He somehow becomes the creatures."[35] Yet, Nicholas's point is much too dialectical to be accommodated by such an insensitive interpretation. Nicholas is perplexed about whether or not God's act of creating is comprehensible. For he cannot understand how from the eternal, the temporal could arise, how from the indistinct, there could come forth a plurality and a succession. He proceeds to make a distinction: insofar as the creation is God's being, it is eternity; insofar as it is subject to time, it is not from God, who is eternal. "Who, then, understands the creation's existing both eternally and temporally?" In the course of his dialectical reasoning Nicholas makes it clear that the creation is God's being—and therefore eternal—only insofar as it exists in God. But as it exists in God, it is God and not something finite and differentiated. In Nicholas's mind, this point is associated with his second comparison with the infinite line—a comparison to which we may now turn.

2. In the infinite line all lines are the infinite line; similarly, in the Absolute Maximum all things are the Absolute Maximum. The word "in" is all-important. For Nicholas nowhere states that all things are the Absolute Maximum, or God, but maintains only that *in* God all things are God:[36] ontologically prior to their creation they are "enfolded" in God as God; and the act of creation is God's act of "unfolding" them from Himself. Since it seems strange to speak, plurally, of *things* existing in God prior to their creation, Nicholas's expression might give rise to confusion. For instead of regarding this as simply another *modus loquendi*, someone might take him to be affirming that things exist in God as the *forms* of their finite selves. Yet, Nicholas takes pains to prevent such a misunderstanding. In I, 24 (77:1–7) he asks rhetorically: "Who could understand the infinite Oneness which infinitely precedes all opposition?—where all things are incompositely enfolded in simplicity of

Oneness, where there is neither anything which is other nor anything which is different, where a man does not differ from a lion, and the sky does not differ from the earth. Nevertheless, in the Maximum they are most truly the Maximum, [though] not in accordance with their finitude; rather, [they are] Maximum Oneness in an enfolded way."[37] The very same point is repeated in *Apologia* 27:2–5; and the rationale for the point is generalized in *DI* II, 5 (119:12–20).

This doctrine of enfolding overlaps with the doctrine that in God opposites coincide, though it is primarily correlated with the theology of creation, whereas the doctrine of *coincidentia* is primarily correlated with the *via negativa* and with God's inconceivability and simplicity. Of course, Nicholas does not hesitate to state that "God is the enfolding of all things, even of contradictories" (I,22), and here the topic is not creation. But it is a topic directly associated with creation; and what is said to be enfolded is *all things*, not simply *contradictories*. These linguistic patterns are matters of idiom, not matters of substance. Since all things are in God as what is caused is in the cause, it is more felicitous to say "the effect is enfolded in its cause" than to say "in the cause the effect coincides with the cause." Moreover, "enfolding" and "unfolding" serve as a balanced couple for portraying the relation between Creator and creation. But what could balance as fittingly with "coinciding"?

It is the height of irony that Nicholas, who thus restricts the use of *"coincidere"* by avoiding it when discussing the Creator-creature relationship should have been accused by Wenck of having taught, *tout simplement*, that all things coincide with God. Wenck's mistake befigured the central mistake that would come to be made by Nicholas's subsequent *frondeurs*: viz., to excerpt from *DI* some key word or key sentence, while ignoring the restrictions and qualifications that had been placed upon its use.

3. As an infinite line is the measure of all lines, so the Absolute Maximum is the Measure of all things. This point about the Absolute Maximum Nicholas illustrates not only by the hypothesized infinite line but also by the relationship between substance and accident: "accidents are more excellent in proportion to their participation in substance; and, further, the more they participate in a more excellent substance, the still more excellent they are" (I, 18). By comparison, God—who orders all things in measure and number and weight, according to Wisdom 11:21, a verse Nicholas is fond of quoting—is variously participated in by various things. A thing's entire perfection derives from God, who created it to exist in the best manner possible for it.[38] But one thing is more perfect than another in accordance with its degree of participation in Divine Perfection.

To say that finite things participate in the Absolute Maximum is tantamount to saying that they owe their existence to the Maximum, which created them and which sustains them for as long as they exist. Their being is therefore dependent being, illustrated by an accident's dependency upon the substance in which it participates—with the proviso that whereas an accident modifies the substance, the universe does not modify God.[39] God is the Measure of all these things in that He alone has bestowed upon each thing its degree of perfection, which He alone knows precisely, though He knows this immediately and apart from any comparative relation to Himself.

Though the Maximum is not of the nature of the things it measures, it nonetheless receives the name of the things it measures—i.e., of the things that participate in it (I, 18). But these transferred names and significations befit God only infinitesimally. Even "Oneness," though it seems to be a quite close name for the Maximum, is still infinitely distant from the true and ineffable name of the Maximum—a name which *is* the Maximum.[40] The same point holds true, a fortiori, for "Substance," "Justice," "Truth," and all the other names traditionally applied to God. In last analysis, Nicholas regards these names as religiously useful metaphors. They are not proper names but are simply words whose significations have been transferred so as to apply figuratively to God. Or better, what is customarily signified by these words can, by a kind of extension, as it were, be considered as "likenesses" of God. And yet, they are not likenesses that correspond to what God is but are only quasi likenesses that direct the mind in its worship of the Deity. Accordingly, *Apologia* 24:19–22 declares: "to all who do not have learned ignorance (i.e., a knowledge of the fact that [the likenesses to God] are altogether disproportional), [the likenesses] are useless rather than useful."

The foregoing names belong to affirmative theology. According to negative theology, however, "there is not found in God anything other than infinity" (I, 26). Thus, according to negative theology God is known only to Himself; the human mind, even in the life to come, will be unable to know Him other than as He shows forth in Christ.

We have now reached the fundamental tension within the entire system of learned ignorance. For if affirmative theology terminates in likenesses that are infinitely remote from Divine Being and if negative theology conceives of God only as Inconceivable Infinity, what entitles Nicholas to refer to creatures as a reflection or an image of God, as he does in II, 2 (103:3–9)?[41] And how, on the basis of the creaticn can he see clearly God's eternal power and divinity, as Paul teaches in Romans 1:20?

The foregoing problem is so philosophically grave that unless it can be dealt with successfully, it threatens to undermine the very basis of learned ignorance. Let us be content to examine here only one small aspect of the network of interlacing difficulties. Wenck reproached Nicholas for tacitly repudiating Wisdom 13:5: "By the greatness of the beauty of creation the Creator can be knowably seen."[42] To this reproach Nicholas responded: "Since there is no comparative relation of the creature to the Creator, no created thing possesses a beauty through which the Creator can be attained. But from the greatness of the beauty and adornment of created things we are elevated unto what is infinitely and incomprehensibly beautiful—just as from a work of craft [we are referred] to the craftsman, although the work of craft bears no comparative relation to the craftsman.''[43]

The first thing for us to notice is Nicholas's reaffirmation of the principle *"non est proportio creaturae ad creatorem."* But a second feature also strikes our attention: viz., that the illustration of the craftsman does not serve Nicholas's purpose. True, a craftsman's work furnishes us with some basis for making inferences about the craftsman himself, even though the work does not *resemble* the craftsman. For example, from a Greek vase we can justifiably make inferences about the Greek potter, even though the vase does not resemble the potter. Similarly, Nicholas wants to say, from the works of God we can justifiably make inferences about God, even though the works of God do not resemble God. Yet, the comparison does not hold: it is defeated by Nicholas's unremitting claim—at the beginning, the middle, and the end of Book One— that God, unlike a craftsman, is inconceivable.[44] We therefore cannot justifiably draw any inferences about what He is like. We remain stranded in the realm of the *as if*.

Had Nicholas throughout his works not emphasized and reemphasized the inconceivability of God (except to Himself), we might have had grounds for construing the principle of *nulla proportio* in a different way. For we might understand it merely to mean that there is no *fully adequate* likeness between God and creation. But in order for *this* interpretation of his words to be plausible, there would have to be found in his works the parallel thesis that we have no *fully adequate* concept of God but only a partially adequate one. But for better or for worse, this latter thesis does not square with the texts.[45]

Throughout his works Nicholas shies away from using the word ''*analogia.*'' This aversion goes so far that it leads him to substitute the word ''*proportio*'' for the word ''*analogia*'' in the passage he cites, in *De Venatione Sapientiae* 30, from Ambrose Traversari's translation of Pseudo-Dionysius's *The Divine Names*; and on folio 65ʳ of Codex Cusanus 106 (works of Heimeric de Campo) he strikes out the word ''*analogae*'' and writes instead ''*proportionalis.*''[46] Many explanations for his having done so would be viable. But it is tempting to view him as simply going further in the direction of disassociating himself from the doctrine of *analogia entis*. For in place of Thomisticlike distinctions between *analogia proportionis* and *analogia proportionalitatis*, we find, in *DI*, the use of infinite geometrical figures to illustrate Divine Infinity and, in later works, ''object lessons,'' such as the lessons learned from the eyeglass in *De Beryllo*, the spinning top in *De Possest*, and the glowing ruby in *De Li Non Aliud*. It would be wrong to suppose that these object lessons and illustrations are variants of the Thomistic doctrine of *analogia*. True, Nicholas does draw various kinds of analogy—e.g., that an infinite line is to finite lines as God is to the world. But he never believes, as does Thomas, that on the basis of analogies something that is really the case can be signified about God's relation to the world—or even about God's nature. Because analogies do not correspond to any reality to be found in Infinite Being or its relations, they are better called illustrations. Nicholas himself calls them *aenigmata*, i.e., symbolisms; and he uses them to direct the mind's reflection so that the mind's ignorance may be learn-ed. For the human intellect is supposed to recognize that though these symbolisms help it to form a lofty conception of God, this conception is nonetheless only an *as if*—infinitely distant from and infinitely other than the Reality itself.[47] Now, since there are alternative—indeed, conflicting—sets of symbolisms, Nicholas needs criteria for deciding which sets are fitting and which unfitting. But if all of these symbolisms and illustrations are infinitely distant from Infinite Reality, then in accordance with Nicholas's own example of an infinite line, a "fitting" symbolism will be no closer to the Reality than an "unfitting" one. For "it is not the case that an infinite line exceeds the length of one foot more than it exceeds the length of two feet";[48] for it exceeds both lengths infinitely.

II. *Maximum Contractum*

As the Maximum Absolutum is infinite, so the maximum contractum is finite. Book One has already taught us the former point. Book Two now develops the latter point. Wherever there can be comparisons of greater and lesser we do not attain to the unqualifiedly Maximum, which escapes all such comparisons. Moreover, wherever there can be such comparisons we cannot by any addition thereto or division thereof reach the infinite. (This is clear, declares Nicholas, from the example of the ascending number series and from the example of the divisibility of a finite line. In neither case do we arrive at the infinitely great or the infinitely small, for we can always keep adding or keep dividing.) Hence, since one quantitative part of the universe (e.g., the moon) can be greater or lesser than another part (e.g., the earth), we do not by adding all the quantitative parts arrive at something infinite (i.e., maximum), than which there could not be a still greater quantity. Similarly, with regard to virtue, perfection, etc.: since one order of perfection (e.g., human beings) can be greater or lesser than another order of perfection (e.g., angels), we do not by increasing the degree or order of perfection arrive at an infinite (i.e., maximum) perfection, than which there could not be a still greater degree. Accordingly, since the quantitative and nonquantitative parts of the universe are finite and comparative, they cannot by being extended become maximum and noncomparative. Hence, the whole of the universe is also finite.

Yet, Nicholas calls the finite universe privatively infinite, distinguishing it from God, who is negatively infinite. And this terminology causes some confusion. To say that God, or Maximum Absolutum, is negatively infinite is to say that nothing at all can limit Him, for He is everything which can be. To say that the universe is privatively infinite is to say that it lacks limits—that it is not, and cannot be, actually limited by any greater thing external to it; for it is by definition, all things other than God. (And God does not delimit it in such way as to be its bound—i.e., a bound which would mark the end of the universe and the beginning of what is not the universe. For such a bound would have to be finite, since it would stand in comparative relation to what it bounded and would be defined partly in contrast to what it bounded). Accordingly, to call the universe privatively infinite amounts to calling it finite but physically unbounded. In order not to be misled by this expression, we must be reminded of two tenets of Nicholas's program: (1) the universe, of itself, does not have the power to expand; (2) to say that God is greater than the universe is not to place God in a comparative relation with the universe, for it is tantamount to saying only that the Infinite is greater than the finite—that whatever is, actually, all that can possibly be surpasses infinitely and disproportionally whatever is not the actuality of all possibility.

Nicholas thinks that, given our understanding of the notion *universe*, we cannot *conceive* of the universe as finite.[49] For to conceive of something as finite is to conceive of it as demarcated by what it is not. But since we understand the universe to be everything there is (other than God), we cannot conceive of there being anything beyond it which delimits it. Any such thing of which we did conceive would itself be a part of the universe. And so, we could conceive of it as delimiting the universe only if we radically misunderstood the notion *universe*. This move allows Nicholas to draw a parallelism between the world and God: just as we judge that God is infinite, so we judge that the world is finite; yet, just as we cannot conceive of God's infinitude, so we cannot conceive of the world's finitude.[50] However, with regard to both aspects of this parallelism, Nicholas needs to provide a penetrating analysis of conceivability.

The universe is not only *infinitum*, or *maximum*: it is also *contractum*. Nowhere in Nicholas's works do we find a definition of *"contractio."* The closest thereto is the statement at the end of II, 4: *"Contraction* means contraction to [i.e., restriction by] something, so as to be this or that." Yet, from this statement, together with various other statements which use the word *"contractio"* or the word *"contractum,"* we obtain an idea of what Nicholas understood by these terms. For he contrasts what is contracted with what is Absolute; and just as he regards the Absolute as in every respect undifferentiated, so he considers the contracted as in some respect differentiated. Thus, God is *Absolute* Maximum[51] in that He is that Maximum in which opposites coincide (as well as in the sense that there *cannot possibly* be anything greater than God); and the universe is a *contracted* maximum in that it is that maximum which is ever a oneness-in-plurality because it is a differentiated oneness, in which opposites cannot coincide. But when we read that "the universe is contracted in each actually existing thing" or that a universal is contracted in a particular, the sense is rather the following: the universe (or some given universal) exists in a restricted way—which Nicholas will have to explain—in each actually existing thing (or in the designated particular).

Over and over again Nicholas states that only God is absolute, that all else is contracted.[52] These clear statements serve to exclude all interpretation of his philosophy as pantheistic. And yet, tragically, John Wenck and a host of others have stigmatized his thinking as pantheistic or as leaning towards pantheism. This misrepresentation occurs both from a neglecting of the emphasis upon the infinite gulf between the contracted and the Absolute[53] and from a confusion about certain other statements which become strange-sounding once their connection with the foregoing distinction is obscured. Sometimes Nicholas's very words are changed, his concepts shifted, so that he is presented as teaching that "everything is, in fact, God himself,"[54] that "the being of a creature is instrinsically constituted by the divine being,"[55] that the world is a contraction of the divine being,[56] that God is the maximum and minimum of creatures,[57] that the universe is *Geist*.[58] Perhaps too the very description of the Maximum as "all that which can be" has confused some readers. For if the Maximum is, actually, all that which can be, then it might seem that the reality of God must in some respect be mingled with the reality of the universe, which is among the things which can be.[59] Let us, then, take a closer look at Nicholas's teachings regarding the distinction between Creator and creature.

Above all, we need to notice that in *DI* Nicholas clearly affirms that the creation is not God.[60] And he reaffirms it in *Apologia* 23:8–9. Indeed, the creation is a *reflection* of God, is the *image* of that Infinite Form.[61] But the reflection of God is not God—any more than an image is the reality of which it is the image. Moreover, the terms "reflection" and "image" will mislead us if we forget that, for Nicholas, the so-called reflection, or image, is not the resemblance of God but is only the work of God—a work from which we can form a useful conception of God, though it be a conception falling infinitely and incommensurably short of the Reality itself. The words "*resplendentia*" and "*imago*" are used chiefly to insist that the creation owes to God all that it positively is, for it was created *ex nihilo* rather than fashioned from some independently preexisting material principle.[62] When Nicholas says that the creature is "something very much like God,"[63] he means to indicate that each creature was created in as perfect a state as it could be and that every created thing qua created thing is perfect (even if it seems less perfect in comparison with some other created thing). Thus, there is a parallelism between the fact that the creation qua creation is perfect and the fact that God is absolutely perfect. And yet, created perfection does not resemble Divine Perfection; nor does the creation's originally being as perfect as it could be preclude its having become imperfect as a result of the Fall. So when Nicholas terms each creature a created god or a god manqué, he does so in order to emphasize that God was not niggardly or envious in creating: He imparted as much being and perfection as could be received. But now the question arises: received by what?, since God created *ex nihilo*. Here Nicholas's response is altogether unsatisfactory: a thing's degree of perfection comes from God; its imperfection and limitation come neither from God nor from any positive cause but only from contingency.[64] And the introducing of the word "contingency"—like Augustine's having introduced the phrase "deficient cause" vis-à-vis Satan's fall—signals that Nicholas has no intelligible explanation to offer. He is thus reduced further and further to unintelligibility: "There remains only to say that the plurality of things arises from the fact that God is present in nothing."[65]

We may now turn to the central metaphysical theme vis-à-vis God's relation to the world—a theme we have already briefly touched upon: "God is the enfolding of all things in that all things are in Him; and He is the unfolding of all things in that He is in all things."[66] In what sense, according to Nicholas, is it true that all things are in God and that God is in all things? Probably no question has generated more conflicting responses among Cusa scholars. For precisely this configuration of themes has led many to see in *DI* a tendency toward pantheism.

We previously observed that, for Nicholas, all things are enfolded in God ontologically prior to their creation and that as thus enfolded in God they are God.[67] And we saw that they are in God as what is caused is in the power of its cause. The universe is not in God *temporally* prior to its creation because "before" creation there was no time. Like Augustine, Nicholas believes that time was created together with the world.[68] Hence, there is a sense in which the world always existed—viz., that it existed from the beginning of time. But there is also a sense in which it did not always exist—viz., that time itself has a beginning. Thus, God is prior to the world in the order of dependency: without God the world would be nothing (i.e., there would be no world); but without the world God would remain the eternal and immutable God.

Accordingly, we may view created things in two different ways: (1) as totally deriving, in an ultimate sense, from God's power (i.e. as enfolded in God); (2) as being parts of an on-going world process in which one thing is interrelated to other things and in which there are secondary causes of existence and change (i.e., as unfolded from God).[69] From the first point of view, all things may be said to be in God's power and to be—in God's power—*God* without differentiation: "in the Maximum they are most truly the Maximum, [though] not in accordance with their finitude; rather, [they are] Maximum Oneness in an enfolded way.''[70] From the second point of view, they may be said to exist according to their finitude and as distinct from God and from one another. Yet, even as distinct from God and unfolded from God they still exist, in some sense, in God. But the sense is now different. For whereas in the first sense they exist in God as God, in the second sense they exist as themselves in God: "Everything which exists actually, exists in God, since He is the actuality of all things. Now, actuality is the perfection and the end of possibility. Hence, since the universe is contracted in each actually existing thing: it is evident that God, who is in the universe, is in each thing and that each actually existing thing is immediately in God, as is also the universe.''[71] The first sense accords with the way things exist in God as enfolded-in-God; the second sense accords with the way they continue to exist in God while existing as unfolded-from-God. The first sense can be illustrated by the way a craftsman's idea of what he will produce exists in his mind *as* his mind (and thus as himself). The second sense can be illustrated by an *as if*: the world is, *as it were*, "an artifact"—but one which depends entirely upon the Divine Craftsman's Idea and which, ultimately speaking, has no other being than dependent being.[72] Of course, the relation between a craftsman's idea and his product is temporal: the idea temporally precedes the production. But the relation between God and His creation is ontological: God ontologically precedes the created world. Still, we can envision a state of affairs in which only God exists; and we can also envision a state of affairs in which both God and the creation exist. And this envisioning enables Nicholas to use the language of enfolding and unfolding, even though the enfolded state does not temporally precede the unfolded state. Viewed, then, as enfolded absolutely in God, each thing *is* God; for *there* it is not its finite self. Viewed as unfolded from God, no thing is God; for *here* it *is* its finite, contracted self and is said to participate in God rather than to be God.

Whatever problems Nicholas has with his language of creation, they are problems shared by Augustine and by all who profess the doctrine that time does not precede the beginning of the world. Nonetheless, let it be clear that Nicholas is not subscribing to a double aspect theory, in terms of which the world and God, though identical, may be viewed according to one aspect as world, according to another as God. This doctrine was reserved for Spinoza to set forth at a later period in the history of philosophy. Nicholas himself teaches something more traditional: the world is not identical with God but is only an image of God. The language of enfolding and unfolding is meant to mark this fundamental ontological distinction.

So then, as unfolded from God, things remain in some sense in God. But it is also true that God is in some sense present in each *unfolded* thing;[73] and thus He may be said to be the *unfolding* of all things. To say this, however, is not to say that the world is God unfolded, for the world is not at all God. The world is unfolded *from* God without being God in His unfolded state, so to speak.

Nicholas attempts to clarify the doctrine of divine presence by means of a comparison: "in all things God is that which they are, just as in an image the reality itself (*veritas*) is present."[74] Of course, the reality (i.e., the original) is not physically present in the image—any more than God is physically present in His creation. The reality is present in the sense that the image is truly an image of the original. In the case of God and the world, Nicholas regards the world as truly an image of God, even though it is not a true image of God. That is, it befigures God[75] but is not an analogue of God. This befiguring is really a kind of parallelism: as God is Absolute Maximum, so the universe is a contracted maximum; as God is Absolute Oneness, so the universe is a oneness-in-plurality; as God is Trinity, so the universe is also a trinity; and so on. Likewise, with regard to the language of image and original, we also have a parallelism: the original gives to the image its identity, insofar as the image is identified in terms of what it is an image of; indeed, the image would not be what it is if the original were not what *it* is. Similarly, no thing in the world would be what it is if God were not what He is. Elsewhere Nicholas reverts to the illustration of the craftsman: God is in the universe as a craftsman's design, which is something abstract, is present in the artifact, which is something concrete.[76] Because Nicholas believes that everything sprang into existence from God's design, he views the world's perfection as an indicator of that design and, consequently, of the presence of Omnipresence.

In stating that in a thing God is, absolutely, what that thing is, Nicholas uses the language of quiddity and of essence: God is the Absolute Quiddity, or Absolute Essence, of that thing.[77]

> Just as God, since He is immense, is neither in the sun nor in the moon, although in them He is, absolutely, that which they are: so the universe is neither in the sun nor in the moon; but in them it is, contractedly, that which they are. Now, the Absolute Quiddity of the sun is not other than the Absolute Quiddity of the moon (since [this] is God Himself, who is the Absolute Being and Absolute Quiddity of all things);[78] but the contracted quiddity of the sun *is* other than the contracted quiddity of the moon (for as the Absolute Quiddity of a thing is not the thing, so the contracted [quiddity of a thing] is none other than the thing). . . . Although the universe is neither the sun nor the moon, nevertheless in the sun it is the sun and in the moon it is the moon. However, it is not the case that God is in the sun sun and in the moon moon; rather, He is that which is sun and moon without plurality and difference.[79]

Hereby Nicholas reaffirms that God is not, in any ordinary sense, present in all things. But in the moon, say, He is, absolutely, that which is moon. To say "absolutely" is to say that in the moon God is the ultimate ground of the moon's being what it is. That is, God is not this finite thing; nor in this finite thing is He this finite thing; rather, in this finite thing He is the ultimate sustaining Power of its contracted being and essence—in which Power its contracted being and essence "participate."

Is Nicholas teaching that each thing, in its being, is God? In order to answer this question satisfactorily we must keep in mind that his thought moves back and forth between two distinct ontological levels: the level of the ultimate and the level of the nonultimate. Thus, when speaking nonultimately, he deals with the contracted quiddity, or contracted essence, of things;[80] he declares that "Aristotle was right in dividing all the things in the world into substance and accident";[81] he proclaims that each thing exists in the best way it can, that it is a union of potentiality and of actuality—and so on. When speaking on the ultimate level, he talks of the Absolute Quiddity of all things, the Essence of all essences, the enfoldedness of all things in God; and he makes statements such as the following: the creation qua creation "does not have even as much being as an accident but is altogether nothing. . . . "[82] This last citation illustrates how radically incoherent—even nonsensical—his entire system would be if we did not distinguish, with him, these two different levels; for otherwise, it would be absurd to affirm that the creation qua creation does not have as much being as an accident, since an accident is itself a part of the creation. Similarly, when he teaches that the universe is only a reflection or that God is the Essence of all things, he is speaking from the point of view of the ultimate.

We are now in a position to understand the following statement from the end of I, 17: "No thing exists in itself except the Maximum; and every thing exists in itself insofar as it exists in its Essence [*ratio*], because its Essence is the Maximum." God is the ultimate Essence in which all things are enfolded; these things qua enfolded in God *are* God and hence exist per se and in se. Nicholas is not claiming that a thing has no being or essence except God; nor is he claiming that is has no positive being or essence except God. Rather, he is maintaining that, ultimately speaking, the creation—both as a whole and with respect to any of its parts—would be nothing without God, since it has no independent ontological status other than the relatively independent status given to it by God (e.g., there are secondary causes; and human beings have free wills). But in granting this status, God has granted to each created substance its own positive, contracted essence, so that those substances which are material objects are other than the contracted mirror images of themselves. At this level it would be just as wrong to call a material object a mere reflection as it would be on the ultimate level not to call the entire universe a mere reflection. Indeed, because there are two different levels Nicholas can meaningfully advance the following proportionality: a face is to its mirror image as God is to the world.[83]

Accordingly, Nicholas does not teach either that the universe is God in a state of contraction[84] or that each thing's being is Divine Being. For, on the one hand, Divine Being cannot at all be contracted; and, on the other, Divine Being is never a created thing's being but is the ultimate Cause and Sustainer of each finite thing's being. In the moon God is not the moon's being, for the moon's being is contracted being and hence different from the sun's being. God's being is never *this* being or *that* being but is undifferentiated Being itself; He is Being only in a sense which is inconceivable to us, for He is Being in such way that Being is not opposed to not-being.

Thus, interpreters such as Vincent Martin[85] have been misled by the illustration of the infinite line in I, 17: "An infinite line is the essence of a finite line. Hence, there is one essence of both lines [i.e., a line of two feet and a line of three feet]; and the difference between the things, or the lines, does not result from a difference of the essence, which is one, but from an accident, because the lines do not participate equally in the essence." From such passages Martin infers that, for Nicholas, "God and the creature have the same proper nature," that a creature's "positive content, i.e., that by which . . . it is constituted, is the divine being."[86] And Martin thinks that Nicholas conceives of creatures as differing from one another only accidentally, because they differ by their degree of participation in their Essence, which is God.[87] Yet, Martin's inferences are too sweeping. For such Cusanian passages as the foregoing teach only the following: that just as the infinite line is the essence of all finite lines, which differ from one another in accordance with their respective degree of participation in it, so the Maximum Essence is the Essence of all finite essences, each of which differs from the others in accordance with its respective degree of participation in the Maximum Essence. From Nicholas's comparison with the infinite line we are not supposed to infer that as all finite lines differ only accidentally, so all finite things differ only accidentally. Had Nicholas meant for us to make this inference, he would not have gone on in I, 18 to classify finite things as substances and accidents. For a substance differs from a finite line by virtue of having an essence of its own. Throughout I, 16–18 Nicholas speaks of essences and substances in the plural. Moreover, throughout *DI* he uses the language of genus, species, common nature. In II, 6 we read that "dogs and other animals of the same species are united by virtue of the common specific nature which is in them" (126:6–8). And in III, 7 we read, apropos of Christ's example of the grain of wheat: "In this example the numerical distinctness of the grain is destroyed, while the specific essence remains intact; by this means nature raises up many grains" (225:2–4). Similarly, III, 8 states: "There is only one indivisible humanity and specific essence of all human beings. Through *it* all individual human beings are numerically distinct human beings, so that Christ and all human beings have the same humanity, though the numerical distinctness of the individuals remains unconfused" (227:12–16). And III, 1 tells us that a particular "contracts, in its own degree, the one nature of its own species" (186:7), that "all things differ from one another—either (1) in genus, species, and number or (2) in species and number or (3) in number—

so that each thing exists with its own number, weight, and measure" (182:14–16). Accordingly, Nicholas teaches that a dog and a human being differ essentially.[88] In differing essentially, they also differ in their degree of participation in Divine Being, or Divine Essence.[89]

The illustration of the infinite line also teaches that substance does not admit of more or less—"even as a finite straight line, insofar as it is straight, does not admit of more and less. But because [it is] finite, one [straight] line is—through a difference of participation in the infinite line—longer or shorter in relation to another; no two [finite lines] are ever found to be equal."[90] By comparison, one dog is not more a dog than is another. And yet, each dog contracts the canine nature in its own degree, for no two dogs are perfect dogs. That is, the different degrees of contraction do not correspond to different degrees of being canine but to different degrees of being more perfectly or less perfectly canine.[91] Thus, it is true both that each individual thing of a given species or genus has its own unique degree of contraction and, at the same time, that it has an essence, or nature, which is its positive principle of determinateness.[92]

We may now return to the question of whether or not the very description of the Maximum entails that the world's being is also God's being. The answer is plainly No. For although the Maximum is, actually, all that which can be, it is it coincidingly—i.e., absolutely and indistinctly. Therefore, the Maximum cannot be the universe, since it cannot be any finite or composite thing. Likewise, the only way that Maximum Being constitutively includes the universe's being is by way of enfolding. But, of course, insofar as the universe is enfolded in God, it is not the universe but is God Himself. The universe qua universe exists only as unfolded from God; and as unfolded from God, it is not at all God, though Nicholas calls every creature a "created god" and a "god manqué" in order to make a special point about created perfection.

A final passage which has been thought to exhibit pantheistic tendencies is the whole of II, 5, where the doctrine of *quodlibet in quolibet* is found. As philosophically bizarre as this doctrine is, Nicholas regards it as implied by what he has already taught. For if (1) all things are in God and (2) God is in all things, then (3) everything is in everything else—i.e., each thing is in each other thing. Nicholas expands these statements by reasoning that God is present in all things by means of the universe, which precedes its own parts, "just as in a craftsman's design the whole (e.g., a house) is prior to a part (e.g., a wall)"; similarly, all things, by means of the universe, are present in God (II,4). This expansion then allows him to make the following restatement: "to say that each thing is in each thing is not other than [to say] that through all things God is in all things and that through all things all things are in God" (II, 5).

Nicholas illustrates his doctrine in two ways: by the example of the infinite line and by the example of the several members of one body. Since neither one of these illustrations is philosophically intelligible, neither one need here be rehearsed. Suffice it to say that both are based upon an altogether dubious notion of the relation between part and whole.

With the foregoing bizarre doctrine Nicholas was seeking to portray another parallelism between God and the world: as (in one way) God is in all things, and all things in God, so (in another way) the universe is in all things, and all things in the universe; indeed, as God is in all things through the mediation of the universe, so through the mediation of the universe all things are in God. But this time the parallelism was of no help to him. For the crux of his doctrine exceeds the parallelism and relies upon a different comparison: just as the hand, the foot, etc., are, in the eye, the eye insofar as the eye is immediately in the man, so the sun, the moon, etc., are, in any given thing, that given thing insofar as that thing is immediately in God. Nicholas thinks that from the proposition "each actually existing thing is immediately in God, as is also the universe" and the proposition "God is in all things" it follows that in each thing each other thing exists as contractedly *that* thing. But since no such conclusion is entailed by these premises, additional premises will be needed. Nicholas's several illustrations become substitutes for the required additional premises. In the end, this elaborate edifice of thought collapses, raising a beclouding dust, so that many readers of *DI* come becloudedly to believe that the expression 'the universe is immediately in God' displays pantheistic leanings.

We have already seen that in I, 18 Nicholas agrees that "Aristotle was right in dividing all the things in the world into substance and accident." Similarly, in II, 6 he commends the Aristotelians when he writes: "In this way the Peripatetics speak the truth [when they say that] universals do not actually exist independently of things. For only what is particular exists actually." Nicholas's theory of universals blends Aristotelianism with his own metaphysic of contraction. Here again we find a parallelism: as God is the enfolding and unfolding of all things,[93] so the universe enfolds and unfolds all univerals. For the universe is the contracted enfolding of three types of universal (each possessing its own respective degree of universality): viz., the ten categories, genera, and species. The categories are unfolded in and exist in the genera; the genera are unfolded in and exist in the species; the species exist only in individual things, i.e., in particulars. In Nicholas's language of oneness: God is the first and absolute Oneness; the universe is a second, but contracted, universal oneness-of-ten-categories; genera are a third universal oneness; species, a fourth. Species have a greater degree of contraction than do genera; and genera have a greater degree of contraction than do the categories. God, of course, is uncontracted; and Nicholas does not hesitate to refer to Him as *Absolute Universal*.

Though universals exist in particulars, which are still more contracted than is any universal, they exist in each particular as that particular. For example, though humanity is neither Socrates nor Plato: in Socrates it is Socrates, and in Plato it is Plato.[94] This statement about universals corresponds to the statement about the universe, which in a given thing is that thing.[95]

Humanity, according to Nicholas, exists in Socrates and in Plato in the following sense: Socrates is a man, and Plato is a man. Similarly, to say that in Socrates humanity is Socrates is tantamount to saying that Socrates's humanity differs numerically from Plato's. It is not tantamount to denying the reality of humanity qua universal. Nicholas is not a nominalist (or a conceptualist) but an Aristotelian-Thomistic realist; for he teaches that universals—i.e., species, or natures—exist in the particulars to which they belong; they are not mere rational entities. Though they do not exist apart from particulars, they are nonetheless ontologically prior (in Nicholas's words "prior in the order of nature") to those particulars in which they are present. Human beings (or dogs or cats, etc.) share a specific nature which is individuated in each human being (in each dog or cat, etc.).[96] These natures are therefore numerically distinct, as Aristotle and Thomas had taught. Nicholas also borrows the Aristotelian-Thomistic view that the intellect, by the process of comparing and abstracting, makes universal concepts which correspond to the specific natures that exist in the various kinds of particulars.

The theory of universals sketched in *DI* cannot without distortion be severed from the doctrine of *quodlibet in quolibet*; in this respect it shares some of the failings of the company it keeps. And yet, no part of *DI* is more basic than is this theory; for the exposition in II, 6 is fundamental to the developments in Book Three, where the role of genus and species looms large vis-à-vis the topic of Christ's humanity.

Having made his peace with the Aristotelians, Nicholas must still contend with those Platonists and Neoplatonists whose metaphysic interposed between God and the cosmos a world-soul in which are found the exemplars of all created things. Allegedly, the world-soul unfolds from God: that which in God is one uncreated Exemplar is in the world-soul an uncreated plurality. The corresponding likenesses of these exemplars, or intelligible forms, are said by these Platonists to exist in matter—though they exist there ontologically (not temporally) subsequent to the existence of the corresponding exemplar in the world-soul. Supposedly, this world-mind, as it is also called, is the cause of motion, to which it is also prior only ontologically.

While never making explicit just who these Platonists might be, Nicholas opposes their configuration of views primarily because it is inconsistent with the metaphysic he has been devising: whatever is is either God or not-God, either Absolute or contracted. If there were a Platonistic-type world-soul, containing a plurality of exemplars, then it would exist contractedly (for wherever there is a plurality, there is contraction). However, "there cannot be many distinct exemplars, for each exemplar would be maximum and most true

26

with respect to the things which are its exemplifications. But it is not possible that there be many maximal and most true things.''[97] Accordingly, there is only one Exemplar, teaches Nicholas: viz., the Word of God, who is God.[98] As the Form of all forms and the Essence of all essences[99] God may not unfittingly be called World-soul, thinks Nicholas. But he would not want our use of this appellative to obscure the fact that the Word of God—"the World-soul"—is neither a contracted nor an uncontracted *unfolding* of God and that the "exemplars" which exist in Him are one indistinct "Exemplar," which He Himself *is* qua God the Son.

The topic of the world-soul naturally gives rise to the topic of motion, since the Platonists of II, 9 regarded the world-soul as the source of mundane motion. Within the Cusanian metaphysic God Himself, who replaces the world-soul, is the ultimate source of the world's motion. But "it is not the case that any [mundane] motion is unqualifiedly maximum motion, for this latter coincides with rest. Therefore, no motion is absolute, since absolute motion is rest and is God. And absolute motion enfolds all motions.''[100] Book One has already made clear that God is really beyond the distinction between motion and rest, so that to call Him Absolute Motion is tantamount to denying that He is motion in any sense comparable to what we ordinarily understand by the term. Yet, He is the cause of the movements of the spheres. The Ptolemaic ordering had depicted the earth as the fixed center of ten concentric spheres, beginning with the moon and proceeding outwards with Mercury, Venus, the sun, Mars, Jupiter, Saturn, the sphere of "fixed" stars (i.e., the firmament), the crystallinum, and the primum mobile—the last three spheres being the three heavens. We may surmise from II, 11 (159:10–13) that Nicholas accepted this ordering. But he did not accept the tenet that the earth or any other body is the fixed center. His reasons for not doing so are mainly metaphysical. A fixed and immovable physical center would be minimum motion (i.e., rest), than which there could not be a lesser motion. "However, it is not the case that in any genus—even [the genus] of motion—we come to an unqualifiedly maximum and minimum" (156:11–12). Given any motion, he thinks, there can always in principle be a greater and a lesser motion. Moreover, if the earth (or some other body) were the fixed, *immovable* physical center of the world, then (because the unqualifiedly minimum coincides with the unqualifiedly maximum) it would also be the circumference—something which it obviously is not. (Indeed, no physical object can be both the smallest thing and the largest thing.) Therefore, the world has neither a fixed physical center nor a fixed physical circumference. Not even the center of the earth can be the center of the world. For the earth, being an imperfect sphere, cannot have an exact center—i.e., a point equidistant from every point on its circumference. According to Nicholas's metaphysic a perfect sphere or a perfect circle does not actually exist, because for any positable sphere or circle a still truer one could be posited. Hence, with respect to any correspondingly posited center a still truer center could be posited.

Since the earth is not the fixed center of the universe, it is not unmoved. Nicholas regards the earth as an approximate sphere that moves with an approximately circular motion around a pole which "we conjecture to be where the center is believed to be." For, by parity of reasoning, there are no fixed and immovable physical poles in the sky. Though the world, the heavens, the earth, and any body whatsoever have no *fixed physical* center or circumference, they do have a center and a circumference. For since such a center would be an unqualifiedly minimum, it can only be God, who was shown in Book One to be the unique Absolute Minimum. And since God is also the Absolute Maximum, with which the Minimum coincides, He is also the circumference of the world, of the earth, and of all things in the world. Thus, the world's center and circumference coincide, for they are not a physical center and circumference but are God Himself.

Having reached this conclusion on the basis of purely metaphysical considerations, Nicholas attempts to render it plausible by other than purely metaphysical considerations. He does so by introducing the notion of perspective, which he develops in accordance with a *Gedankenexperiment*. Suppose person *A* were on the earth somewhere below the north pole of the heavens and person *B* were at the north pole of the heavens. In that case, to *A* the pole would appear to be at the zenith, and *A* would believe himself to be at the center; to *B* the earth would appear to be at the zenith, and *B* would believe himself to be at the center. Thus, *A*'s zenith would be *B*'s center, and *B*'s zenith would be *A*'s center.

> And wherever anyone would be, he would believe himself to be at the center. Therefore, merge these different imaginative pictures so that the center is the zenith and vice versa. Thereupon you will see—through the intellect, to which only learned ignorance is of help—that the world and its motion and shape cannot be apprehended. For [the world] will appear as a wheel in a wheel and a sphere in a sphere—having its center and circumference nowhere. . . .[101]

In Nicholas's paradoxical language: the world's center and circumference are nowhere because they are everywhere,[102] depending upon the perspective. The center and the circumference coincide for God, because God is equally near to, and equally far from all things[103]—presumably in the sense that the Divine Mind encompasses infinite perspectives.

So in *DI* II, 11 Nicholas first of all derives—from metaphysical principles already accredited in Book One—the conclusion that the world has no center and circumference but God; only thereafter does he provide the *Gedankenexperiment* to help us envision the corollary that this center and this circumference are everywhere and nowhere.[104] The thought experiment is never intended to establish the conclusion.[105] Nor is it indispensable for supporting the corollary; for once we grant that *God* is the center and the circumference, then it follows from the theological doctrine of divine omnipresence that the center and the circumference are everywhere and nowhere. And indeed this theological route is explicitly taken by Nicholas in II, 12: "The world-machine will have its center everywhere and its circumference nowhere, so to speak; for God, who is everywhere and nowhere, is its circumference and center" (162:15–17). Like the recurring illustration of the infinite line, so the presence of the quasi-empirical thought experiment gives witness to the era in which Nicholas lived—an era which still wanted to safeguard many of the received theological traditions but which felt the need to reexpound them and reexplain them in more up-to-date terms.

The updating is often more suggestive than detailed. For example, in *DI* Nicholas actually says very little about perspectivism; but the little he says is rich with implication. "It would always seem to each person," he says, "(whether he were on the earth, the sun, or another star)[106] that he was at the 'immovable' center, so to speak, and that all other things were moved. . . ."[107] This statement implies that if someone were on the sun, he would regard the earth as revolving around the sun just as from his present vantage point on earth he regards the sun as revolving around the earth. Nowhere however, does Nicholas develop this implication. Yet, his relativizing of motion and the measure of motion, together with his repudiation of the view that the earth is immobile and is the lowliest of all the "stars," dimly foreshadowed—but did not anticipate—the future Copernican Revolution.

Nicholas's relativization is not thoroughgoing, for he is still willing to believe, through learned ignorance, that the world has a motion and a shape.[108] Later in the history of philosophy Leibniz, in his correspondence with Clarke, exposed the strangeness of the affirmation that the world as a whole is moved; and he went on thoroughly to relativize the notions of space and time by defining them as relations. Nicholas's speculation falls far short of such tenets, not being as revolutionary. Yet, for its own day it was bold and innovative—for example, in its surmise that the earth and the moon have a light, a heat, and an influence of their own.

In judging that the earth is larger than the moon—a judgment which startled Wenck—Nicholas appealed, for confirmation, to evidence from our experience of eclipses. But such a direct empirical appeal is rare in his works—the notable exception being *De Staticis Experimentis*. When he asserts that the earth and the moon have a heat of their own or that there is life on every other "star," he does not point to any direct or indirect empirical confirmation thereof. What can be discerned most of all in his speculative cosmology is what can also be discerned principally in his metaphysic: viz., a burning desire for *nouveautés*. This is the desire that drives him to view every created thing as a finite infinity[109] and to view the universe as "neither finite nor infinite."[110] He lived in an age in which the old ways of looking at things were beginning to be experienced as confining. A world whose celestial motions were supposed to be precisely measurable and whose sole living inhabitants were to be found exclusively at its center no longer seemed sufficiently adventurous. *DI*'s own venturesome picture of the world testifies to the fact that as early as 1440 the dawn of the Renaissance had commenced for German intellectuality.

III. *Maximum simul Contractum et Absolutum*

The innovativeness of Nicholas's theory of redemption strikingly surpasses, in significance, the novelty of his cosmological speculation. For this theory is more centrally linked to the originality and distinctiveness of his entire program of learned ignorance than are the "corollaries of motion" and the "conditions of the earth" found in Book Two, chapters eleven and twelve. Indeed, without some such theory, the labors of Books One and Two could not have come to fruition. And the unity-of-thought which was being sought would have remained hauntingly unattained. Still, for all its uniqueness, the theory of redemption does not veer from orthodoxy, as certain isolated expressions might induce us to believe. Instead, in its broad sweep, it retains the dogmas of Christ's virginal and sinless birth, the hypostatic union of His two natures, the dispensing of His merit to all believers, the final resurrection of the dead through His power, and the last judgment, before His throne, of all human and angelic beings. Thus, what is innovative is not the dogmas themselves but the understanding of them in terms of the metaphysic of contraction.

According to this metaphysic no contracted thing or series of contracted things can become infinite, or unqualifiedly maximum. Thus, no individual thing attains unto the maximum of its species, since for any given species God can always create a more perfect individual within that species. Similarly, for any given species within a genus, or any given genus within the universe, God can create a more perfect species within that genus, or a more perfect genus within the universe. And the universe itself does not exhaust the power of God; for God could have created a more perfect universe, even though He could not have created *this* universe with *these* creatures more perfect than it existed in its state before the Fall. "Therefore, all contracted things exist between a maximum and a minimum, so that there can be posited a greater and a lesser degree of contraction than [that of] any given thing. Yet, this process does not continue actually unto infinity, because an infinity of degrees is impossible, since to say that infinite degrees actually exist is nothing other than to say that no degree exists. . . ."[111]

Having thus reaffirmed that in general there is no actually maximum individual of any species, no actually maximum species of any genus, no actually maximum genus within the universe, and that the universe itself is not a maximum in the unqualified sense of being all that which can be, Nicholas now begins to reason hypothetically: what if there were an actually existing contracted maximum individual of some species? In that case, it would be actually everything that is in the possibility of that species, just as a maximum line is "actually" whatever is in the possibility of any finite line. Thus, it would enfold in itself the entire perfection of that species. And in being both the maximum and the minimum of the species, it would be beyond all comparative relation and would be the measure of everything within the species, as the maximum line is the measure of all finite lines.

But since no merely contracted individual thing can attain unto the limit of its species: this maximum individual thing, if it exists, will not be a purely contracted thing existing in itself; rather, since it will be maximum because it exists in Absolute Maximality, it will exist in union with what is Absolute. The divine and uncontracted maximum nature will be united to the creaturely and contracted maximum nature in such way that the being who is both Absolute and contracted will not be (1) only God or (2) only a creature or (3) a composite of the divine and the creaturely. Rather, the created nature will be subsumed in the divine person—as, in our own cognitive being, what is perceptual is subsumed in what is intellectual—so that the one being will be both a creature and the Creator. Neither nature will pass over into the other; for the uncontracted nature cannot become contracted, nor can the contracted nature lose its contractedness. Instead, the two natures will be united to such an extent that if they were more united, there would not remain two distinct natures. Who, then, asks Nicholas rhetorically, can conceive of such a union?

But within which species would the Absolute Maximum unite itself to a contracted maximum? In answering this question Nicholas adopts the following guideline: "If Absolute Maximality is in the most universal way the Being of all things, so that it is not more of one thing than of another: clearly, that being which is more common to the totality of beings is more unitable with the [Absolute] Maximum."[112] Now, in the order of contracted natures some natures are higher or lower than others. For example, living beings are higher than nonliving beings; intelligent beings are higher than nonintelligent beings; living and intelligent beings are higher than living but nonintelligent beings. If there is a middle nature—one which is the highest of the lower natures and the lowest of the higher natures—then this would be the nature with which God would unite. For such a nature would enfold within itself all natures, so that if it were to ascend wholly to a union of itself with God, then in and through it "all natures and the entire universe" would reach the supreme gradation.[113] Now, human nature, thinks Nicholas, is just such an intermediate nature; created a little lower than the angels, it enfolds both the sensible and the intellectual and is a microcosm enclosing all things.

But since humanity exists only contractedly as this or that human nature, only this or that human nature—and not humanity as such—is elevated to the point that it is the maximum human nature existing in maximum union with the Absolute Maximum.

> And, assuredly, this being would be a man in such way that He was also God and would be God in such way that He was also a man. [He would be] the perfection of the universe and would hold preeminence in all respects. In Him the least, the greatest, and the in-between things of the nature that is united to Absolute Maximality would so coincide that He would be the perfection of all things; and all things, qua contracted, would find rest in Him as in their own perfection. The measure of this man would also be the measure of an angel (as John says in the Book of Revelation) and of each thing; for through union with Absolute [Maximality], which is the Absolute Being of all things, He would be the universal contracted being of each creature. Through Him all things would receive the beginning and the end of their contraction, so that through Him who is the contracted maximum [individual] all things would go forth from the Absolute Maximum into contracted being and would return unto the Absolute [Maximum] through this same Medium. . . .[114]

Nicholas identifies the contracted maximum individual within the species of humanity as the human nature of Jesus. This human nature, he believes, is elevated into a hypostatic union with the divine nature, so that through this maximal union Jesus is both human and divine. Nicholas bases his identification upon the authority of Scripture and the witness of the Church. A number of observations are now called for.

1. Earlier in the history of theology Anselm of Canterbury had attempted to establish that God's justice, mercy, and honor, together with the fact of the Fall and its consequences, theologically necessitated the advent of a God-man; through this God-man there would be made a satisfaction sufficient to pay the debt of all men's sins. The main lines of Anselm's magnificent theory are well known and need not here be rehearsed.[115] Let us simply be reminded that Anselm begins, in the *Cur Deus Homo*, by reasoning *Christo remoto*; and then, having exhibited by "rational necessity" (*rationibus necessariis*) that a God-man is required, he turns to identify the required individual with Jesus and to assert that what has been established rationally proves the truth of the Old and the New Testaments. Since Nicholas, in his sermons,[116] appropriates portions of the Anselmian theory, it is tempting to view his procedure in III, 1–3 as analogous to Anselm's *Christo remoto* methodology. But, in fact, any such comparison with Anselm would be misleading. For Nicholas does not aim to show *rationibus necessariis* that the advent of a contracted maximum individual who is also God is theologically required—i.e., is implied by the theological principles and premises that he presupposes as true. Instead, his reasoning moves with a reverse emphasis. For the *Christo remoto* portion of it

32

is presented without any appeal to the theological need for the *existence* of such an individual, whereas the identification portion of it emphatically appeals to the *evidential* witness of the Evangelists and the Apostles "regarding the fact that Jesus is God and man."[117]

2. Indeed, the very sentence "Jesus is God and man" is striking. For throughout the discussion Nicholas prefers the expression "God and man" to the expression "the God-man." This way of speaking, together with certain other sentences containing the word *"homo,"* fosters the impression that Nicholas adheres to a Nestorian Christology, which affirms a merely moral unity of two persons. For example, in III, 12 he speaks of "the true man Christ Jesus" as "united, in supreme union, with the Son of God" (260:2–3). And in III, 3 he states: "It would not be possible that more than one true human being [*homo*] could ascend to union with Maximality. And, assuredly, this being would be a man in such way that He was also God and would be God in such way that He was also a man" (199:2–4). But these passages must be interpreted in the light of Nicholas's clear exclusion of Nestorianism: "The maximum man, Jesus, was not able to have in Himself a person that existed separately from the divinity. For He is the maximum [human being]. And, accordingly, there is a sharing of the respective modes of speaking [about the human nature and the divine nature], so that the human things coincide with the divine things;[118] for His humanity—which on account of the supreme union is inseparable from His divinity (as if it were put on and assumed by the divinity)—cannot exist as separate in person."[119] This passage, together with the consideration that *DI* nowhere speaks of a human person in Christ, means that we are obligated to view his Nestorian-sounding statements as primarily the result of imprecise uses of the notoriously ambiguous word *"homo."* For example, at 198:5-6 he speaks of *ipsa* (=*humana natura*) as elevated unto a union with Maximality.[120] A few lines later (199:2-3) he talks about the impossibility of more than *unus verus homo* ascending to union with Maximality. But for him to say that only one true *homo* ascends to union with Maximality sounds as if he meant that a human being—consisting of both a nature and a person—was united with the divine person, i.e., with the Word of God. But though *homo* qua united with God is *a man*, it is not the case that the *homo* which ascends to this union is *a man*. Rather, it is a human nature which Nicholas already thinks of as a man because he believes that the human nature and the Word of God were united beyond all time.[121] Indeed, he employs the verb "ascends" to indicate an ontological rather than a temporal difference.[122] The true man Christ Jesus is "ever" one with the Son of God, for the Son of God was nontemporally united with the human nature He assumed. Nicholas would agree with Augustine's statement in *Enchiridion* 35.10 to the effect that Jesus is God without beginning, man with a beginning. But he would insist that the beginning of Jesus as a

man is not a temporal beginning, even though His historical birth was subject to time.

So we see that although in many respects Nicholas's Christology is quite different from Anselm's, it resembles Anselm's in at least the following way: both Christologies teach that in the incarnation God the Son assumed a human nature into a unity of person with the divine nature. That is, they do not teach that He assumed a man (i.e., an individual human being consisting of a nature and a person) or that He became Man (by assuming unindividuated human nature, human nature as such); instead, they maintain that He became *a man* by assuming *a human nature*. Of course, Nicholas goes on to develop the idea that the humanity of Jesus is the contracted maximum individual (indeed, is the maximum creature) and that therefore Jesus is the fullness of perfection of the human species (indeed, is—qua maximum humanity, which is an intermediate nature—the enfolding of all creatable things). But this further development takes nothing away from his view that humanity exists contractedly and in individual men[123] and that in these different men it is differently individuated.[124] Even the *maximum* human nature is individuated—so that Jesus was a man distinct from every other man, for other men do not have a maximum nature. Because Jesus's human nature was maximal, its perfection transcends all comparative relation with the degrees of perfection of other human natures.[125]

So when Nicholas says that Jesus is God and man or that He is God and creature, he means that He is a man, or a creature, who is also God.

3. Jesus is said to be the perfection of all things[126] and the universal contracted being of each creature,[127] as well as "the means, form, essence, and truth of all the things which are possible in the species."[128] These and other such statements led Wenck to denounce *DI* as heretical—as negating the doctrine of the individuality of Christ's humanity and as teaching that "Christ was not an individual man but was universal man," "that the being of Christ is the being of each man."[129] In the *Apologia* Nicholas does not deign to respond to these particular charges, regarding them as too obviously distorted. Thereby he signals to us that however the foregoing statements from *DI* are to be interpreted, they are not to be construed radically and heretically, à la Wenck. Indeed, Nicholas specified in what sense Jesus is the universal contracted being of each creature: viz., in the double sense that (1) His humanity, which is both a *natura maxima* and a *natura media*, "enfolds within itself all natures"[130] and that (2) through His humanity, as united to His deity, all things receive "the beginning and the end of their contraction."[131]

Although, for Nicholas, then, Jesus is the maximum human being, He is nonetheless the maximum *individual*, with an *individuated* maximum human nature. He is the *universal* contraction of all things not because His humanity is unindividuated but because it enfolds all things. And His humanity is the *essence* of all the things which are possible in the species not because it is numerically identical with the respective human nature of other men (for, as was said, they do not have a maximum nature) but because it is, actually, whatever can exist within the species, just as the Absolute Maximum, which is the Essence of all things, is, actually, whatever can at all exist.

4. Someone might now ask: 'If, as is taught in Book Two, everything is present in everything else (*quodlibet in quolibet*), then why could God not have united Himself to anything whatsoever, e.g., to a nonrational animal or to an angel? For in so doing He also would have united all things to Himself.' Anselm of Canterbury, in his *Cur Deus Homo*, had reasoned that the divine program of human redemption required that someone of the same race (viz., the human race) make satisfaction for the sin and debt of Adam: "For just as it is right that human nature make satisfaction for human nature's guilt, so it is necessary that the one who makes satisfaction be either the sinner himself or someone of his race. Otherwise, neither Adam nor his race would make satisfaction for themselves."[132] Judging from the sermon *"Hoc Facite,"*[133] we may infer that Nicholas would have accepted Anselm's line of argument. Nonetheless, in *DI* he reasons differently, not appealing to the doctrine of atonement in order to fix his doctrine of incarnation. Instead, he bases his argument on the metaphysic of contraction, and he appeals to the illustration of the maximum line to help render plausible his position:

> If the nature of lower things is considered and if one of these lower beings were elevated unto [Absolute] Maximality, such a being would be both God and itself. An example is furnished with regard to a maximum line. Since the maximum line would be infinite through Absolute Infinity and maximal through [Absolute] Maximality (to which, necessarily, it is united if it is maximal): through [Absolute] Maximality it would be God; and through contraction it would remain a line. And so, it would be actually everything which a line can become. But a line does not include [the possibility of] life or intellect. Therefore, if the line would not attain to the fullness of [all] natures, how could it be elevated to the maximum gradation? For it would be a maximum which could be greater and which would lack [some] perfections (III, 3).

Just as lower natures lack some of the perfections of higher natures, so higher natures lack some of the perfections of lower natures. Accordingly, God willed to elevate a *natura media*—which would in some respect contain the perfections of higher and of lower natures—into a maximum union with the Absolute Maximum.

We may put the foregoing point in a slightly different form: Although everything is present in everything else, not everything is *enfolded* in everything else, according to Nicholas's account; in this respect the doctrine of *quodlibet in quolibet* is different from the doctrine of enfolding. For if all perfections are enfolded in human nature, it makes sense to think of them as also unfolded from human nature. But from the supposed fact that each thing is in each other thing, it does not follow that from a given thing all things can emanate. Now, on Nicholas's Christology, Jesus—the maximum human nature, united with the Absolute Maximum—is the one from whom the whole of creation emanates. All things qua existing are from Him qua Word of God; and all things qua contracted are from Him qua universal contraction.[134]

So because God the Son unites a human nature to His own divine person,[135] He may be said to be—through and in the humanity—all things contractedly.[136] Yet, this statement must not obscure the fact that not the divine nature or the divine person, but only the human nature, is contracted.

5. A final network of problems surfaces regarding Nicholas's Christology: (a) a pedagogical problem, (b) a semantical problem, and (c) a theological problem.

a. In order better to explain how it is that Jesus's maximal human intellect exists in the divine intellect in such way that it is God, Nicholas offers a further illustration:

> Assume that a polygon inscribed in a circle were the human nature and the circle were the divine nature. Then if the polygon were to be a maximum polygon, than which there cannot be a greater polygon, it would exist not through itself with finite angles but in the circular shape. Thus, it would not have its own shape for existing—[i.e., it would not have a shape which was] even intellectually separable from the circular and eternal shape.[137]

Yet, far from proving clarificatory, this illustration engenders bafflement. According to I, 20 the only polygonal figure which can be infinite is the triangle. In an ingenious argument Nicholas there "proves" that whenever "x" stands for any polygonal shape other than triangular (e.g., when it stands for *quadrangular shaped*) the expression "to be maximum and to be x" implies a contradiction. So in the foregoing quotation from III, 4, the inscribed polygon is not understood to be maximal in the same sense of "maximum" as in I, 20; for if it were, the expression "maximum polygon" would either refer to a maximum triangle or else would imply a contradiction (or else Nicholas's point in I, 20 would not be consistent with his point above). But as used above, this expression neither indicates such a triangle nor implies anything contradictory. Instead, it indicates a finite polygon having infinitely many angles. And this is where the perplexity begins. For according to I, 3 an inscribed polygon of infinite angles would not be equal to the inscribing circle unless it were identical with the circle. (And, of course, in the case of an identity the polygon would no longer rightly be said to be *inscribed*.) Now, in the above quotation from III, 4 we are told that the inscribed maximum polygon would not retain its own shape but would have a shape inseparable from the circular shape—inseparable even for the intellect. This claim, together with the passage in I, 3, implies that the polygon of infinite angles would *be* the circle rather than merely being in the circle. For if it were merely in the circle its shape would, according to I, 3, only very closely approximate the circle's shape and some infinitesimal difference would always remain; and thus the two shapes would be both distinguishable and separable. So either Nicholas's point in the illustration is that the polygon would be the circle or else the illustration is inconsistent with I, 3. Assume the former alternative. Then, drawing the comparison with the two natures of Christ, we would have to say that Christ's maximum human nature is not merely in the divine nature but *is* the divine nature and is not even conceivably separable from it, i.e., is not distinct from it. But this consequence is inconsistent with his earlier point that though the human nature is subsumed in the divine nature, the two remain distinct because what is contracted does not become uncontracted and vice versa.[138] The upshot is, then, that though Nicholas wants to safeguard the distinction between the human and the divine natures in Christ, he can do so consistently only if he either abandons the foregoing illustration or else changes his mind about his position in I, 3. But the point made in the passage cited from I, 3 is so central to his program that he cannot afford to reverse it. He must therefore abandon the foregoing illustration.

b. If the illustration in II, 4 is misleading, then so also at times is Nicholas's very choice of words. For example, difficulties are created by the use of the word "coincide" in the following sentence from III, 7: "There is [with regard to Jesus] a sharing of the respective modes of speaking [about the human nature and the divine nature], so that the human things coincide with the divine things. . . ."[139] But "coincide" suggests, by its very nuances, that the human properties and the divine properties are indistinct and indistinguishable in Christ—just as when opposites coincide in God, rest is no longer distinct from motion, and so on. Yet, what Nicholas means by his doctrine of *communicatio idiomatum* is that the human nature and the divine nature are inseparably and hypostatically united and that the properties of the one nature may sometimes be spoken of as if they were also properties of the other nature. To express this idea clearly, he needs to choose a word other than the verb "coincide."

c. These first two difficulties—the pedagogical and the semantical ones—appear to be easily surmountable. And so, we are tempted to imagine that both of them could have, and would have, been dealt with satisfactorily had they been brought to Nicholas's attention. Yet, when they are recognized to be linked to the third difficulty—the theological one—they will not seem so readily surmountable, for this latter difficulty will appear to be much more devastating to the central enterprise of Book Three. Let us consider the following passage:

With respect to the fact that the humanity of Jesus is considered as contracted to the man Christ, it is likewise understood to be united also with His divinity. As united with the divinity, [the humanity] is fully absolute; [but] as it is considered to be that true man Christ, [the humanity] is contracted, so that Christ is a man through the humanity. And so, Jesus's humanity is a medium between what is purely absolute and what is purely contracted.[140]

Preliminarily, we may note that here and elsewhere the name "Jesus" is used interchangeably with the name "Christ" and that "humanity" is simply an alternative name for human nature. Another example of a simple interchange of expressions is the switch between saying, as above, that the humanity is united to the divinity and saying, as elsewhere,[141] that it is united to the divine person. (Since the divine nature is in the divine person, the humanity could not be united to the latter without also being united to the former.)[142] These interchanges are not objectionable as long as we recognize them as simply that. Indeed, the use of "divinity" instead of "divine person" is not the source of trouble in the troublesome sentence "As united with the divinity, [the humanity] is fully absolute. . . ." Only if the humanity were united to the divinity in such way as to be in some respect identical with it could it be in any respect fully absolute (*humanitas plurimum absoluta*). But what sense would it make to assert that the humanity is in one respect identical to the divinity and in another respect not identical to it? By comparison, how could the human properties rightly be affirmed both to coincide and not to coincide with the divine properties? Or how could a polygon with infinite angles be consistently alleged both to be and not to be the inscribing circle? The theological, the semantical, and the pedagogical assertions are inextricably interlinked, so that either some sense must be found in each of them or else all three must be rejected. Yet, it is not clear what this sense could be. We might suppose Nicholas to mean that because in God everything is God (a principle advanced in Book Two),[143] the human nature is, *in the divine nature*, the divine nature—though the human nature qua not in the divine nature is not the divine nature. But if this is what he means, then his argument will be the following:

(1) Jesus's humanity qua in the divinity is the uncontracted God.

(2) Jesus's humanity qua not in the divinity is a contracted creature.

So (3) Jesus's humanity is a medium between the uncontracted and the contracted.

And such an argument is strange by virtue of its first premise. For humanity qua in the divinity would no longer be humanity; and therefore the premise would not conduce to entailing the conclusion.

Let us recast the objection. A more traditional-sounding way for Nicholas to have put his point would have been for him to assert that Jesus is both absolute and contracted: with respect to His divine nature He is absolute; with respect to His human nature He is contracted. Nicholas agrees to this more traditional-sounding statement. For at the end of III, 2 he states that in the hypostatic union there is no confusion of the natures and that what is contracted does not pass over into what is absolute.[144] In III, 7 the word "unconfusedly" ("*absque confusione*'') is again used to describe how the two natures are united.[145] But in further theologizing, Nicholas goes beyond the theological conservatism of this point and asserts that Jesus's *humanity* is both contracted and uncontracted. If we ask how what is asserted would be possible, he answers that the humanity qua the human Jesus is contracted but that the humanity as united to the divinity is uncontracted. If we ask why humanity as united to the divinity is not still contracted humanity, he introduces in reply an example from our cognitive being: "Perceptual knowledge is a certain contracted knowledge because the senses attain only to particulars; intellectual knowledge is universal knowledge because in comparison with the perceptual it is free from contraction to the particular. . . . In the intellect the perceptual contractedness is somehow subsumed in the intellectual nature, which exists as a certain divine, separate, abstract being, while the perceptual remains temporal and corruptible in accordance with its own nature."[146] That is, as the perceptual is subsumed in the intellectual, so Jesus's humanity is subsumed in His divinity. Moreover, the essence of the humanity is the intellect,[147] and since Jesus's intellect is a maximum intellect, it "cannot at all exist without being intellect in such way that it is also God. . . ,"[148] as is illustrated by the example of a maximum polygon inscribed in a circle. But at this point Nicholas has gone too far; and it now becomes obvious how ad hoc his examples are. To exemplify the relationship between the human nature and the divine nature he introduces the example of the relationship between the perceptual and the intellectual. But when the example will not support his further point, about the intellect's being God, he simply supplements it by a further illustration. But the trouble with the further point is that both it and the accompanying illustration produce an incoherence. Although Nicholas sees that humanity qua the human Jesus cannot be uncontracted, he does not see that so-called humanity qua uncontracted (*humanitas plurimum absoluta*) could not in any respect be humanity. And hence his reasoning will not have shown that the humanity of Jesus is in different respects both contracted and uncontracted.

Nicholas's Christology depends in an essential way upon his taking the foregoing further step beyond theological conservatism. For, on his view, the humanity of Jesus can be maximum only if it exists in Absolute Maximality, i.e., in the divine nature. And, according to his metaphysic, whatever exists in the divine nature is the divine nature. Thus, Nicholas must conclude that Jesus's humanity is in some respect divinity. But, at the same time, his orthodoxy requires him to maintain that Jesus is fully human by virtue of His humanity. So he infers, though invalidly, that Jesus's humanity is a medium between what is purely absolute and what is purely contracted (in addition to being a medium between the higher and the lower orders of contracted natures). This doctrine allows him to preserve his orthodoxy by affirming that in Jesus the contracted nature does not pass over into identity with the uncontracted nature. But he preserves the orthodoxy at the expense of introducing an incoherence into his Christology. Moreover, he veers from the more traditional forms of orthodoxy in teaching that God the Son *assumed* a human nature by *subsuming* the human nature in the divine nature, thereby "maximizing" it.

Nicholas proceeds to explain that the birth of the maximum human being could not have been by natural means and that it was most appropriate that such a maximum individual be born of a virgin. He deems that Mary "ought rightfully to have been free of whatever could have hindered the purity or the vigor, and likewise the uniqueness, of such a most excellent birth."[149] But he does not develop any of these points. Similarly, in preference to elaborating a theory of atonement, he merely indicates the direction that such a theory might take:

> The maximality of human nature brings it about that in the case of each man who cleaves to Christ through formed faith Christ is this very man by means of a most perfect union—each's numerical distinctness being preserved. Because of this union the following statement of Christ is true: "Whatever you have done to one of the least of my [brethren], you have done to me." And, conversely, whatever Christ Jesus merited by His suffering, those who are one with Him also merited— different degrees of merit being preserved in accordance with the different degree of each [man's] union with Christ through faith formed by love.[150]

Scandalized by the statement that "Christ is this very man by means of a most perfect union," Wenck referred to Nicholas as a pseudo-apostle and a universalizer. To be sure, Nicholas's theological expressions do have an initially startling quality; and yet, a reflective reading discloses nothing intrinsically shocking about the foregoing statement. The believer is united to Christ by faith rather than by his membership in the human race. That he is "of the same humanity with Christ"[151] means that his humanity and Christ's are one in species, not that they are one in number. Accordingly, what Christ has merited He has merited not for each individual of the species but only for the faithful. And the sense in which Christ *is* each of the faithful is the very sense in which each of the faithful is united to Christ—as the branches are in the vine, as the members of the body are in the body.[152] Of course, Nicholas is here adopting the language of Scripture.[153] But in some contexts he metaphysicizes this language, construing it as more than metaphorical: each member of the body is, through the mediation of the body, in each other member. Yet, in other contexts he spiritualizes: in this life believers are united to Christ spiritually through faith and love; in the next life they shall be thus united through attainment and enjoyment.[154] Though all human beings shall arise through Christ, only believers shall arise "as Christ and in Christ through union."[155] Moreover, Nicholas unabashedly speaks of *absorption*: "As someone's flesh is progressively and gradually mortified by faith, he progressively ascends to oneness with Christ, so that he is absorbed into Christ by a deep union—to the extent that this is possible on [this pilgrim's] pathway.''[156] Of course, the clause ''he is absorbed into Christ'' is theologically explosive. And on the basis of such statements Wenck hastens to associate Nicholas with the much maligned Meister Eckhart.

Sometimes, at first glance, Nicholas seems to be deliberately provocative; for the inflaming word ''absorbed'' need not have been used. In last analysis, however, Wenck's judgment of condemnation reflects more adversely upon himself than upon Nicholas. For Wenck mistook the language of mysticism for the language of metaphysics. Such statements as ''We shall arise as Christ,'' ''We are absorbed into Christ,'' ''We exist in the flesh as a spirit for whom this world is death,'' ''We see in each believer Jesus,'' and ''The truth of our body exists in the truth of Christ's body'' are redolent with the spirit of mysticism. They pervade Book Three and set it in contrast to the pervasive use of mathematical language in Book One and to the pronouncedly metaphysical disquisitions of Book Two. In the program of learned ignorance the mathematical and the metaphysical are impulses motivating the mind in its ascent toward the mystical. On this pilgrim's pathway Nicholas desires to be engulfed by Christ—engulfed spiritually, not ontologically. If he wants to lose himself in Christ in this lifetime, it is not in order to lose his individual identity but in order to transcend the intellectual, moral, and emotional constrictions which are the consequences of sin.

In accordance with the mystical themes of Book Three Nicholas emphasizes the need for faith:

> Since God is not knowable in this world (where by reason and by opinion or by doctrine we are led, with symbols, through the more known to the unknown), He is apprehended only where persuasive considerations cease and faith appears. Through faith we are caught up, in simplicity, so that being in a body incorporeally (because in spirit) and in the world not mundanely but celestially we may incomprehensibly contemplate Christ above all reason and intelligence, in the third heaven of most simple intellectuality. Thus, we see even the following: viz., that because of the immensity of His excellence God cannot be comprehended. And this is that learned ignorance through which most blessed Paul, in ascending, saw that when he was being elevated more highly to Christ, he did not know Christ, though at one time he had known only Christ.[157]

Nicholas believes that the *visio dei* is given by grace to some believers even during their earthly lifetime; but it is a vision of God as He is manifested in the glorified Christ. As Moses of old was unable to gaze upon the resplendent countenance of God and live,[158] so in the mystical ascent the believer will behold the divine glory only through the shielding cloud that renders forever inaccessible God's inmost abode. This beholding may well be fuller, more joyous, and more ecstatic than was Moses's; but it will nonetheless remain a veiled viewing of God by means of the glorified Christ and through a more rarefied beveiling cloud.[159] It will not be a knowing; for what is beheld with "the intellectual eye"[160] will be too boundlessly immense to become an object of knowledge.

The *intellectual* eye, to be sure, is the eye of the *intellect*. In Book Three Nicholas distinguishes the intellect (*intellectus*) from reason (*ratio*), as he had not explicitly done in Books One and Two. The intellect is higher than reason and "is not temporal and mundane but is free of time and of the world."[161] In the *Apologia, ratio* is said to be the domain of discursive reasoning, *intellectus* the domain of mental seeing.[162] Only the intellect attains unto the coincidence of opposites—a coincidence which, because it cannot be conceived, is not within the reach of reason. Though in the *Apologia* Nicholas speaks of the *evidence* that comes from seeing, he does not mean evidence in any sense that requires (1) a weighing of data in support of premises or (2) an inference from premises to a conclusion. The eye of the intellect is that power by which the mind intuitively apprehends that which it is unable to conceptualize and is therefore unable to know. And thus even in the future *visio dei*, on the part of all resurrected believers, God will be seen only insofar as He is present in the glorified Christ, who is God and man; the God of gods in Zion, who dwelleth in light inaccessible, will remain eternally unintuited. Therefore, learned ignorance is as much an abiding condition as a speculative method. As a method it is associated with the *via negativa* and involves the recognition that God cannot be *known* as He is, that our symbolic representations of His nature must fall infinitely short of the reality itself. As an abiding condition it is associated with the believer's perpetual hungering after God, so that Nicholas can boldly proclaim the blessedness of God, "who has given us an intellect which cannot be filled in the course of time."[163] In the resurrected state the believer's intellect will be, paradoxically, both filled with truth and desirous of more truth; for each truth learned will, while it satisfies, whet the intellectual desire. Though never apprehending all truths, the believer will apprehend Him who is all truth. Until the coming of this resurrection day the believer's understanding is to be guided by faith; for "where there is no sound faith, there is no true understanding."[164]

DI began with a discussion of the Absolute Maximum, which was shown to be Absolute Oneness. From out of Oneness there arose a oneness in plurality, viz., the created universe, which was discussed in Book Two. Book Three then took as its theme the return of the creation to God through Christ. But in its return the creation is not *reenfolded* in God, is not merged with Absolute Oneness, for each finite thing retains its individuality; rather, the creation is *reunited* to God. The closing chapter of this last book distinguishes between three unions: the Absolute Union, the hypostatic union, and the ecclesiastical union. The first of these is Absolute Oneness; the second is the union, in Jesus, of the two natures in one person; the third is the union of the blessed with the deity of Christ. Since each of the three unions is a maximum union, than which there can be no greater union, they all coincide and are one Maximum Union—one Union of all unions. (As used here the word "coincide" does not preclude the distinctness either of the unions or of the things united.) Moreover, the ecclesiastical union includes both redeemed human beings and unfallen angels—all of whom, having their own identities preserved, exist "in Christ Jesus as Christ and—through Christ—in God as God."[165] Since unfallen angels have never turned from God, they cannot, strictly speaking, return to God. Nicholas views them as united—not reunited—to God through Christ, whose humanity is a union of the higher and the lower orders of created being. The human beings who do not belong to the ecclesiastical union, i.e., to the church of the triumphant, are returned to God through sharing in Christ's resurrection and immortality. But though they shall arise through the power of Christ, they shall not arise "as Christ and in Christ through union."[166] And though they are returned to God, they are returned for the judgment of condemnation and for banishment from the presence of Him whose love they have freely spurned.

A balanced interpretation of the thought of the man from Cusa must take account of both its original and its traditional aspects. The Aristotelian–Thomistic terminology is not mere window dressing, any more than is the language of Absolute Maximality, Absolute Quiddity, Absolute Possibility. Even the various *modi loquendi* are not mere matters of adornment but are integral parts of the profound program of learned ignorance. This program does *not* teach that we know *only* that we do not know; indeed, we have just finished considering many of the truths that *DI* purports to disclose. Rather, the program of learned ignorance attempts to show the limitations of human knowledge by exhibiting the cognitive limits for various domains. In attempting to demarcate the bounds of knowledge—to draw the line between what can and what cannot be humanly known—Nicholas is not thoroughgoing enough to be called a precursor of Kant.[167] But by generalizing the notion of learned ignorance into the formula "the seeing that precision cannot be seen," he leans in the direction of modernity.

In the Prologue to Book One Nicholas ritualistically displays humility by referring to his work—being presented to the Italian Cardinal Cesarini—as his "foreigner's foolishness." Wenck was quick to stigmatize it as ignorance. Yet, whatever may be its shortcomings, it is not *foolish* ignorance but *learn-ed* ignorance. And whoever scrutinizes it more carefully than did Wenck will feel obliged to pay tribute to it as a landmark in fifteenth-century theorizing.

ON LEARNED IGNORANCE

(*De Docta Ignorantia*)

by

Nicholas of Cusa

CHAPTER TITLES FOR BOOK I

1. How it is that knowing is not-knowing.
2. Preliminary clarification of what will follow.
3. The precise truth is incomprehensible.
4. The Absolute Maximum,with which the Minimum coincides, is understood incomprehensibly.
5. The Maximum is one.
6. The Maximum is Absolute Necessity.
7. The trine and one Eternity.
8. Eternal generation.
9. The eternal procession of union.
10. An understanding of trinity in oneness transcends all things.
11. Mathematics assists us very greatly in apprehending various divine [truths].
12. The way in which mathematical signs ought to be used in our undertaking.
13. The characteristics of a maximum, infinite line.
14. An infinite line is a triangle.
15. The maximum triangle is a circle and a sphere.
16. In a symbolic way the Maximum is to all things as a maximum line is to [all] lines.
17. Very deep doctrines from the same [symbolism of an infinite line].
18. From the same [symbolism] we are led to an understanding of the participation in being.
19. The likening of an infinite triangle to maximum trinity.
20. Still more regarding the Trinity. There cannot be fourness, [fiveness], etc., in God.
21. The likening of an infinite circle to oneness.
22. How God's foresight unites contradictories.
23. The likening of an infinite sphere to the actual existence of God.
24. The name of God; affirmative theology.
25. The pagans named God in various ways in relation to created things.
26. Negative theology.

CHAPTER TITLES FOR BOOK II

1. Corollaries preliminary to inferring one infinite universe.
2. Created being derives from the being of the First in a way that is not understandable.
3. In a way that cannot be understood the Maximum enfolds and unfolds all things.
4. The universe, which is only a contracted maximum, is a likeness of the Absolute [Maximum].
5. Each thing in each thing.
6. The enfolding, and the degrees of contraction, of the universe.
7. The trinity of the universe.
8. The possibility, or matter, of the universe.
9. The soul, or form, of the universe.
10. The spirit of all things.
11. Corollaries regarding motion.
12. The conditions of the earth.
13. The admirable divine art in the creation of the world and of the elements.

CHAPTER TITLES FOR BOOK III

1. The maximum which is contracted to this or that, and than which there cannot be a greater, cannot exist without the Absolute [Maximum].
2. The maximum contracted [to a species] is also the Absolute [Maximum; it is both] Creator and creature.
3. Only in the case of the nature of humanity can there be such a maximum [individual].
4. Blessed Jesus, who is God and man, is the [contracted maximum individual].
5. Christ, conceived through the Holy Spirit, was born of the Virgin Mary.
6. The mystery of the death of Jesus Christ.
7. The mystery of the Resurrection.
8. Christ, the Firstfruits of those who sleep, ascended to Heaven.
9. Christ is judge of the living and the dead.
10. The Judge's sentence.
11. The mysteries of faith.
12. The church.

BOOK I

Prologue

[Nicholas of Cusa] to his own venerable teacher, the divinely beloved and most
reverend father, Lord Julian,[1] most worthy cardinal of the holy Apostolic See.

Your very great and indeed very proven Genius will rightly wonder what to
make of the following fact: viz., that when, quite imprudently, I endeavor to
publish my foreigner's-foolishness, I select you as a judge. [You will wonder
about my treating you] as if you retained some leisure (you, who by virtue of
your cardinal's duties at the Holy See are extremely busy with especially
important public affairs) and as if, given your most thorough knowledge of all
the Latin writers who have hitherto become illustrious (and [your] recent
[knowledge] of the Greek writers as well), you could be drawn by the novelty of
its title to this presumably very foolish production of mine—I, whose quality of
intellect is already very well known to you. This wondering shall, I hope,
induce your knowledge-hungry mind to take a look. [You will wonder] not
because you think that something prevously unknown might be presented here;
rather, [you will marvel] at the boldness by which I was led to deal with learned
ignorance. For the naturalists state that a certain unpleasant sensation in the
opening of the stomach precedes the appetite in order that, having been
stimulated in this way, the nature (which endeavors to preserve itself) will
replenish itself. By comparison, I consider *wondering* (on whose account there
is philosophizing)[2] to precede the desire-for-knowing in order that the intellect
(whose understanding is its being) will perfect itself by the study of truth.[3]
Unusual things, even if they be monstrous, are accustomed to move us. For this
reason, O unparalleled Teacher, deem, according to your kindness, that something worthwhile lies hidden herein; and in regard to divine matters receive
from a German a mode of reasoning such as the following—a mode which great
labor has rendered very pleasing to me.

Chapter One: How it is that knowing is not-knowing.

We see that by the gift of God there is present in all things a natural desire to
exist in the best[4] manner in which the condition of each thing's nature permits

this. And [we see that all things] act toward this end and have instruments adapted thereto. They have an innate sense of judgment which serves the purpose of knowing. [They have this] in order that their desire not be in vain but be able to attain rest in that [respective] object which is desired by the propensity of each thing's own nature. But if perchance affairs turn out otherwise, this [outcome] must happen by accident—as when sickness misleads taste or an opinion misleads reason. Wherefore, we say that a sound, free intellect knows to be true that which it insatiably desires to attain (while it surveys all things by means of its innate faculty of inference), that which is apprehended by its affectionate embrace. That from which no sound mind can withhold assent is, we have no doubt, most true. However, all those who make an investigation judge the uncertain proportionally, by means of a comparison with what is taken to be certain.[5] Therefore, every inquiry is comparative and uses the means of comparative relation.[6] Now, when the things investigated are able to be compared by means of a close proportional tracing back to what is taken to be [certain], our judgment apprehends easily; but when we need many intermediate steps, difficulty arises and hard work is required. These points are recognized in mathematics, where the earlier propositions are quite easily traced back to the first and most evident principles but where later propositions [are traced back] with more difficulty because [they are traced back] only through the mediation of the earlier ones.

3   Therefore, every inquiry proceeds by means of a comparative relation, whether an easy or a difficult one. Hence, the infinite, qua infinite, is unknown; for it escapes all comparative relation.[7] But since *comparative relation* indicates an agreement in some one respect and, at the same time, indicates an otherness, it cannot be understood independently of number. Accordingly, number encompasses all things related comparatively. Therefore, number, which is a necessary condition of comparative relation, is present not only in quantity but also in all things which in any manner whatsoever can agree or differ either substantially or accidentally. Perhaps for this reason Pythagoras deemed all things to be constituted and understood through the power of numbers.

4   Both the precise combinations in corporeal things and the congruent relating of known to unknown surpass human reason—to such an extent that Socrates seemed to himself to know nothing except that he did not know. And the very wise Solomon maintained that all things are difficult and unexplainable in words.[8] And a certain other man of divine spirit says that wisdom and the seat of understanding are hidden from the eyes of all the living.[9] Even the very profound Aristotle, in his *First Philosophy*, asserts that in things most obvious by nature such difficulty occurs for us as for a night owl which is trying to look at the sun.[10] Therefore, if the foregoing points are true, then since the desire in us is not in vain, assuredly we desire to know that we do not know. If we can

fully attain unto this [knowledge of our ignorance], we will attain unto learned ignorance. For a man—even one very well versed in learning—will attain unto nothing more perfect than to be found to be most learned in the ignorance which is distinctively his. The more he knows that he is unknowing, the more learned he will be. Unto this end I have undertaken the task of writing a few things about learned ignorance.

5   *Chapter Two*:   Preliminary clarification of what will follow.

Since I am going to discuss the maximum learning of ignorance, I must deal with the nature of Maximality.[11] Now, I give the name "Maximum" to that than which there cannot be anything greater. But fulness befits what is one. Thus, oneness—which is also being—coincides with Maximality. But if such oneness is altogether free from all relation and contraction, obviously nothing is opposed to it, since it is Absolute Maximality. Thus, the Maximum is the Absolute One which is all things. And all things are in the Maximum (for it is the Maximum); and since nothing is opposed to it, the Minimum likewise coincides with it, and hence the Maximum is also in all things. And because it is absolute, it is, actually, every possible being; it contracts nothing from things, all of which [derive] from it. In the first book I shall strive to investigate— incomprehensibly above human reason—this Maximum, which the faith of all nations indubitably believes to be God. [I shall investigate] with the guidance of Him "who alone dwells in inaccessible light."[12]

6   Secondly, just as Absolute Maximality is Absolute Being, through which all things are that which they are, so from Absolute Being there exists a universal oneness of being which is spoken of as "a maximum deriving from the Absolute [Maximum]"—existing from it contractedly and as a universe. This maximum's oneness is contracted in plurality, and it cannot exist without plurality. Indeed, in its universal oneness this maximum encompasses all things, so that all the things which derive from the Absolute [Maximum] are in this maximum and this maximum is in all [these] things. Nevertheless, it does not exist independently of the plurality in which it is present, for it does not exist without contraction, from which it cannot be freed. In the second book I will add a few points about this maximum, viz., the universe.

7   Thirdly, a maximum of a third sort will thereafter be exhibited. For since the universe exists-in-plurality only contractedly, we shall seek among the many things the one maximum in which the universe actually exists most greatly and most perfectly as in its goal. Now, such [a maximum] is united with the Absolute [Maximum], which is the universal end; [it is united] because it is a most perfect goal, which surpasses our every capability. Hence, I shall add some points about this maximum, which is both contracted and absolute and

which we name *Jesus*, blessed forever. [I shall add these points] according as Jesus Himself will provide inspiration.

8 However, someone who desires to grasp the meaning must elevate his intellect above the import of the words rather than insisting upon the proper significations of words which cannot be properly adapted to such great intellectual mysteries. Moreover, it is necessary to use guiding illustrations in a transcendent way and to leave behind perceptible things, so that the reader may readily ascend unto simple intellectuality. I have endeavored, for the purpose of investigating this pathway, to explain [matters] to those of ordinary intelligence as clearly as I could. Avoiding all roughness of style,[13] I show at the outset that learned ignorance has its basis in the fact that the precise truth is inapprehensible.[14]

9 *Chapter Three*: The precise truth is incomprehensible.[15]

It is self-evident that there is no comparative relation of the infinite to the finite.[16] Therefore, it is most clear that where we find comparative degrees of greatness, we do not arrive at the unqualifiedly Maximum; for things which are comparatively greater and lesser are finite; but, necessarily, such a Maximum is infinite. Therefore, if anything is posited which is not the unqualifiedly Maximum, it is evident that something greater can be posited. And since we find degrees of equality (so that one thing is more equal to a second thing than to a third, in accordance with generic, specific, spatial, causal, and temporal agreement and difference among similar things), obviously we cannot find two or more things which are so similar and equal that they could not be progressively more similar *ad infinitum*.[17] Hence, the measure and the measured—however equal they are—will always remain different.[18]

10 Therefore, it is not the case that by means of likenesses a finite intellect can precisely attain the truth about things. For truth is not something more or something less but is something indivisible. Whatever is not truth cannot measure truth precisely. (By comparison, a noncircle [cannot measure] a circle, whose being is something indivisible.) Hence, the intellect, which is not truth, never comprehends truth so precisely that truth cannot be comprehended infinitely more precisely. For the intellect is to truth as [an inscribed] polygon is to [the inscribing] circle.[19] The more angles the inscribed polygon has the more similar it is to the circle. However, even if the number of its angles is increased *ad infinitum*, the polygon never becomes equal [to the circle] unless it is resolved into an identity with the circle. Hence, regarding truth, it is evident that we do not know anything other than the following: viz., that we know truth not to be precisely comprehensible as it is. For truth may be likened unto the most absolute necessity (which cannot be either something more or something less

than it is), and our intellect may be likened unto possibility. Therefore, the quiddity of things,[20] which is the truth of beings, is unattainable in its purity; though it is sought by all philosophers, it is found by no one as it is. And the more deeply we are instructed in this ignorance, the closer we approach to truth.

11   *Chapter Four*:   The Absolute Maximum, with which the Minimum coincides, is understood incomprehensibly.

Since the unqualifiedly and absolutely Maximum (than which there cannot be a greater) is greater than we can comprehend (because it is Infinite Truth), we attain unto it in no other way than incomprehensibly. For since it is not of the nature of those things which can be comparatively greater and lesser, it is beyond all that we can conceive. For whatsoever things are apprehended by the senses, by reason, or by intellect differ both within themselves and in relation to one another—[differ] in such way that there is no precise equality among them. Therefore, Maximum Equality, which is neither other than[21] nor different from anything, surpasses all understanding. Hence, since the absolutely Maximum *is* all that which can be,[22] it is *altogether* actual. And just as there cannot be a greater, so for the same reason there cannot be a lesser, since it is all that which can be. But the Minimum is that than which there cannot be a lesser. And since the Maximum is also such, it is evident that the Minimum coincides with the Maximum. The foregoing [point] will become clearer to you if you contract maximum and minimum to quantity. For maximum quantity is maximally large; and minimum quantity is maximally small. Therefore, if you free *maximum* and *minimum* from *quantity*—by mentally removing *large* and *small* —you will see clearly that maximum and minimum coincide.[23] For *maximum* is a superlative just as *minimum* is a superlative. Therefore, it is not the case that absolute quantity is maximum quantity rather than minimum quantity; for in it the minimum is the maximum coincidingly.

12   Therefore, opposing features belong only to those things which can be comparatively greater and lesser; they befit these things in different ways; [but they do] not at all [befit] the absolutely Maximum, since it is beyond all opposition. Therefore, because the absolutely Maximum is absolutely and actually all things which can be (and is so free of all opposition that the Minimum coincides with it), it is beyond both all affirmation and all negation. And it is not, as well as is, all that which is conceived to be; and it is, as well as is not, all that which is conceived not to be. But it is a given thing in such way that it is all things; and it is all things in such way that it is no thing; and it is maximally a given thing in such way that it is it minimally. For example, to say "God, who is Absolute Maximality, is light" is [to say] no other than "God is

maximally light in such way that He is minimally light.'' For Absolute Maximality could not be actually all possible things unless it were infinite and were the boundary of all things and were unable to be bounded by any of these things—as, by the graciousness of God, I will explain in subsequent sections. However, the [absolutely Maximum] transcends all our understanding. For our intellect cannot, by means of reasoning,[24] combine contradictories in their Beginning, since we proceed by means of what nature makes evident to us. Our reason falls far short of this infinite power and is unable to connect contradictories, which are infinitely distant. Therefore, we see incomprehensibly, beyond all rational inference, that Absolute Maximality (to which nothing is opposed and with which the Minimum coincides) is infinite. But "maximum" and "minimum," as used in this [first] book, are transcendent terms of absolute signification, so that in their absolute simplicity they encompass—beyond all contraction to quantity of mass or quantity of power—all things.

13   *Chapter Five*:   The Maximum is one.

From these [considerations] it is most clearly evident that the absolutely Maximum is both incomprehensibly understandable and unnameably nameable. (I will later present a fuller version of this doctrine.)[25]Anything than which a greater or a lesser cannot be posited cannot be named. For by the movement of our reason names are assigned to things which, in terms of comparative relation, can be comparatively greater or lesser. And since all things exist in the best way they are able to exist, there cannot be a plurality of beings independently of number. For if number is removed, the distinctness, order, comparative relation, and harmony of things cease; and the very plurality of beings ceases. But if number itself were infinite—in which case it would be actually maximal and the minimum would coincide with it—all of these would likewise cease, since to be infinite number and to be minimally number [i.e., not at all to be number] amount to the same thing. Therefore, if in ascending the scale of numbers we actually arrive at a maximum number, since number is finite, still we do not come to a maximum number than which there can be no greater number; for such a number would be infinite. Therefore, it is evident that the ascending number-scale is actually finite,[26] and that the [arrived at maximum number] would be in potentiality relative to another [greater] number. But if on the descending scale a similar thing held true of number, so that for any actually posited small number a smaller number were always positable by subtraction just as on the ascending scale a larger number [is always positable] by addition, [then the outcome] would still be the same [as in the case where number were infinite]. For there would be no distinction of things; nor would any order or any plurality or any degrees of comparatively greater and lesser be found among numbers; indeed there would not be number.[27] Therefore, in numbering, it is neccessary to come to a minimum than which there cannot be a lesser, viz., oneness. And since there cannot be anything lesser than oneness,[28] oneness will be an unqualifiedly minimum, which, by virtue of the considerations just presented, coincides with the maximum.

14   However, oneness cannot be number; for number, which can be comparatively greater, cannot at all be either an unqualifiedly minimum or an unqualifiedly maximum. Rather, oneness is the beginning of all number,[29] because it is the minimum; and it is the end of all number, because it is the maximum. Therefore, [by comparison] Absolute Oneness, to which nothing is opposed, is Absolute Maximality, which is the Blessed God. Since this Oneness is maximal, it cannot be multiple (for it is all that which can be). Therefore, it cannot become number.

See that by means of number we have been led to understanding (1) that "Absolute Oneness" quite closely befits the unnameable God and (2) that God is so one that He is, actually, everything which is·possible. Accordingly, Absolute Oneness cannot be comparatively greater or lesser; nor can it be multiple. Thus, Deity is Infinite Oneness. Therefore, he who said "Hear, O Israel, your God is one"[30] and "Your Father and Teacher in Heaven is one"[31] could not have spoken more truly. And whoever would say that there are many gods would deny, most falsely, the existence not only of God but also of all the things of the universe—as will be shown in what follows. For the pluralities of things, which descend from Infinite Oneness, are related to Infinite Oneness [in such way] that they cannot exist independently of it (just as number, which is an entity-of-reason produced by our [power of] relational discrimination, necessarily presupposes oneness as such a beginning of number that without this beginning there could not possibly be number). For how could they exist independently of being? Absolute Oneness is being, as we shall see later.[32]

15   *Chapter Six*:   The Maximum is Absolute Necessity.

In the preceding[33] I indicated that everything except the one unqualifiedly Maximum is—in contrast to it—limited and bounded. Now, what is finite and bounded has a beginning point and an end point. And we cannot make the following claim: viz., that "one given finite thing is greater than another given finite thing, [the series of finite things] always proceeding in this way unto infinity." (For there cannot actually be an infinite progression of things which are comparatively greater and lesser, since in that case the Maximum would be of the nature of finite things). Accordingly, it follows that the actually Maximum is the Beginning and the End of all finite things. Moreover, nothing could exist if the unqualifiedly Maximum did not exist. For since everything non-maximal is finite, it is also originated. But, necessarily, it will exist from another. Otherwise—i.e., if it existed from itself—it would have existed when it did not exist. Now, as is obviously the rule, it is not possible to proceed to infinity in beginnings and causes. So it will be the case that the unqualifiedly Maximum exists, without which nothing can exist.

16   Furthermore, let us contract maximum to being,[34] and let us say: it is not the case that anything is opposed to maximum being; hence, neither not-being nor minimally being [are opposed to it]. How, then—since minimally being is maximally being—could we rightly think that the Maximum is able not to exist?[35] Moreover, we cannot rightly think that something exists in the absence of being. But Absolute Being cannot be other than the absolutely Maximum. Hence, we cannot rightly think that something exists in the absence of the [absolutely] Maximum.

Moreover, the greatest truth is the absolutely Maximum. Therefore, either (1) it is most greatly true that the unqualifiedly Maximum either exists or does not exist, or (2) [it is most greatly true that it] both exists and does not exist, or (3) [it is most greatly true that it] neither exists nor does not exist. Now, no more [alternatives] can be either asserted or thought. No matter which one of them you say to be most greatly true, my point is made. For I have the greatest truth, which is the unqualifiedly Maximum.

17   Wherefore, although it is evident through the aforesaid that the name "being" (or any other name) is not a precise name for the Maximum (which is beyond every name),[36] nevertheless it is necessary that being befit it maximally (but in a way not nameable by the name "maximum") and above all nameable being.

By such considerations, as well as by an infinity of similar ones, learned ignorance sees most clearly from the aforesaid that the unqualifiedly Maximum exists necessarily, so that it is Absolute Necessity. But I indicated[37] that the unqualifiedly Maximum cannot exist except as one. Therefore, it is most true that the Maximum exists as one.

18   *Chapter Seven*:   The trine and one Eternity.

There has never been a nation which did not worship God and did not believe Him to be the absolutely Maximum. We find that Marcus Varro, in his book *Antiquities* noted that the Sissennii worshipped Oneness as the Maximum. [38] But Pythagoras, a very famous man of undeniable authority in his own time, added that this Oneness is trine.[39] As we investigate the truth about this [matter] and elevate our intellects more highly, let us assert (in accordance with the aforesaid): No one doubts that that which precedes all otherness is eternal. For otherness is identical with mutability. Now, everything which naturally precedes mutability is immutable and, hence, eternal. But otherness consists of one thing and another. Hence, otherness is subsequent to oneness, just as is number. Therefore, oneness is by nature prior to otherness; and since oneness naturally precedes otherness, it is eternal.

19   Moreover, every inequality is composed of an equal and a greater. Therefore, inequality is by nature subsequent to equality—something which can be proven very cogently by means of analysis. For every inequality is analyzable into an equality. For the equal is between the greater and the lesser. So if you remove that [portion] which is greater, there will be an equal. But if there is a lesser, remove from the other that [portion] which is greater, and an equal will result. And you can continue to do this until, in the process of removing, you come to things simple.[40] Clearly, then, every inequality is, by removing, analyzable into an equality. Therefore, equality naturally precedes inequality.

But inequality and otherness are by nature concomitant. For wherever there is inequality there is, necessarily, otherness—and conversely. For between two things there will at least be otherness;[41] now, the fact that they are two will mean that one of them is a duplicate;[42] therefore, there will be inequality. Hence, otherness and inequality will, by nature, be concomitant—especially since the number two is the first otherness and the first inequality. Now, I have already proved that by nature equality precedes inequality. Hence, [it] also [precedes] otherness. Therefore, equality is eternal.

20   Moreover, if there are two causes one of which is by nature prior to the other, the effect of the prior [cause] will be by nature prior to [the effect] of the subsequent [cause]. Now, oneness (*unitas*) is both union[43] and a cause of union; for the reason things are said to be in union is that they are united (*unita*) together.[44] Likewise, the number two is both separation and a cause of separation; for two is the first separation. Therefore, if oneness is a cause of union and if the number two is [a cause] of separation, then just as oneness is by nature prior to two, so union is by nature prior to separation. But separation and otherness are by nature concomitant. Hence, union is eternal (just as is oneness), since it is prior to otherness.

21   Thus, I have proved that oneness is eternal, equality eternal, and union also eternal. But there cannot be more than one eternal thing. For if there were more than one eternal thing, then since oneness precedes all plurality, something [viz., oneness] would by nature be prior to eternity—an impossibility. Furthermore, if there were more than one eternal thing, the one eternal thing would lack the other eternal things; and so, none of them would be perfect. Thus, something would be eternal which would not be eternal, because it would not be perfect. Since this is not possible, there cannot be more than one eternal thing. But since oneness is eternal, equality eternal, and union also eternal: oneness, equality, and union are one.[45] And this is that trine Oneness which

Pythagoras, the first philosopher of all and the glory of Italy and of Greece, affirmed to be worthy of worship.

But let me add, still more explicitly, some further points about the generation of equality from oneness.

22   *Chapter Eight*:   Eternal generation.

Let me now show very briefly that equality of oneness is begotten from oneness but that union proceeds from oneness and from equality of oneness. *"Unitas"* (or *"ὤντας,"* so to speak) is derived from the Greek word *"ὤν,"* which is rendered in Latin as *"ens"*; and *unitas* [oneness] is *entitas* [being], as it were. For, indeed, God is the being of things; for He is the Form of being[46] and, hence, is also being. Now, equality of oneness is equality of being, as it were (i.e., equality of existing (*essendi sive exsistendi*)). But equality of existing [i.e., of being] is that which is present in a thing neither too much nor too little, neither excessively nor deficiently. For if it were present too much in a thing, [that thing] would be something monstrous; and if it were present too little, [that thing] would not even exist.

23   When we pay attention to what generation is, we view clearly the generation of equality from oneness. For generation is the repetition of oneness or the multiplication of the same nature as it proceeds from a father to a son. This latter generation is found only in transient things. However, the generation of oneness from oneness is one repetition of oneness—i.e., is oneness once [i.e., oneness times one]. But if I multiply oneness two times or three times, and so on, oneness will beget from itself another—e.g., the number two or the number three or some other number. But oneness once repeated [i.e., oneness times one] begets only equality of oneness; this [repeating] can only be understood as oneness begetting oneness. And this generation is eternal.

24   *Chapter Nine*:   The eternal procession of union.

Just as generation of oneness from oneness is one repetition of oneness, so the procession from both is oneness of the repetition of this oneness—or (if you prefer the expression) is oneness of oneness and of the equality of this oneness. However, "procession" signifies an "extension," as it were, from one thing to another—just as in the case where two things are equal,[47] a certain equality (which conjoins and unites them in a certain way) is extended, as it were, from the one to the other. Therefore, union is rightly said to proceed from oneness and from equality of oneness. For union is not merely of one [of these]; rather it proceeds from oneness to equality of oneness[48] and from equality of oneness to oneness. Therefore [union] is rightly said to proceed from both, since it is extended, as it were, from the one to the other.

25   But we do not say that union is *begotten* from oneness or from equality of oneness, since union is not from oneness either through repetition or through multiplication. And although equality of oneness is begotten from oneness and although union proceeds from both [of these], nevertheless oneness, equality of oneness, and the union proceeding from both are one and the same thing—as if we were to speak of [one and] the same thing as *this, it, the same.*⁴⁹ The fact of our saying "it" is related to a first thing; but our saying "the same" unites and conjoins the related thing to the first thing. Assume, then, that from the pronoun "it" there were formed the word "itness," so that we could speak of oneness, itness, and sameness: itness would bear a relation to oneness, but sameness would designate the union of itness and oneness. [In this case, the names "Oneness," "Itness," and "Sameness"] would nearly enough befit the Trinity.

26   As for our most holy teachers having called Oneness *Father*, Equality *Son*, and Union *Holy Spirit*: they have done so because of a certain likeness to these transient things.⁵⁰ For in a father and a son there is a common nature which is one, so that with regard to this nature the son is equal to the father; for humanity is not present more greatly or less greatly in the son than in the father. And between a father and a son there is a certain union. For a natural love unites the one with the other, and does so because of the similarity of the same nature which is in them and which passes down from the father to the son. Wherefore, a father loves his son more than [he loves] someone else who agrees with him in humanity. Because of such a likeness—though it is a very remote likeness— Oneness is called Father, Equality is called Son, and Union is called Love or Holy Spirit. [Yet they are given these names] only in relation to creatures, as I shall show more clearly hereafter,⁵¹ when the time comes. And, in my judgment, this is a very clear investigation (in accord with the Pythagorean investigation) of the ever adorable Trinity in oneness and Oneness in trinity.

27   *Chapter Ten:*   An understanding of trinity in oneness transcends all things.

Let us now inquire about what Martian is getting at when he says⁵² that Philosophy, desiring to ascend unto a knowledge of this Trinity, left behind circles and spheres.

In the preceding [passages] I have shown the sole and very simple Maximum. And [I have shown]⁵³ that [the following] are not this Maximum: the most perfect corporeal figure (viz., the sphere), the most perfect surface figure (viz., the circle), the most perfect rectilineal figure (viz., the triangle), the most perfect figure of simple straightness (viz., the line). Rather, the Maximum itself is beyond all these things. Consequently, we must leave behind the things which, together with their material associations, are attained through the senses, through the imagination, or through reason—[leave them behind] so that we may arrive at the most simple and most abstract understanding,[54] where all things are one, where a line is a triangle, a circle, and a sphere, where oneness is threeness (and conversely), where accident is substance, where body is mind (*spiritus*), where motion is rest, and other such things. Now, there is understanding when (1) anything whatsoever in the One is understood to be the One, and the One [is understood to be] all things, and, consequently, (2) anything whatsoever in the One [is understood to be] all things. And you have not rightly left behind the sphere, the circle, and the like, unless you understand that maximal Oneness is necessarily, trine—since maximal Oneness cannot at all be rightly understood unless it is understood to be trine.

28   To use examples suitable to the foregoing [point]: We see that oneness of understanding is not anything other than that which understands, that which is understandable, and the act of understanding. So suppose you want to transfer your reflection from that which understands to the Maximum and to say that the Maximum is, most greatly, that which understands; but suppose you do not add that the Maximum is also, most greatly, that which is understandable,[55] together with being the greatest actual understanding. In that case, you do not rightly conceive of the greatest and most perfect Oneness. For if Oneness is the greatest and most perfect understanding (which without these three mutual relations cannot be either understanding or the most perfect understanding), then whoever does not attain to the trinity of this Oneness does not rightly conceive of oneness. For oneness is only threeness, since oneness indicates indivision, distinctness, and union. Indeed, indivision is from oneness—as is also distinctness and union (*unio sive conexio*). Hence, the greatest Oneness is not other than indivision, distinctness, and union. Since it is indivision, it is eternity and without beginning. (The eternal is not divided by anything.) Since it is distinctness, it is from immutable eternity. And since it is union (*conexio sive unio*), it proceeds from both [indivision and distinctness].

29   Moreover, when I say "Oneness is maximal," I indicate threeness. For when I say "oneness," I indicate a beginning without a beginning; when I say "maximal," I indicate a beginning from a beginning; when I conjoin and unite these two through the word "is," I indicate a procession from both. Therefore, if from earlier[56] [considerations] I have proven very clearly that the One is maximal: since the Minimum, the Maximum, and their Union are one (so that Oneness is minimal Oneness, maximal Oneness, and their Union), then it is evident that Philosophy (which endeavors to comprehend, by a very simple understanding, that the maximal Oneness is only trine) must leave behind all things imaginable and rational.[57]However, you are wondering about what I said: viz., that someone who by means of a simple understanding desires to

apprehend the Maximum must pass beyond the differences and varieties of things and beyond all mathematical figures. (For I said that in the Maximum a line is a surface, a circle, and a sphere.)[58] Hence, so that your understanding may be sharpened, I will try to convey you more readily, and by sure guidance, toward seeing these necessary and very true points. They will suitably lead you (provided you rise from the sign upward to the truth, by understanding [the meaning of] words symbolically) unto wondrous delight. For you will proceed on this pathway by means of learned ignorance, so that you will be able to see (to the extent granted to an ardent [seeker who is] elevated in accordance with the powers of human intelligence)[59] the one and incomprehensible Maximum, the ever-blessed one and trine God.

30   *Chapter Eleven:*   Mathematics assists us very greatly in
                          apprehending various divine [truths].

All our wisest and most divine teachers agree that visible things are truly images of invisible things and that from created things the Creator can be knowably seen as in a mirror and a symbolism.[60] But the fact that spiritual matters (which are unattainable by us in themselves) are investigated *symboli-cally* has its basis in what was said earlier. For all things have a certain comparative relation to one another ([a relation which is], nonetheless, hidden from us and incomprehensible to us), so that from out of all things there arises one universe and in [this] one maximum all things are this one. And although every image seems to be like its exemplar, nevertheless except for the Maximal Image (which is, in oneness of nature, the very thing which its Exemplar is) no image is so similar or equal to its exemplar that it cannot be infinitely more similar and equal. (These [doctrines] have already been made known from the preceding [remarks]).[61]

31   Now, when we conduct an inquiry on the basis of an image, it is necessary that there be no doubt regarding the image, by means of whose symbolical comparative relation we are investigating what is unknown. For the pathway to the uncertain can be only through what is presupposed and certain.[62] But all perceptible things are in a state of continual instability because of the material possibility abounding in them. In our considering of objects, we see that those which are more abstract than perceptible things,[63] viz., mathematicals, (not that they are altogether free of material associations, without which they cannot be imagined, and not that they are at all subject to the possibility of changing) are very fixed and are very certain to us. Therefore, in mathematicals the wise wisely sought illustrations of things that were to be searched out by the intellect.[64] And none of the ancients who are esteemed as great approached difficult matters by any other likeness than mathematics. Thus, Boethius,[65] the most learned of the Romans, affirmed that anyone who altogether lacked skill

in mathematics could not attain a knowledge of divine matters.

32   Did not Pythagoras, the first philosopher both in name and in fact, consider all investigation of truth to be by means of numbers? The Platonists and also our leading [thinkers] followed him to such an extent that our Augustine,[66] and after him Boethius,[67] affirmed that, assuredly, in the mind of the Creator number was the principal exemplar of the things to be created. How was Aristotle[68] (who by refuting his predecessors wanted to appear as someone without parallel) able in the *Metaphysics* to teach us about the difference of species otherwise than by comparing the species to numbers? And likewise when, regarding natural forms, he wanted to teach how the one form is in the other, he resorted of necessity to mathematical forms, saying: "Just as a triangle is in a quadrangle, so the lower [form] is in the higher [form]."[69] I will not mention innumerable other similar examples of his. Also, when the Platonist Aurelius Augustine[70] made an investigation regarding the quantity of the soul and its immortality, and regarding other very deep matters, he had recourse to mathematics as an aid. This pathway seemed to please our Boethius[71] to such an extent that he repeatedly asserted that every true doctrine is contained in [the notions of] multitude and magnitude. And to speak more concisely, if you wish: was not the opinion of the Epicureans about atoms and the void—[an opinion which] denies God and is at variance with all truth— destroyed by the Pythagoreans and the Peripatetics only through mathematical demonstration?[72] [I mean the demonstration] that the existence of indivisible and simple atoms—something which Epicurus took as his starting point—is not possible.

Proceeding on this pathway of the ancients, I concur with them and say that since the pathway for approaching divine matters is opened to us only through symbols, we can make quite suitable use of mathematical signs because of their incorruptible certainty.

33   *Chapter Twelve*:   The way in which mathematical signs ought to be used in our undertaking.

But since from the preceding [points] it is evident that the unqualifiedly Maximum cannot be any of the things which we either know or conceive: when we set out to investigate the Maximum symbolically, we must leap beyond simple likeness. For since all mathematicals are finite and otherwise could not even be imagined: if we want to use finite things as a way for ascending to the unqualifiedly Maximum, we must first consider finite mathematical figures together with their characteristics and relations. Next, [we must] apply these relations, in a transformed way, to corresponding infinite mathematical figures. Thirdly, [we must] thereafter in a still more highly transformed way, apply the relations of these infinite figures to the simple Infinite, which is altogether independent even of all figure. At this point our ignorance will be taught incomprehensibly how we are to think more correctly and truly about the Most High as we grope by means of a symbolism.

34   Operating in this way, then, and beginning under the guidance of the maximum Truth, I affirm what the holy men and the most exalted intellects who applied themselves to figures have stated in various ways. The most devoted Anselm[73] compared the maximum Truth to infinite rectitude. (Let me, following him, have recourse to the figure of rectitude, which I picture as a straight line.) Others who are very talented compared, to the superblessed Trinity, a triangle consisting of three equal right angles.[74] Since, necessarily, such a triangle has infinite sides, as will be shown, it can be called an infinite triangle. (These men I will also follow.) Others who have attempted to befigure infinite oneness have spoken of God as an infinite circle.[75] But those who considered the most actual existence of God affirmed that He is an infinite sphere, as it were.[76] I will show that all of these [men] have rightly conceived of the Maximum and that the opinion of them all is a single opinion.

35   *Chapter Thirteen*:   The characteristics of a maximum, infinite line.

I maintain, therefore, that if there were an infinite line, it would be a straight line, a triangle, a circle, and a sphere. And likewise if there were an infinite sphere, it would be a circle, a triangle, and a line. And the same thing must be said about an infinite triangle and an infinite circle.

First of all, it is evident that an infinite line would be a straight line: The diameter of a circle is a straight line, and the circumference is a curved line which is greater than the diameter. So if the curved line becomes less curved in proportion to the increased circumference of the circle, then the circumference of the maximum circle, which cannot be greater, is minimally curved and therefore maximally straight. Hence, the minimum coincides with the maximum—to such an extent that we can visually recognize that it is necessary for the maximum line to be maximally straight and minimally curved. Not even a scruple of doubt about this can remain when we see in the figure here at the side that arc CD of the larger circle is less curved than arc EF of the smaller circle, and that arc EF is less curved than arc GH of the still smaller circle. Hence, the straight line AB will be the arc of the maximum circle, which cannot be greater. And thus we see that a maximum, infinite line is, necessarily, the straightest; and to it no curvature is opposed. Indeed, in the maximum line curvature is straightness. And this is the first thing [which was] to be proved.

36   Secondly, I said that an infinite line is a maximum triangle, a maximum circle, and a [maximum] sphere. In order to demonstrate this, we must in the case of finite lines see what is present in the potency of a finite line. And that which we are examining will become clearer to us on the basis of the fact that an infinite line is, actually, whatever is present in the potency of a finite line. To begin with, we know that a line finite in length can be longer and straighter; and I have just proved that the maximum line is the longest and straightest. Next, if while point A remains fixed, line AB is rotated until B comes to C, a triangle is formed. And if the rotation is continued until B returns to where it began, a circle is formed. Furthermore, if, while A remains fixed, B is rotated until it

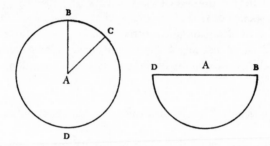

comes to the place opposite to where it began, viz., to D, then from lines AB and AD one continuous line is produced and a semicircle is described. And if while the diameter BD remains fixed the semicircle is rotated, a sphere is formed.[77] And the sphere is the termination of the potency of the line. The sphere exists in complete actuality since it is not in potency with respect to any further derivable figure. Therefore, if these figures are present in the potency of a finite line and if an infinite line is actually all the things with respect to which a finite line is in potency, then it follows that an infinite line is a triangle, a circle, and a sphere. Q.E.D.

    And because, presumably, you would like to see more clearly how it is that the infinite is actually those things which are present in the potency of the finite, I will now make you very certain thereof.

37   *Chapter Fourteen*:   An infinite line is a triangle.

Since in the case of quantitative things a line and a triangle differ incomparably, the imagination, which does not transcend the genus of perceptible things, does not apprehend that the former can be the latter. However, this [apprehending] will be easy for the intellect. It is already evident[78] that there can be only one maximum and infinite thing. Moreover, since any two sides of any triangle cannot, if conjoined, be shorter than the third: it is evident that in the case of a triangle whose one side is infinite, the other two sides are not shorter [i.e., are together infinite]. And because each part of what is infinite is infinite: for any triangle whose one side is infinite, the other sides must also be infinite. And since there cannot be more than one infinite thing, you understand transcendently that an infinite triangle cannot be composed of a plurality of lines, even though it is the greatest and truest triangle, incomposite and most simple. And because it is the truest triangle—something which it cannot be without three lines—it will be necessary that the one infinite line be three lines and that the three lines be one most simple line. And similarly regarding the angles; for there will be only one infinite angle; and this angle is three angles, and the three angles are one angle. Nor will this maximum triangle be composed of sides and angles; rather, the infinite line and the [infinite] angle are one and the same thing, so that the line is the angle, because the triangle is the line.

38   Furthermore, you can be helped to understand the foregoing if you ascend from a quantitative triangle to a nonquantitative triangle. Clearly, every quantitative triangle has three angles equal to two right angles. And so, the larger the one angle is, the smaller are the other two. Now, any one angle can be increased almost but (in accordance with our first premise) not completely up to the size of two right angles. Nevertheless, let us hypothesize that it is increased completely up to the size of two right angles while the triangle remains [nonetheless a triangle]. In that case, it will be obvious that the triangle has one angle which is three angles and that the three angles are one.

39   In like manner, you can see that a triangle is a line. For any two sides of a quantitative triangle are, if conjoined, as much longer than the third side as the angle which they form is smaller than two right angles. For example, because the angle BAC is much smaller than two right angles, the lines BA and AC, if conjoined, are much longer than BC. Hence, the larger the angle, e.g., BDC, the less the lines BD and DC exceed the line BC, and the smaller is the surface. Therefore, if, by hypothesis, an angle could be two right angles, the whole triangle would be resolved into a simple line.

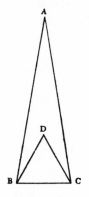

Hence, by means of this hypothesis, which cannot hold true for quantitative things, you can be helped in ascending to nonquantitative things; that which is impossible for quantitative things, you see to be altogether necessary for nonquantitative things. Hereby it is evident that an infinite line is a maximum triangle. Q.E.D.

40   *Chapter Fifteen*:   The maximum triangle is a circle and a sphere.

Next, we shall see more clearly that a triangle is a circle. Let us postulate the triangle ABC, formed by rotating the line AB—A remaining stationary—until B comes to C. There is no doubt that if line AB were infinite and B were rotated until it came all the way back to the start-ing point, a maximum circle would be formed, of which BC would be a portion. Now, because BC is a portion of an infi-nite arc, BC is a straight line.[79] And since every part of what is infinite is infinite, BC is not shorter than the whole arc of infinite circumference. Hence, BC will be not only a portion but the most complete cir-cumference. Therefore, it is necessary that the triangle ABC be a maximum circle. And because the circumference BC is a straight line, it is not greater than the infi-nite line AB;[80] for there is nothing greater than what is infinite. Nor are there two lines, because there cannot be two infinite things. Therefore, the infinite line, which is a triangle, is also a circle. And [this is] what was proposed [for proof].

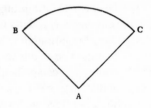

41   Moreover, that an infinite line is a sphere becomes very obvious in the following way: The line AB is the circumference of the maximum circle—indeed, it *is* the [maximum] circle, as was just proved.[81] And, in the triangle ABC, AB was brought from B to C, as was previously stated. But BC is an infinite line, as was also just proved. Hence, AB [which is the maximum circle] reached C by a complete coming around upon itself.[82] And since this is the case, it follows of necessity that from such a coming around of a circle upon itself a sphere is originated. And given that we previously proved that ABC is a circle, a triangle, and a line, we have now proved that it is also a sphere. And these are [the results] we set out to find.

42   *Chapter Sixteen*:   In a symbolic way the Maximum is to all things as
                          a maximum line is to [all] lines.

Now that we have seen how it is that an infinite line is actually and infinitely all that which is in the possibility of a finite line: we likewise have a symbolism for seeing how it is that, in the case of the simple Maximum, this Maximum is actually and maximally all that which is in the possibility of Absolute Simplicity. For whatever is possible, this the Maximum is actually and maximally. [I do] not [mean] that it is *from* what is possible but rather that it is [what-is-possible] maximally. By comparison, a triangle is educed from a line; but an infinite line, [though a triangle], is not a triangle as [a triangle] is educed from a finite [line]; rather, [the infinite line] is *actually* an infinite triangle, which is identical with the [infinite] line. Moreover, absolute possibility is, in the Maximum, not other than actually the Maximum—just as an infinite line is actually a sphere. The situation is otherwise in the case of what is nonmaximum. For in that case the possibility is not the actuality—even as a finite line is not a triangle.

43   Hence, we notice here an important speculative consideration which, from the foregoing, can be inferred about the Maximum: viz., that the Maximum is such that in it the Minimum is the Maximum, and thus the Maximum infinitely and in every respect transcends all opposition. From this principle there can be elicited about the Maximum as many negative truths as can be written or read; indeed, all humanly apprehensible theology is elicited from this very great principle. Accordingly, the greatest seeker of God, Dionysius the Areopagite,[83] declares in his *Mystical Theology* that most blessed Bartholomew marvelously understood theology, having called it the greatest and the least. For whoever understands this [point] understands all things; he transcends all created understanding. For God, who is this Maximum, "is not *this* thing and is not any *other* thing; He is not *here* and is not *there*," as the same Dionysius says regarding the divine names; for just as He is all things, so He is not any of all the things.[84] For, as Dionysius concludes at the end of *The Mystical Theology*: "above all affirmation God is the perfect and unique Cause of all things; and the excellence of Him who is unqualifiedly free from all things and is beyond all things is above the negation of all things."[85] Hence, he concludes in his *Letter to Gaius* that God is known above every mind and all intelligence.[86]

44   And in harmony with this [verdict] Rabbi Solomon states that all the wise agreed that the sciences do not apprehend the Creator. Only He Himself apprehends what He is; our apprehension of Him is a defective approximation of His apprehension.[87] Accordingly, Rabbi Solomon elsewhere says by way of conclusion: "Praised be the Creator! When His existence (*essentia*) is apprehended, the inquiry of the sciences is cut short, wisdom is reckoned as ignorance, and elegance of words as fatuity." And this is that learned ignorance which we are investigating. Dionysius [himself] endeavored to show in many ways that God can be found only through learned ignorance—[found] by no other principle, it seems to me, than the aforesaid.

45   Therefore, let our speculative consideration (which we elicit from the fact that infinite curvature is infinite straightness) be applied symbolically to the

Maximum as regards the Maximum's most simple and most infinite Essence: [We see] (1) that this Essence is the most simple Essence of all essences; (2a) that in this Essence all the essences of past, present, and future things are—ever and eternally—actually this Essence; and so, [it is] all essences, even as it is the Essence of all [essences]; (2b) that the Essence of all [essences] is each essence in such way that it is all of them together and none of them in particular; (3) that as an infinite line is the most congruent measure of all lines, so the Maximum Essence is likewise the most congruent measure of all essences. For, necessarily, the Maximum, to which the Minimum is not opposed, is the most congruent measure of all things; [it is] not a greater [measure than anything], because it is the Minimum; nor [is it] a lesser [measure than anything], because it is the Maximum. But everything measurable falls between the maximum and the minimum. Therefore, the Infinite Essence is the most congruent and most precise measure of all essences.[88]

46   Furthermore, so that you may see this [point] more clearly, consider [the following]: If an infinite line were constituted by an infinite number of one-foot sections and if another infinite line were constituted by an infinite number of two-foot sections, these lines would nevertheless have to be equal, since the infinite is not greater than the infinite. Therefore, just as in an infinite line one foot is not shorter than two feet, so it is not the case that an infinite line exceeds the length of one foot more than it exceeds the length of two feet. Rather, since any part of the infinite is infinite, one foot of an infinite line is convertible with the whole infinite line, just as are two feet. Similarly, since in the Maximum Essence every essence is the Maximum Essence, the Maximum is none other than the most congruent measure of all essences. Nor is there found to be any other precise measure of every essence than that Essence; for all others fall short and can be more precise, as was shown very clearly earlier.[89]

47   *Chapter Seventeen*:   Very deep doctrines from the same [symbolism of an infinite line].

Still more on the same topic: A finite line is divisible, and an infinite line is indivisible; for the infinite, in which the maximum coincides with the minimum, has no parts. However, a finite line is not divisible to the point that it is no longer a line, because in the case of magnitude we do not arrive at a minimum than which there cannot be a lesser—as was indicated earlier.[90] Hence, a finite line is indivisible in its essence [*ratio*]; a line of one foot is not less a line than is a line of one cubit. It follows, then, that an infinite line is the essence of a finite line. Similarly, the unqualifiedly Maximum is the Essence of all things. But the essence is the measure. Hence, Aristotle[91] rightly says in the *Metaphysics* that the First is the measure [*metrum et mensura*] of all things because it is the Essence of all things.

48   Furthermore: Just as an infinite line, which is the essence of a finite line, is indivisible and hence immutable and eternal, so also the Essence of all things, viz., Blessed God, is eternal and immutable. And herein is disclosed an understanding of the great Dionysius, who says that the Essence [*essentia*] of things is incorruptible,[92] and of others who have said that the Essence [*ratio*] of things is eternal. For example, [let me mention] the divine Plato, who, as Chalcidius reports,[93] stated in the *Phaedo* that, as it exists in itself, there is one Form or Idea of all things but [that] with respect to things, which are plural, there seems to be a plurality of forms. For example, when I consider a two-foot line, a three-foot line, and so on, two things appear: (1) the line's essence, which is one and equal in each and every line and (2) the difference which there is between a line of two feet and a line of three feet. And so, the essence of a two-foot line and the essence of a three-foot line seem to be different. However, it is obvious that in an infinite line a line of two feet and a line of three feet do not differ. Now, an infinite line is the essence of a finite line. Hence, there is one essence of both lines; and the difference between the things, or the lines, does not result from a difference of the essence, which is one, but from an accident, because the lines do not participate equally in the essence. Hence, there is only one essence of all lines, and it is participated in in different ways.

49   But as for there being differences of participation: this occurs because (as we proved earlier)[94] there cannot be two things which are exactly similar and which, consequently, participate precisely and equally in one essence. For only the Maximum, which is Infinite Essence, can participate with supreme equality in essence.[95] Just as there is only one Maximum Oneness, so there can be only one Equality of Oneness. Because it is Maximum Equality, it is the Essence of all things. By comparison, there is only one infinite line, which is the essence of all finite lines; and because of the fact that a finite line necessarily falls short of an infinite line, it cannot be the essence of itself, even as it cannot be both finite and infinite. Hence, just as no two finite lines can be precisely equal (since only the Maximum is precise Equality, which is Maximum Equality), so also there are not found to be two lines which participate equally in the one essence of all [lines].

50   Moreover, in a line of two feet an infinite line is neither longer nor shorter than the two-foot line, as was stated earlier.[96] And similarly regarding lines of three feet and more. Now, since an infinite line is indivisible and one, it is present as a whole in each finite line. But it is not present as a whole in each finite line according to participation and limitation; otherwise, when it was present as a whole in a line of two feet, it could not be present in a line of three feet, since a line of two feet is not a line of three feet. Therefore, it is present as a

whole in each line in such way that it is not present in any line insofar as one line is distinct from the others through limitation. Therefore, the infinite line is present as a whole in each line in such way that each line is present in it. Now, this [point] must be considered in both its aspects; for then we will see clearly how it is that the Maximum is in each thing and in no thing. This [symbolism of a line] symbolizes none other than the Maximum, since by similar reasoning the Maximum is [seen to be] in each thing, even as each thing [is seen to be] in it; moreover, [this symbolism] displays the reason that the Maximum exists in itself. Accordingly, the fact that the Maximum is the measure [*metrum et mensura*] of all things is not other than the fact that the unqualifiedly Maximum exists in itself—i.e., that the Maximum is the Maximum. Therefore, no thing exists in itself except the Maximum; and everything exists in itself insofar as it exists in its Essence [*ratio*], because its Essence (*ratio*) is the Maximum.

51   From these [considerations] the intellect can be helped; and by the illustration of an infinite line, the intellect can in sacred ignorance very greatly advance beyond all understanding and toward the unqualifiedly Maximum. For here we have now seen clearly how we can arrive at God through removing the participation of beings. For all beings participate in Being. Therefore, if from all beings participation is removed, there remains most simple Being itself, which is the Essence (*essentia*) of all things. And we see such Being only in most learned ignorance; for when I remove from my mind all the things which participate in Being, it seems that nothing remains. Hence, the great Dionysius says[97] that our understanding of God draws near to nothing rather than to something. But sacred ignorance teaches me that that which seems to the intellect to be nothing is the incomprehensible Maximum.

52   *Chapter Eighteen*:   From the same [symbolism] we are led to an understanding of the participation in being.

Furthermore, our insatiable intellect, stimulated by the aforesaid, carefully and with very great delight inquires into how it can behold more clearly this participation in the one Maximum. And being once again aided by the illustration of an infinite straight line, it remarks: A curve, which admits of more or less, cannot be a maximum or a minimum. Nor is a curve, qua curve, anything—since it is a deficiency of what is straight. Therefore, the being which is in a curve derives from participation in straightness, since a curve, considered maximally and minimally, is only something straight. Therefore, the less a curve is a curve (e.g., the circumference of a quite large circle), the more it participates in straightness. [I do] not [mean] that it takes a part of it, because infinite straightness is not partible. Now, the longer a straight finite line is, the more it seems to participate in the infinity of an infinite, maximum line.

A finite straight line, insofar as it is straight (minimal curvature is a reduction to that which is straight) participates in the infinite line according to a more simple participation, and a curve [participates in the infinite line] not [according to] a simple and immediate participation but rather [according to] a mediate and remote participation; for [it participates] through the medium of the straightness in which it participates. (Similarly, some beings—viz., simple finite substances—participate more immediately in Maximum Being, which exists in itself. And other beings—viz., accidents—participate in [Maximum] Being not through themselves but through the medium of substances.) Hence— the difference in participation notwithstanding—the straight is the measure of itself and of the not-straight, as states Aristotle.[98] Just as an infinite line [is the measure] of a straight line and of a curved line, so the Maximum [is the measure] of all things which participate [in it], no matter how differently.

53   In this [illustration] is disclosed an understanding of the statement that substance does not admit of more or less. This statement is true—even as [it is true that] a finite straight line, insofar as it is straight, does not admit of more and less. But because [it is] finite, one [straight] line is—through a difference of participation in the infinite line—longer or shorter in relation to another; no two [finite lines] are ever found to be equal. But a curve admits of more and less, according as it participates in straightness. Consequently, as being something straight through participated straightness, the curve admits of more and less. By analogous reasoning: accidents are more excellent in proportion to their participation in substance; and, further, the more they participate in a more excellent substance, the still more excellent they are.

Moreover, through this [illustration] we see how it is that there can be only beings which participate in the being of the First either through themselves or through other than themselves—just as there are only lines, either straight or curved. Wherefore, Aristotle[99] was right in dividing all the things in the world into substance and accident.

54   There is, then, one most congruent measure of substance and of accident— viz., the most simple Maximum. Although the Maximum is neither substance nor accident, nevertheless from the foregoing we see clearly that it receives the name of those things which participate in it immediately, viz., substances, rather than [the name] of accidents. Hence, the very great Dionysius[100] calls it more-than-substance, or supersubstantial, rather than superaccidental. Since to say "supersubstantial" is to say more than [to say] "superaccidental," the former is more fittingly predicated of the Maximum. Now, we say *supersub-*

stantial—i.e., not substantial but above substance (for the substantial is lower than it). And so, "supersubstantial" is a negation, quite truly befitting the Maximum, as I shall later teach regarding the names of God.[101]

On the basis of the foregoing considerations someone could make an extensive inquiry regarding the difference between, and the excellence of, accidents and substances. But this is not the place for dealing with these matters.

55   *Chapter Nineteen:*   The likening of an infinite triangle to maximum trinity.

Regarding what was stated and shown, viz., that a maximum line is a maximum triangle: let us now become instructed in ignorance. We have seen[102] that a maximum line is an [infinite] triangle; and because [this] line is most simple, it will be something most simple and three. Every angle of the triangle will be the line, since the triangle as a whole is the line. Hence, the infinite line is three. But there cannot be more than one infinite thing. Therefore, this trinity is oneness.

Moreover, as is shown in geometry: the angle opposite the longer side is the larger. Now, the [maximum triangle] is a triangle which has no side except an infinite side. Hence, the angles will be maximum and infinite. Therefore, one angle is not smaller than the others, nor are two of them larger than the third. Rather, because there could not be any quantity outside of infinite quantity, there cannot be any angles outside of the one infinite angle. Therefore, the angles will be in one another; and all three angles [will be] one maximum.

56   Furthermore, a maximum line is just as much a triangle, a circle, and a sphere as it is a line; it is truly and incompositely all these, as was shown.[103] Similarly, the unqualifiedly Maximum can be likened to the linear maximum, which we can call essence; it can be likened to the triangular maximum and can be called trinity; it can be likened to the circular maximum and can be called oneness; it can be likened to the spherical maximum and can be called actual existence. Therefore, the Maximum is actually one trine essence, although it is most true that the Maximum is these identically and most simply; the essence is not other than the trinity; and the trinity is not other than the oneness; and the actuality is not other than the oneness, the trinity, or the essence. Therefore, just as it is true that the Maximum exists and is one, so it is true that it is three in a way in which the truth of the trinity does not contradict the most simple oneness but is the oneness.

57   The foregoing is not possible otherwise than as is recognizable through the correspondence with the maximum triangle. Hence, when from the aforesaid we acquire knowledge of the true triangle and the most simple line, in the way

in which this [knowledge] is possible for man, we will attain, in learned ignorance, unto the Trinity. For we [shall] see that we do not find first one angle and then another and then still another, as in the case of finite triangles; for there cannot be numerically different angles in the oneness of an incomposite triangle. Rather, one thing exists trinely without numerical multiplication. Therefore, most learned Augustine was right in saying that when you begin to number the Trinity, you depart from the truth.[104] For in the case of God we must, as far as possible, precede contradictories and embrace them in a simple concept. For example, in God we must not conceive of distinction and indistinction as two contradictories but [must conceive of] them as antecedently present in their own most simple Beginning, where distinction is not anything other than indistinction; and then we will conceive more clearly that the trinity and the oneness are the same thing. For where distinction is indistinction, trinity is oneness; and, conversely, where indistinction is distinction, oneness is trinity. And similarly about the plurality of persons and the oneness of essence: for where plurality is oneness, trinity of persons is the same as oneness of essence; and, conversely, where oneness is plurality, oneness of essence is trinity of persons.

58   The foregoing points are clearly seen in our illustration, where the most simple line is a triangle, and, conversely, the simple triangle is linear oneness. In our illustration we also see that the angles of the triangle cannot be numbered through *one*, *two*, *three*, since each angle is in each angle—as the Son says, "I am in the Father, and the Father is in me."[105] Yet, the truth of a triangle requires that there be three angles. Hence, in our illustration there are most truly three angles; and each one is a maximum angle; and all are one maximum. Moreover, the truth of a triangle requires that no one angle be the other; and, in like manner, in the illustration the truth of the oneness of the most simple essence requires that these three angles not be three distinct things but be one thing. And this requirement, too, is met in the illustration.

    Therefore, join together antecedently, as I said, these things which seem to be opposites, and you will have not one thing and three things, or three things and one thing, but the Triune, or Unitrine. And this is Absolute Truth.

59   *Chapter Twenty*:   Still more regarding the Trinity. There cannot be fourness, [fiveness], etc., in God.

Furthermore, the truth of the Trinity—a Trinity which is Triunity—requires that the trine be one, because [the trine] is spoken of as triune. But the triune comes under a concept only in the manner in which a mutual relationship unites distinct things and an order distinguishes them. Now, when we construct a finite triangle there is first one angle, then another, and then a third from the first two; and these angles bear a mutual relationship to one another, so that from them there is one triangle. By comparison, then, [this mutual relationship obtains] infinitely in the infinite. Nevertheless, we must view this [mutual relationship] in the following way: viz., that priority is conceived to be in the eternity in such way that posteriority does not contradict it. For priority and posteriority could not belong in any other way to the infinite and eternal. Hence, it is not the case that the Father is prior to the Son, and the Son posterior [to the Father]; rather, the Father is prior in such way that the Son is not posterior. The Father is the first person in such way that the Son is not subsequently the second person; rather, just as the Father is the first person without priority, so the Son is the second person without posteriority; and, in a similar way, the Holy Spirit is the third person. Let this [discussion] suffice, since [the topic] was dealt with more fully earlier.[106]

60   However, you might like to note, regarding this ever-blessed Trinity, that the Maximum is three and not four or five or more. This point is surely noteworthy. For [fourness or fiveness, etc.] would be inconsistent with the simplicity and the perfection of the Maximum. For example, every polygonal figure has a triangular figure as its simplest element; moreover, a triangular figure is the minimal polygonal figure—than which there cannot be a smaller figure. Now, we proved[107] that the unqualifiedly minimum coincides with the maximum. Therefore, just as one is to numbers, so a triangle is to polygonal figures. Therefore, just as every number is reducible to oneness, so [all] polygons are [reducible] to a triangle. Therefore, the maximum triangle, with which the minimum triangle coincides, encompasses all polygonal figures. For just as maximum oneness is to every number, so the maximum triangle is to every polygon. But, as is obvious, a quadrangular figure is not the minimum figure, because a triangular figure is smaller than it. Therefore, a quadrangular figure—which cannot be devoid of composition, since it is greater than the minimum—cannot at all be congruent with the most simple maximum, which can coincide only with the minimum. Indeed, "to be maximum and to be quadrangular" involves a contradiction. For [a quadrangle] could not be a congruent measure of triangular figures, because it would always exceed them. Hence, how could that which would not be the measure of all things be the maximum? Indeed, how could that which would derive from another and would be composite, and hence finite, be the maximum?

61   It is now evident why from the potency of a simple line there first arises a simple triangle (as regards polygons), then a simple circle, and then a simple sphere; and we do not arrive at other than these elemental figures which are disproportional to one another in finite things and which enfold within themselves all figures. Hence, if we wanted to conceive of the measures of all measurable quantities: first we would have to have, for length, a maximum, infinite line, with which the minimum would coincide; then, similarly, for

rectilinear size [we would have to have] a maximum triangle; and for circular size, a maximum circle; and for depth, a maximum sphere; and with other than these four we could not attain to all measurable things. And because all these measures would have to be infinite and maximum measures, with which the minimum would coincide, and since there cannot be more than one maximum: we say that the one maximum, which is supposed to be the measure of all quantities, *is* those things[108] without which it could not be the maximum measure. Yet, considered in itself, without relation to what is measurable, it neither is nor can be truly called any of these things; rather, it is infinitely and disproportionally above them.

By comparison, then, since the unqualifiedly Maximum is the measure of everything, we predicate of it those attributes without which we do not consider it to be able to be the measure of everything. Hence, although the Maximum is infinitely above all trinity, we call it trine; for otherwise we would not be considering it to be the simple Cause and Measure of the things whose oneness of being is a trinity—even as, with regard to figures, triangular oneness consists of a trinity of angles. Yet, in truth: if this consideration is eliminated, then neither the name "trinity" nor our concept of trinity at all befit the Maximum; rather, they fall infinitely short of this maximal and incomprehensible Truth.

62   And so, we regard the maximum triangle as the simplest measure of all trinely existing things—even as activities are actions existing trinely (1) in potency, (2) in regard to an object, and (3) in actuality. The case is similar regarding perceptions, thoughts, volitions, likenesses, unlikenesses, adorn-ments, comparative relations, mutual relations, natural appetites, and all other things whose oneness of being consists of plurality—e.g., especially a nature's being and activity, which consist of a mutual relationship between what acts, what is acted upon, and what derives commonly from these two.

63   *Chapter Twenty-one*:   The likening of an infinite circle to oneness.

We considered a few points regarding a maximum triangle. Let us likewise add [a few points] about an infinite circle. A circle is a perfect figure of oneness and simplicity. Earlier[109] I showed that a [maximum] triangle is a circle; and so, trinity is oneness. But this oneness is infinite, just as the circle is infinite. Therefore, it is infinitely more one, or more identical, than any oneness[110] expressible and apprehensible by us. For the identity in an infinite circle is so great that it precedes all oppositions—even relative oppositions. For in an infinite circle *other* and *different* are not opposed to identity.

Therefore, [by comparison]: since the Maximum is of infinite oneness, all the things which befit it are it, without difference and otherness. Thus, its goodness is not different from its wisdom but is the same thing; for in the

Maximum all difference is identity. Hence, since the Maximum's power is most one, its power is also most powerful and most infinite. The Maximum's most one duration is so great that in its duration the past is not other than the future, and the future is not other than the present; rather, they are the most one duration, or eternity, without beginning and end. For in the Maximum the beginning is so great that even the end is—in the Maximum—the beginning.

64   All these [points] are exhibited by the infinite circle, which is eternal,[111] without beginning and end, indivisibly the most one and the most encompassing. Because this circle is maximum, its diameter is also maximum. And since there cannot be more than one maximum, this circle is most one to such an extent that the diameter is the circumference. Now, an infinite diameter has an infinite middle. But the middle is the center. Therefore, it is evident that the center, the diameter, and the circumference are the same thing.

Accordingly, our ignorance is taught that the Maximum, to which the Minimum is not opposed, is incomprehensible. But in the Maximum the center is the circumference. You see that because the center is infinite, the whole of the Maximum is present most perfectly within everything as the Simple and the Indivisible; moreover, it is outside of every being—surrounding all things, because the circumference is infinite, and penetrating all things, because the diameter is infinite. It is the Beginning of all things, because it is the center; it is the End of all things, because it is the circumference; it is the Middle of all things, because it is the diameter. It is the efficient Cause, since it is the center; it is the formal Cause, since it is the diameter; it is the final Cause, since it is the circumference. It bestows being, for it is the center; it regulates being, for it is the diameter; it conserves being, for it is the circumference. And many similar such things.

65   And so, your intellect apprehends that the Maximum is neither identical with nor different from anything and that all things are in it, from it, and through it, because it is the circumference, the diameter, and the center. [I do] not [mean] that it really is the circle, the circumference, the diameter, or the center; rather, it is only the most simple Maximum, which is investigated by means of these symbolisms. And it is found to surround all existing and nonexisting things, so that in it not-being is maximum being, just as the Minimum is the Maximum. It is the measure (1) of all circular movement from potentiality to actuality and back again from actuality to potentiality, (2) of the composition from first principles to individuals and of the resolution of individuals to first principles, (3) of perfect forms of circular things, (4) of circular activities and motions which turn back on themselves and return to their [respective] beginning, and (5) of all such [motions] whose oneness consists of a perpetual circularity.

66   From this circular figure many [points] might here be elicited about the perfection of oneness. For the sake of brevity I will pass over them, for on the basis of the aforesaid they can be readily inferred by anyone. I call attention

only to the following: that all theology is circular and is based upon a circle.[112] [This is true] to such an extent that the names for the [divine] attributes are predicated truly of one another in a circular manner. For example, supreme justice is supreme truth, and supreme truth is supreme justice; and similarly for all the others. Accordingly, if you want to prolong the inquiry, an infinite number of theological [points] which are now hidden from you can be made very obvious to you.

67   *Chapter Twenty-two*:   How God's foresight unites contradictories.

But so that we may also come to see how through the previous points we are led to a deep understanding, let us direct our inquiry to [the topic of] God's foresight. Since it is evident from the foregoing that God is the enfolding of all things, even of contradictories, [it is also evident that] nothing can escape His foresight. For whether we do some thing or its opposite or nothing, the whole of it was enfolded in God's foresight. Therefore, nothing will occur except in accordance with God's foreseeing.

68   Hence, although God could have foreseen many things which He did not foresee and will not foresee and although He foresaw many things which He was able not to foresee, nevertheless nothing can be added to or subtracted from divine foresight. By way of comparison: Human nature is simple and one; if a human being were born who was never even expected to be born, nothing would be added to human nature. Similarly, nothing would be subtracted from human nature if [the human being] were not born—just as nothing [is subtracted] when those who have been born die. This [holds true] because human nature enfolds not only those who exist but also those who do not exist and will not exist, although they could have existed. In like manner, even if what will never occur were to occur, nothing would be added to divine foresight, since it enfolds not only what does occur but also what does not occur but can occur. Therefore, just as in matter many things which will never occur are present as possibilities so, by contrast, whatever things will not occur but can occur: although they are present in God's foresight, they are present not possibly but actually.[113] Nor does it follow herefrom that these things exist actually.

Accordingly, we say that "human nature enfolds and embraces an infinite number of things" because it [enfolds] not only the human beings who did exist, do exist, and will exist but also those who can exist, though they never will (and so, human nature embraces mutable things immutably, just as infinite oneness [embraces] every number). In a similar way, God's infinite foresight enfolds not only the things which will occur but also the things which will not occur but can occur (and it enfolds contraries, even as a genus enfolds contrary differentiae). Those things which [infinite foresight] knows, it knows without a difference of times; for it is not the case that it knows future things as future, and past things as past; rather, it [knows] mutable things eternally and immutably.

69   Hence, divine foresight is inescapable and immutable. Nothing can transcend it. Hence, all things related to it are said to have necessity—and rightly so, since in God all things are God,[114] who is Absolute Necessity. And so, it is evident that the things which will never occur are present in God's foresight in the aforesaid manner, even if they are not foreseen to occur. It is necessary that God foresaw what He foresaw, because His foresight is necessary and immutable, even though He was able to foresee even the opposite of that which He did foresee. For if enfolding is posited, it is not the case that the thing which was enfolded is posited; but if unfolding is posited, enfolding is [also] posited. For example, although I am able to read or not to read tomorrow: no matter which of these I shall do, I will not escape [God's] foresight, which embraces [i.e., enfolds] contraries. Hence, whatever I shall do will occur in accordance with God's foresight.

And so, the following is evident: how it is that through the foregoing points (which teach us that the Maximum precedes all opposition since it somehow embraces and enfolds all things), we apprehend what is true about God's foresight and other such matters.

70   *Chapter Twenty-three*:   The likening of an infinite sphere to the actual existence of God.

It is fitting to reflect upon still a few more points regarding an infinite sphere. In an infinite sphere we find that three maximum lines—of length, width, and depth—meet in a center. But the center of a maximum sphere is equal to the diameter and to the circumference.[115] Therefore, in an infinite sphere the center is equal to these three lines; indeed, the center is all three: viz., the length, the width, and the depth. And so, [by comparison], the Maximum will be—infinitely and most simply—all length, width, and depth; in the Maximum these are the one most simple, indivisible Maximum. As a center, the Maximum precedes all width, length, and depth; it is the End and the Middle of all these; for in an infinite sphere the center, the diameter, and the circumference are the same thing. And just as an infinite sphere is most simple and exists in complete actuality, so the Maximum exists most simply in complete actuality. And just as a sphere is the actuality of a line, a triangle, and a circle, so the Maximum is the actuality of all things. Therefore, all actual existence has from the Maximum whatever actuality it possesses; and all existence exists actually insofar as it exists actually in the Infinite. Hence, the Maximum is the Form of forms and the Form of being,[116] or maximum actual Being.

71   Hence, Parmenides,[117] reflecting most subtly, said that God is He for whom to be anything which is is to be everything which is. Therefore, just as a sphere

is the ultimate perfection of figures and is that than which there is no more perfect [figure], so the Maximum is the most perfect perfection of all things. [It is perfection] to such an extent that in it everything imperfect is most perfect— just as an infinite line is [an infinite] sphere, and in this sphere[118] curvature is straightness, composition is simplicity, difference is identity, otherness is oneness, and so on. For how could there be any imperfection in that in which imperfection is infinite perfection, possibility is infinite actuality, and so on?

72   Since the Maximum is like a maximum sphere, we now see clearly that it is the one most simple and most congruent measure of the whole universe and of all existing things in the universe;[119] for in it the whole is not greater than the part, just as an infinite sphere is not greater than an infinite line. Therefore, God is the one most simple Essence (*ratio*) of the whole world, or universe.[120] And just as after an infinite number of circular motions an [infinite] sphere arises, so God (like a maximum sphere) is the most simple measure of all circular motions. For all animation, motion, and understanding are from Him, in Him, and through Him.[121] With God one revolution of the eighth sphere is not smaller than [one revolution] of an infinite [sphere], because He in whom as in an end all motion finds rest is the End of all motions. For He is maximal rest, in which all motion is rest. And so, maximum rest is the measure of all motions, just as maximum straightness [is the measure] of all circumferences, and as maximum presence, or eternity, [is the measure] of all times.

73   Therefore, in God as in an end all natural movements find rest; and in Him as in infinite actuality all possibility is realized. And because He is the Being of all being and because all motion is toward being, He who is the End of motion, viz., the Form and the Actuality of being, is the cessation of motion.

Therefore, all beings tend toward Him. And because they are finite and cannot participate equally in this End relatively to one another, some participate in it through the medium of others. Analogously, a line, through the medium of a triangle and of a circle, is transformed into a sphere; and a triangle [is transformed into a sphere] through the medium of a circle; and through itself a circle [is transformed] into a sphere.[122]

74   *Chapter Twenty-four*:   The name of God; affirmative theology.

Now that in our ignorance we have striven—with divine assistance and by means of mathematical illustration—to become more knowledgeable about the First Maximum, let us inquire about the name of the Maximum, in order that our learning may be still more complete. If we rightly keep in mind the points already frequently made, this inquiry will easily lead to discovery.

Since the Maximum is the unqualifiedly Maximum, to which nothing is opposed, it is evident that no name can properly befit it. For all names are bestowed on the basis of a oneness of conception [*ratio*] through which one thing is distinguished from another. But where all things are one, there can be

75 no proper name. Hence, Hermes Trismegistus rightly says: "Since God is the totality of things, no name is proper to Him; for either He would have to be called by every name or else all things would have to be called by His name";[123] for in His simplicity He enfolds the totality of things. Hence, as regards His own name, which we say to be ineffable and which is "tetragrammaton" (i.e., "of four letters") and which is proper because it befits God according to His own essence, not according to any relation to created things: He ought to be called "One-and-all," or better, "All-in-one." And in like manner we previously[124] discovered [the name] "Maximum Oneness," which is the same thing as "All-in-one"; indeed, the name "Oneness" seems still closer and still more suitable than the name "All-in-one." Wherefore the prophet says: "On that day there will be one God, and His name will be one."[125] And elsewhere: "Hear, O Israel ('Israel' means 'one who sees God with the understanding'), that your God is one."[126]

76 However, it is not the case that "Oneness" is the name of God in the way in which we either name or understand oneness; for just as God transcends all understanding, so, a fortiori, [He transcends] every name. Indeed, through a movement-of-reason which is much lower than the intellect,[127] names are bestowed for distinguishing between things. But since reason cannot leap beyond contradictories: as regards the movement of reason, there is not a name to which another [name] is not opposed. Therefore, as regards the movement of reason: plurality or multiplicity is opposed to oneness. Hence, not "oneness" but "Oneness to which neither otherness nor plurality nor multiplicity is opposed" befits God. This is the maximum name, which enfolds all things in its simplicity of oneness; this is the name which is ineffable and above all

77 understanding.[128] For who could understand the infinite Oneness which infinitely precedes all opposition?—where all things are incompositely enfolded in simplicity of Oneness, where there is neither anything which is other nor anything which is different, where a man does not differ from a lion, and the sky does not differ from the earth. Nevertheless, in the Maximum they are most truly the Maximum, [though] not in accordance with their finitude; rather, [they are] Maximum Oneness in an enfolded way. Hence, if anyone were able to understand or to name such Oneness—which, since it is Oneness is all things and since it is the Minimum is the Maximum—he would attain to the name of God. But since the Name-of-God *is* God, His Name is known only by [that] Understanding which is the Maximum and is the Maximum Name. Therefore, in learned ignorance we attain unto [the following]: Although "Oneness" seems to be a quite close name for the Maximum, nevertheless it is still infinitely distant from the true Name of the Maximum—[a Name] which *is* the Maximum.

78   And so, from these considerations it is evident that the affirmative names we
ascribe to God befit Him [only] infinitesimally. For such [names] are ascribed
to Him in accordance with something found in created things. Therefore, since
any such particular or discrete thing, or thing having an opposite, can befit God
only very minutely: affirmations are scarcely fitting, as Dionysius says.[129] For
example, if you call God "Truth," falsity is the contradistinction; if you call
Him "Virtue," vice is the contradistinction; if you call Him "Substance,"
accident is the contradistinction; and so on. But since God is not a substance
which is not all things and to which something is opposed, and is not a truth
which is not all things without opposition, these particular names cannot befit
Him except very infinitesimally. For it is not the case that any affirmations—
which posit in Him, as it were, something of what they signify—can befit Him
who is not some particular thing more than He is all things.

79   Therefore, if affirmative names befit God, they befit Him only in relation to
created things. [I do] not [mean] that created things are the cause of [these
names'] befitting Him, for the Maximum can have nothing from created things;
rather, [I mean that these names] befit Him on the basis of His infinite power in
relation to created things. For God was eternally able to create, because unless
He had been able, He would not have been supreme power. Therefore,
although the name "Creator" befits Him in relation to created things, it also
befit Him before there was a created thing, since He was eternally able to
create. The case is similar with "justice" and all the other affirmative names
which we symbolically ascribe to God on the basis of created things because of
a certain perfection signified by these names. Nonetheless, even before we
ascribed all these names to God, they were eternally and truly enfolded in His
supreme perfection and in His infinite name—as were all the things (1) which
are signified by such names and (2) from which we transfer [the names] to God.

80   The aforesaid is so true of all affirmations that even the names of the Trinity
and of the persons—viz., "Father," "Son," and "Holy Spirit"—are be-
stowed on God in relation to created things. For because God is Oneness, He is
Begetter and Father; because He is Equality of Oneness, He is Begotten, or
Son; because He is Union of both [Oneness and Equality-of-Oneness], He is
Holy Spirit.[130] Accordingly, it is clear that the Son is called Son because He is
Equality of Oneness, or of Being, or of existing.[131] Hence, from the fact that
God was eternally able to create things—even had He not created them—it is
evident [that] He is called Son in relation to these things. For He is Son because
He is the Equality of being [these] things; things could not be more than, or less
than, this Equality. Thus, He is Son because He is the Equality of the being of
the things which God was able to make, even had He not been going to make
them. Were God not able to make these things, He would not be Father, Son, or
Holy Spirit; indeed, He would not be God. Therefore, if you reflect quite
carefully, [you will see that] for the Father to beget the Son was [for Him] to

81

create all things in the Word.[132] Wherefore, Augustine[133] maintains that the
81 Word is both the Art and the Idea in relation to created things. Hence, God is
Father because He begets Equality of Oneness; but He is Holy Spirit because
He is the Love common to both [Oneness and Equality of Oneness]; and He is
all these[134] in relation to created things. For created things begin to be by virtue
of the fact that God is Father; they are perfected by virtue of the fact that He is
Son; they harmonize with the universal order of things by virtue of the fact that
He is Holy Spirit. And in each thing these are traces of the Trinity. Moreover,
this is the opinion of Aurelius Augustine when he expounds the following
passage from Genesis: "In the beginning God created heaven and earth." For
he says that by virtue of the fact that God is Father He created the beginnings of
things.[135]
82   Therefore, whatever is said about God through affirmative theology is based
upon a relationship to created things. [This is true] even with respect to those
most holy names in which the greatest mysteries of divine knowledge lie
hidden. These names are found among the Hebrews and the Chaldees; all of
them signify God only according to some individual property—[all] except for
the name from four letters, viz., *ioth, he, vau, he*. (This is the proper and
ineffable [name], previously commented on.)[136] Jerome and also Rabbi Solomon (in his book *Dux Neutrorum*)[137] deal extensively with these names. They
can be consulted.

83   *Chapter Twenty-five:*   The pagans named God in various ways in
                                   relation to created things.

The pagans likewise named God from His various relationships to created
things. [They named Him] Jupiter because of marvelous kindness (for Julius
Firmicus[138] says that Jupiter is a star so auspicious that had he reigned alone in
the heavens, men would be immortal); similarly, [they named Him] Saturn
because of a profundity of thoughts and inventions regarding the necessities of
life; Mars because of military victories; Mercury because of good judgment in
counseling; Venus because of love which conserves nature; Sun because of the
force of natural movements; Moon because of conservation of the fluids upon
which life depends; Cupid because of the unity of the two sexes (for which
reason they also called Him Nature, since through the two sexes He conserves
the species of things). Hermes[139] said that not only all [species of] animals but
also all [species of] nonanimals have two sexes; wherefore, he maintained that
the Cause of all things, viz., God, enfolds within Himself both the masculine
and the feminine sex, of which he believed Cupid and Venus to be the
unfolding. Valerius,[140] too, the Roman, making the same affirmation, profes-
sed that Jupiter is the omnipotent Divine Father and Mother. Hence, in

accordance with one thing's desiring (*cupit*) another, they gave to the daughter of Venus, i.e., of natural beauty, the name "Cupid." But they said that Venus is the daughter of omnipotent Jupiter, from whom Nature and all its accompaniments derive.

84   Even the temples—viz., the Temple of Peace, the Temple of Eternity, the Temple of Harmony, and the Pantheon (in which there was in the middle, under the open air, the altar of the Limit of the Infinite, of which there is no limit)—and other such [edifices] inform us that the pagans named God in various ways in accordance with His relationship to created things. All these names are unfoldings of the enfolding of the one ineffable name.[141] And as accords with [this] proper name's being infinite, it enfolds an infinite number of such names of particular perfections. Therefore, the unfolded [names] could be many without being so many and so great that there could not be more of them. Each of them is related to the proper and ineffable name [i.e., to the tetragrammaton] as what is finite is related to what is infinite.

The ancient pagans derided the Jews, who worshipped one infinite God of whom they were ignorant. Nevertheless, these pagans themselves worshipped Him in unfolded things—i.e., worshipped Him where they beheld His divine works. In those days there was the following difference among all men: viz., [although] all believed that God is the one Maximum, than which there cannot be a greater, some of them (e.g., the Jews and the Sissennii)[142] worshipped Him in His most simple oneness (as the Enfolding of all things is); but others worshipped Him in the things in which they found the unfolding of His divinity, construing what was perceptually observed as guidance toward the Cause and Beginning. In this last-mentioned way the simple populace was deceived; for they construed the unfolded things not as images but as the reality itself. As a result thereof, idolatry was introduced to the people—though, for the most part, the wise continued rightly to believe in the oneness of God. These points can be known to anyone who will carefully examine Cicero *On the Nature of the Gods*,[143] as well as the ancient philosophers.

85   I do not deny, however, that certain of the pagans did not understand that since God is the being of things, He exists independently of things in a way other than through abstraction. (By comparison, prime matter exists independently of things only through the abstracting intellect). Such men worshipped God in created things; they also provided idolatry with supporting reasons. Certain men even thought that God can be summoned forth.[144] For example, the Sissennii summoned Him in angels. But the pagans summoned Him in trees, as we read regarding the Tree of the Sun and the Moon. Others summoned Him, with fixed incantations, in air, water, or temples. My earlier remarks show how deceived all these men were and how far they were from the truth.

83

86   *Chapter Twenty-six*:   Negative theology.

The worshipping of God, who is to be worshipped in spirit and in truth,[145] must be based upon affirmations about Him. Accordingly, every religion, in its worshipping, must mount upward by means of affirmative theology. [Through affirmative theology] it worships God as one and three, as most wise and most gracious, as inaccessible Light, as Life, Truth, and so on. And it always directs its worship by faith, which it attains more truly through learned ignorance. It believes that He whom it worships as one is all in one, and that He whom it worships as inaccessible light is not light as is corporeal light, to which darkness is opposed, but is infinite and most simple Light, in which darkness *is* Infinite Light; and [it believes] that Infinite Light always shines within the darkness of our ignorance but [that] the darkness cannot comprehend it.[146] And so, the theology of negation is so necessary for the theology of affirmation that without it God would not be worshipped as the Infinite God but, rather, as a creature. And such worship is idolatry; it ascribes to the image that which befits only the reality itself. Hence, it will be useful to set down a few more things about negative theology.

87   Sacred ignorance has taught us that God is ineffable. He is so because He is infinitely greater than all nameable things. And by virtue of the fact that [this] is most true, we speak of God more truly through removal and negation—as [teaches] the greatest Dionysius, who did not believe that God is either Truth or Understanding or Light or anything which can be spoken of.[147] (Rabbi Solomon[148] and all the wise follow Dionysius.) Hence, in accordance with this negative theology, according to which [God] is only infinite, He is neither Father nor Son nor Holy Spirit. Now, the Infinite qua Infinite is neither Begetting, Begotten, nor Proceeding. Therefore, when Hilary of Poitiers distinguished the persons, he most astutely used the expressions "Infinity in the Eternal," "Beauty in the Image," and "Value in the Gift."[149] He means that although in eternity we can see only infinity, nevertheless since the infinity which *is* eternity is negative infinity, it cannot be understood as Begetter but [can] rightly [be understood as] eternity, since "eternity" is affirmative of oneness, or maximum presence. Hence, [Infinity-in-the-Eternal is] the Beginning without beginning. "Beauty in the Image" indicates the Beginning from the Beginning. "Value in the Gift" indicates the Procession from these two.

88   All these things are very well known through the preceding [discussion]. For although eternity is infinity, so that eternity is not a greater cause of the Father than is infinity: nevertheless, in a manner of considering, eternity is attributed to the Father and not to the Son or to the Holy Spirit; but infinity is not [attributed] to one person more than to another. For according to the consideration of oneness infinity is the Father; according to the consideration of equality of oneness it is the Son; according to the consideration of the union [of the two it

is] the Holy Spirit. And according to the simple consideration of itself infinity is neither the Father nor the Son nor the Holy Spirit. Yet, infinity (as also eternity) is each of the three persons, and, conversely, each person is infinity (and eternity)—not, however, according to [the simple] consideration [of itself], as I said. For according to the consideration of infinity God is neither one nor many. Now, according to the theology of negation, there is not found in God anything other than infinity. Therefore, according to this theology [God] is not knowable either in this world or in the world to come (for in this respect every created thing is darkness, which cannot comprehend Infinite Light), but is known only to Himself.

89   From these [observations] it is clear (1) that in theological matters negations are true and affirmations are inadequate, and (2) that, nonetheless, the negations which remove the more imperfect things from the most Perfect are truer than the others. For example, it is truer that God is not stone than that He is not life or intelligence; and [it is truer that He] is not drunkenness than that He is not virtue. The contrary [holds] for affirmations; for the affirmation which states that God is intelligence and life is truer than [the affirmation that He is] earth or stone or body. All these [points] are very clear from the foregoing. Therefrom we conclude that the precise truth shines incomprehensibly within the darkness of our ignorance. This is the learned ignorance we have been seeking and through which alone, as I explained, [we] can approach the maximum, triune God of infinite goodness—[approach Him] according to the degree of our instruction in ignorance, so that with all our might we may ever praise Him, who is forever blessed above all things,[150] for manifesting to us His incomprehensible self.[151]

BOOK II

Prologue

Through certain symbolic signs we have in the foregoing way discussed instruction in ignorance as it regards the nature of the Absolute Maximum. Through [the assistance of] this Nature, which shines forth a bit to us in a shadow, let us by the same method inquire a bit more about those things which are all-that-which-they-are from the Absolute Maximum.

Since what is caused derives altogether from its cause and not at all from itself and since it conforms as closely (*propinquius et similius*) as it can to the Fount and Form [*ratio*] from which it is that which it is: clearly, the nature of contraction is difficult to attain if the Absolute Exemplar remains unknown. Therefore, it is fitting that we be learned-in-ignorance beyond our understanding [*apprehensio*], so that (though not grasping the truth precisely as it is) we may at least be led to seeing that there is a precise truth which we cannot now comprehend. This is the goal of my work in this part. May Your Clemency[1] judge this work and find it acceptable.

91   *Chapter One*:   Corollaries preliminary to inferring one infinite universe.

It will be very advantageous to set forth, from out of our beginning, the preliminary corollaries of our instruction in ignorance. For they will furnish a certain facility regarding an endless number of similar points which in like manner can be inferred; and they will make clearer the points to be discussed.

I maintained, at the outset of my remarks, that with regard to things which are comparatively greater and lesser we do not come to a maximum in being and in possibility. Hence, in my earlier [remarks] I indicated that precise equality befits only God.[2] Wherefore, it follows that, except for God, all positable things differ. Therefore, one motion cannot be equal to another; nor can one motion be the measure of another, since, necessarily, the measure and the thing measured differ. Although these points will be of use to you regarding an infinite number of things, nevertheless if you transfer them to astronomy, you will recognize that the art of calculating lacks precision, since it presupposes that the motion of all the other planets can be measured by reference to the motion of the sun. Even the ordering of the heavens—with respect to whatever kind of place or with respect to the risings and settings of the constellations or to the elevation of a pole and to things having to do with these—is not precisely knowable. And since no two places agree precisely in time and setting, it is evident that judgments about the stars are, in their specificity, far from precise.

92 If you subsequently adapt this rule to mathematics, you will see that equality is *actually* impossible with regard to geometrical figures and that no thing can precisely agree with another either in shape or in size. And although there are true rules for describing the equal of a given figure as it exists in its definition, nonetheless equality between different things is *actually* impossible.[3] Wherefore, ascend to [the recognition] that truth, freed from material [conditions], sees, as in a definition, the equality which we cannot at all experience in things, since in things equality is present only defectively.

93   Press onward: Conformably to the rule,[4] there is no precision in music. Therefore, it is not the case that one thing [perfectly] harmonizes with another in weight or length or thickness. Nor is it possible to find between the different sounds of flutes, bells, human voices, and other instruments comparative relations which are precisely harmonic—so [precisely] that a more precise one could not be exhibited. Nor is there, in different instruments [of the same kind]—just as also not in different men—the same degree of true comparative relations; rather, in all things difference according to place, time, complexity, and other [considerations] is necessary. And so, precise comparative relation is seen only formally; and we cannot experience in perceptible objects a most agreeable, undefective harmony, because it is not present there. Ascend now to [the recognition] that the maximum, most precise harmony is an equality-of-comparative-relation which a living and bodily man cannot hear. For since [this harmony] is every proportion (*ratio*), it would attract to itself our soul's reason [*ratio*]—just as infinite Light [attracts] all light—so that the soul, freed from perceptible objects, would not without rapture hear with the intellect's ear this supremely concordant harmony. A certain immensely pleasant contemplation could here be engaged in—not only regarding the immortality of our intellectual, rational spirit (which harbors in its nature incorruptible reason, through which the mind attains, of itself, to the concordant and the discordant likeness in musical things), but also regarding the eternal joy into which the blessed are conducted, once they are freed from the things of this world. But [I will deal] with this [topic] elsewhere.[5]

94   Furthermore: If we apply our rule to arithmetic, we see that no two things can agree in number. And since with respect to a difference of number there is also a difference of composition, complexity, comparative relation, harmony, motion, and so on *ad infinitum*, we hereby recognize that we are ignorant.

No one [human being] is as another in any respect—neither in sensibility, nor imagination, nor intellect, nor in an activity (whether writing or painting or an art). Even if for a thousand years one [individual] strove to imitate another in any given respect, he would never attain precision (though perceptible difference sometimes remains unperceived). Even art imitates nature as best it can; but it can never arrive at reproducing it precisely. Therefore, medicine as well[1] as alchemy, magic, and other transmutational arts lacks true precision, although one art is truer in comparison with another (e.g., medicine is truer than the transmutational arts, as is self-evident).

95   Let me say, still making inferences from the same basis: Since with regard to opposites (e.g., with regard to the simple and the composite, the abstract and the concrete, the formal and the material, the corruptible and the incorruptible, etc.) we also find degrees of comparative greatness, we do not come to the pure oppositeness of the opposites—i.e., to that wherein they agree precisely and equally. Therefore, it is with a difference of degree that all things are from opposites; they have more from one [of the opposites] and less from the other, and they receive the nature of one of them through the triumph of one [of them] over the other. Wherefore, we pursue the knowledge of things rationally, so that we may know that in one thing composition is present in a certain simplicity and in another thing simplicity is present in composition, [that] in one thing corruptibility [is present] in incorruptibility and in another the reverse, and so on, as I shall expound in the book of *Conjectures*, where I will discuss this [matter] more fully.[6] Let these few remarks suffice for showing the marvelous power of learned ignorance.

96   Descending more to the [present] topic, I say more fully: Since neither an ascent to the unqualifiedly Maximum nor a descent to the unqualifiedly Minimum is possible, and thus (as is evident regarding number and regarding the division of a continuum) no transition is made to the infinite:[7] clearly, there must always be positable a greater and a lesser—whether in quantity or virtue or perfection, etc.—than any given finite thing, since the unqualifiedly Maximum or Minimum is not positable in [finite] things. But [this] progression does not continue unto the infinite,[8] as was just indicated. Since each part of the infinite is infinite, a contradiction is implied [by the following]: that where we reach the infinite, there we find more and less. For just as more and less cannot befit the infinite, so [they cannot befit] something having any kind of comparative relation to the infinite, since, necessarily, this latter would also be infinite. For example, in the infinite number the number two would not be smaller than the number one hundred—if through ascending we could actually arrive at the infinite number.[9] Similarly, an infinite line composed of an infinite number of lines of two feet would not be shorter than an infinite line composed of an infinite number of lines of four feet. And so, [by comparison] there is not

positable anything which would limit the Divine Power. Therefore, the Divine Power can posit a greater and a lesser than any given thing, unless this given thing is also the Absolute Maximum—as will be demonstrated in the third book.[10]

97   Therefore, only the absolutely Maximum is negatively infinite. Hence, it alone is whatever there can at all possibly be. But since the universe encompasses all the things which are not God, it cannot be negatively infinite, although it is unbounded and thus privatively infinite. And in this respect it is neither finite nor infinite. For it cannot be greater than it is. This results from a defect. For its possibility, or matter, does not extend itself farther. For to say "The universe can always be actually greater" is not other than saying "Possible being passes over into actually infinite being." But this latter [statement] cannot hold true, since infinite actuality—which is absolute eternity, which is *actually* all possibility of being—cannot arise from possibility.[11] Therefore, although with respect to God's infinite power, which is unlimitable, the universe could have been greater: nevertheless, since the possibility-of-being, or matter, which is not actually extendable unto infinity, opposes, the universe cannot be greater. And so, [the universe is] unbounded; for it is not the case that anything actually greater than it, in relation to which it would be bounded, is positable. And so, [it is] privatively infinite. Now, the universe exists actually only in a contracted manner, so that it exists in the best[12] way in which the condition of its nature allows. For it is the creation, which, necessarily, derives from Absolute and unqualifiedly Divine Being—as subsequently and by means of learned ignorance I will very briefly show, as clearly and simply as possible.

98   *Chapter Two*:   Created being derives from the being of the First in a way that is not understandable.

Sacred ignorance has already[13] taught us that nothing exists from itself except the unqualifiedly Maximum (in which *from itself, in itself, through itself*, and *with respect to itself* are the same thing: viz., Absolute Being) and that, necessarily, every existing thing is that which it is, insofar as it is, from Absolute Being. For how could that which is not from itself exist in any other way than from Eternal Being? But since the Maximum is far distant from any envy, it cannot impart diminished being as such. Therefore, a created thing, which is a derivative being, does not have everything which it is (e.g., [not] its corruptibility, divisibility, imperfection, difference, plurality, and the like) from the eternal, indivisible, most perfect, indistinct, and one Maximum—nor from any positive cause.

99   An infinite line is infinite straightness, which is the cause of all linear being. Now, with respect to being a line, a curved line is from the infinite line; but with

respect to being curved, it is not from the infinite line. Rather, the curvature follows upon finitude, since a line is curved because it is not the maximum line. For if it were the maximum line, it would not be curved, as was shown previously.[14] Similarly with things: since they cannot be the Maximum, it happens that they are diminished, other, distinct, and the like—none of which [characteristics] have a cause. Therefore, a created thing has from God the fact that it is one, distinct, and united to the universe; and the more it is one, the more like[15] unto God it is. However, it does not have from God (nor from any positive cause but [only] contingently[16]) the fact that its oneness exists in plurality, its distinctness in confusion, and its union in discord.

100   Who, then, can understand created being by conjoining, in created being, the absolute necessity from which it derives and the contingency without which it does not exist? For it seems that the creation, which is neither God[17] nor nothing, is, as it were, after God and before nothing and in between God and nothing—as one of the sages says: "God is the opposition to nothing by the mediation of being."[18] Nevertheless, [the creation] cannot be composed of being and not-being. Therefore, it seems neither to be (since it descends from being) nor not to be (since it is before nothing) nor to be a composite of being and nothing.

Now, our intellect, which cannot leap beyond contradictories,[19] does not attain to the being of the creation either by means of division or of composition, although it knows that created being derives only from the being of the Maximum. Therefore, derived being is not understandable, because the Being from which [it derives] is not understandable—just as the adventitious being of an accident is not understandable if the substance to which it is adventitious is not understood.[20] And, therefore, the creation as creation cannot be called one, because it descends from Oneness; nor [can it be called] many, since its being derives from the One; nor [can it be called] both one and many conjunctively. But its oneness exists contingently and with a certain plurality. Something similar, it seems, must be said about simplicity and composition and other opposites.

101   But since the creation was created through the being of the Maximum and since—in the Maximum—being, making, and creating are the same thing: creating seems to be not other than God's being all things. Therefore, if God is all things and if His being all things is creating: how can we deem the creation not to be eternal, since God's being is eternal—indeed, is eternity itself? Indeed, insofar as the creation is God's being no one doubts that it is eternity. Therefore, insofar as it is subject to time, it is not from God, who is eternal. Who, then, understands the creation's existing both eternally and temporally? For in[21] Being itself the creation was not able not to exist eternally; nor was it able to exist before time, since "before" time there was no *before*.[22] And so, the creation always existed, from the time it was able to exist.

102   Who, in fact, can understand that God is the Form of being and nevertheless
is not mingled with the creation? For from an infinite line and a finite curved
line there cannot arise a composite, which cannot exist without comparative
relation; but no one doubts that there can be no comparative relation between
the infinite and the finite.[23] How, then, can the intellect grasp the following?:
that the being of a curved line is from an infinite straight line, though the infinite
straight line does not inform the curved line as a form but rather as a cause and
an essence. The curved line cannot participate in this essence either by taking a
part of it (since the essence is infinite and indivisible) or as matter participates in
form (e.g., as Socrates and Plato [participate] in humanity), or as a whole is
participated in by its parts (e.g., as the universe [is participated in] by its parts),
or as several mirrors [partake of] the same face in different ways (for it is not the
case that as a mirror is a mirror before it receives the image of a face, so created
being exists prior to derivative, [participating] being; for created being *is*
103 derivative being). Who is he, then, who can understand how it is that the one,
infinite Form is participated in in different ways by different created things? For
created being cannot be anything other than reflection—not a reflection received positively in some other thing but a reflection which is contingently
different. Perhaps [a comparison with an artifact is fitting]: if the artifact
depended entirely upon the craftman's idea and did not have any other being
than dependent being, the artifact would exist from the craftsman and would be
conserved as a result of his influence—analogously to the image of a face in a
mirror (with the proviso that before and after [the appearance of the image] the
mirror be nothing in and of itself).

Nor can we understand how it is that God can be made manifest to us through
visible creatures. For [God is] not [manifest] analogously to our intellect,
which is known only to God and to ourselves and which, when it commences to
think, receives from certain images in the memory a form of a color, a sound, or
something else. Prior [to this reception] the intellect was without form, and
subsequently thereto it assumes another form—whether of signs, utterances, or
letters—and manifests itself to others [besides itself and God]. Although
God—whether in order to make His goodness known (as the religious maintain), or because of the fact that [He is] maximum, absolute Necessity, or for
some other reason—created the world, which obeys Him (so that there are
those who are compelled and who fear Him and whom He judges), it is evident
that He neither assumes another form (since He is the Form of all forms) nor
appears through positive signs (since these signs themselves, in regard to their
own being, would likewise require other things through which [to appear], and
so on *ad infinitum*).

104   Who could understand the following?: how all things are the image of that
one, infinite Form and are different contingently—as if a created thing were a
god manqué, just as an accident is a substance manqué, and a woman is a man

92

manqué.[24] For the Infinite Form is only received finitely, so that every created thing is, as it were, a finite infinity or a created god,[25] so that it exists in the way in which this can best occur.[26] [Everything is] as if the Creator had said, "Let it be made," and as if because a God (who is eternity itself) could not be made, there was made that which could be made: viz., something as much like God as possible.[27] Wherefore, we infer that every created thing qua created thing is perfect—even if it seems less perfect in comparison with some other [created thing]. For the most gracious God imparts being to all things, in the manner in which being can be received. Therefore, since He imparts without difference and envy and since [what is imparted] is received in such way that contingency does not allow it to be received otherwise or to a greater degree: every created being finds satisfaction in its own perfection, which it has from the Divine Being freely. It does not desire to be another created thing—as if [the other were] more perfect.[28] Rather, it prefers that which it itself has, as a divine gift, from the Maximum; and it wishes for this [gift] to be incorruptibly perfected and preserved.

105   *Chapter Three*:   In a way that cannot be understood the Maximum enfolds and unfolds all things.

Nothing not enfolded in the first part [i.e., Book One] can be stated or thought about the ascertainable truth. For, necessarily, everything that agrees with what was there stated about the First Truth is true; the rest, which disagrees, is false. Now, in Book One we find it indicated [29] that there can be only one Maximum of all maxima. But the Maximum is that to which nothing can be opposed and in which even the Minimum is the Maximum.[30] Therefore, Infinite Oneness is the enfolding of all things. *Oneness*, which unites all things, bespeaks this [enfolding of all things]. Oneness is maximal not simply because it is the enfolding of number but because [it is the enfolding] of all things.[31] And just as in number, which is the unfolding of oneness, we find only oneness, so in all existing things we find only the Maximum.

With respect to quantity, which is the unfolding of oneness, oneness is said to be a point. For in quantity only a point is present. Just as everywhere in a line—no matter where you divide it—there is a point, so [the same thing holds true] for a surface and a material object. And yet, there is not more than one point. This one point is not anything other than infinite oneness; for infinite oneness is a point which is the end, the perfection, and the totality of line and quantity, which it enfolds. The first unfolding of the point is the line, in which only the point is present.

106   In like manner, if you consider [the matter] carefully: rest is oneness which enfolds motion, and motion is rest ordered serially. Hence, motion is the

93

unfolding of rest. In like manner, the present, or the now, enfolds time. The past was the present, and the future will become the present. Therefore, nothing except an ordered present is found in time. Hence, the past and the future are the unfolding of the present. The present is the enfolding of all present times; and the present times are the unfolding, serially, of the present; and in the present times only the present is found. Therefore, the present is one enfolding of all times. Indeed, the present is. oneness. In like manner, identity is the enfolding of difference; equality [the enfolding] of inequality; and simplicity [the enfolding] of divisions, or distinctions.

107   Therefore, there is one enfolding of all things. The enfolding of substance, the enfolding of quality or of quantity, and so on, are not distinct enfoldings. For there is only one Maximum, with which the Minimum coincides and in which enfolded[32] difference is not opposed to enfolding identity. Just as oneness precedes otherness,[33] so also a point, which is a perfection, [precedes] magnitude. For what is perfect precedes whatever is imperfect. Thus, rest [precedes] motion, identity [precedes] difference, equality [precedes] inequality, and so on regarding the other perfections. These are convertible with Oneness, which is Eternity itself (for there cannot be a plurality of eternal things).[34] Therefore, God is the enfolding of all things in that all things are in Him; and He is the unfolding of all things in that He is in all things.

108   To explain my meaning by numerical examples: Number is the unfolding of oneness. Now, number bespeaks reasoning. But reasoning is from a mind. Therefore, the brutes, which do not have a mind, are unable to number.[35] Therefore, just as number arises from our mind by virtue of the fact that we understand what is commonly one as individually many: so the plurality of things [arises] from the Divine Mind (in which the·many are present without plurality, because they are present in Enfolding Oneness). For in accordance with the fact that things cannot participate equally in the Equality of Being: God, in eternity, understood one thing in one way and another thing in another way. Herefrom arose plurality, which in God is oneness. Now, plurality or number does not have any other being than as comes from oneness. Therefore, oneness, without which number would not be number,[36] is present in the plurality. And, indeed, this [is what it] is for oneness to unfold all things: viz., for it to be present in the plurality.[37]

109   However, the mode of enfolding and unfolding surpasses [the measure of] our mind. Who, I ask, could understand how it is that the plurality of things is from the Divine Mind? For God's understanding is His being; for God is Infinite Oneness. If you proceed with the numerical comparison by considering that number is the multiplication, by the mind, of the common one: it seems as if God, who is Oneness, were multiplied in things, since His understanding is His being.[38] And, yet, you understand that this Oneness, which is infinite and maximal, cannot be multiplied. How, then, can you understand there to be a

plurality whose being comes from the One without [there occurring] any multiplication of the One? That is, how you can understand there to be a multiplication of Oneness without there being a multiplication [of Oneness]? Surely, [you can] not [understand it as you understand the multiplication] of one species or of one genus in many species or many individuals; outside of these [individuals] a genus or a species does not exist except through an
110 abstracting intellect.[39] Therefore, no one understands how God (whose oneness of being does not exist through the understanding's abstracting from things and does not exist as united to, or merged with, things) is unfolded through the number of things. If you consider things in their independence from God, they are nothing—even as number without oneness [is nothing]. If you consider God in His independence from things, He exists and the things are nothing. If you consider Him as He is in things, you consider things to be something in which He is. And in this regard you err, as was evident in the preceding chapter.[40] For it is not the case that the being of a thing is another thing, as a different thing is [another thing]; rather, its being is derivative being. If you consider a thing as it is in God, it *is* God and Oneness.

There remains only to say that the plurality of things arises from the fact that God is present in nothing. For take away God from the creation and nothing remains. Take away substance from a composite and no accident remains; and so, nothing remains. How can our intellect fathom this? For although an accident perishes when the substance is removed, an accident is not therefore nothing. However, the accident perishes because its being is adventitious being. And hence, a quantity, for example, exists only through the being of a substance; nevertheless, because quantity is present, the substance is quantitative by virtue of quantity. But [the relationship between God and the creation is] not similar. For the creation is not adventitious to God in a correspondingly similar manner; for it does not confer anything on God, as an accident [confers something] on a substance. Indeed, an accident confers [something] on a substance to such an extent that, as a result, the substance cannot exist without some accident, even though the accident derives its own being from the
111 substance. But with God a similar thing cannot hold true. How, then, can we understand the creation qua creation?—[a creation] which is from God but which cannot as a result thereof contribute anything at all to Him, who is the greatest. And if qua creation it does not have even as much being as an accident but is altogether nothing, how can we understand that the plurality of things is unfolded by virtue of the fact that God is present in nothing? For nothing [or not-being] is without any being. You might reply: "God's omnipotent will is the cause; His will and omnipotence are His being; for the whole of theology is circular."[41] If so, then you will have to admit that you are thoroughly ignorant of how enfolding and unfolding occur and that you know only that you do not know the manner, even if you know (1) that God is the enfolding and the

unfolding of all things, (2) that insofar as He is the enfolding, in Him all things are Himself, and (3) that insofar as He is the unfolding, in all things He is that which they are, just as in an image the reality itself (*veritas*) is present.[42] [It is] as if a face were present in its own image, which, depending upon its repeatedness, is a close or a distant multiple of the face. (I do not mean according to spatial distance but according to a progressive difference from the real face, since [the image] cannot be repeated in any other way [than with a difference].) [It is as if] the one face—while remaining incomprehensibly above all the senses and every mind—were to appear differently and manifoldly in the different images multiplied from it.

112   *Chapter Four*:   The universe, which is only a contracted maximum, is a likeness of the Absolute [Maximum].

If by careful consideration we extend what was previously manifested to us through learned ignorance: from the sole fact of our knowing that all things are either the Absolute Maximum or from the Absolute Maximum, many points can become clear to us regarding the world, or universe, which I affirm to be only a contracted maximum. Since what is contracted, or concrete, has from the Absolute whatever it is, that which is the [contracted] maximum imitates the maximally Absolute as much as it can. Therefore, [regarding] those things which in Book One were made known to us about the Absolute Maximum: as they befit the maximally Absolute absolutely,[43] so I affirm that they befit in a contracted way what is contracted.

113   Let me present some examples in order to prepare an inroad for one who is inquiring. God is Absolute Maximality and Oneness, who precedes and unites absolutely different and separate things—i.e., contradictories—between which there is no middle ground. Absolute Maximality is, absolutely, that which all things are (in all things it is the Absolute Beginning of things, the [Absolute] End of things, and the [Absolute] Being of things; in it[44] all things are— indistinctly, most simply, and without plurality—the Absolute Maximum), just as an infinite line is all figures.[45] So likewise the world, or universe,[46] is a contracted maximum and a contracted one. The world precedes contracted opposites—i.e., contraries. And it is, contractedly, that which all things are (in all things it is the contracted beginning of things, the contracted end of things, and the contracted being of things; it is a contracted infinity and thus is contractedly infinite; in it all things are—with contracted simplicity and contracted indistinction and without plurality[47]—the contracted maximum), just as a contracted maximum line is contractedly all figures.

114   Hence, when one rightly considers contraction, the whole matter becomes clear. For contracted infinity, simplicity, or indistinction is, with regard to its

contraction, infinitely lower than what is absolute, so that the infinite and eternal world[48] falls disproportionally short of Absolute Infinity and Absolute Eternity,[49] and [so that] the one [falls disproportionally short] of Oneness. Hence, Absolute Oneness is free of all plurality. But although contracted oneness (which is the one universe) is one maximum: since it is contracted, it is not free of plurality, even though it is only one contracted maximum. Therefore, although it is maximally one, its oneness is contracted through plurality, just as its infinity [is contracted] through finitude, its simplicity through composition, its eternity through succession, its necessity through possibility, and so on—as if Absolute Necessity communicated itself without any intermingling and yet necessity were contractedly restricted in something opposed to it. [For example, it is] as if whiteness had, in itself, absolute being apart from any abstracting on the part of our intellect, and as if what is white were contractedly white from whiteness; in this case whiteness would be restricted by nonwhiteness in something actually white, so that that which would not be white without whiteness is white through whiteness.

115   From these [observations] an inquirer can infer many points. For example, just as God, since He is immense, is neither in the sun nor in the moon, although in them He is, absolutely, that which they are: so the universe is neither in the sun nor in the moon; but in them it is, contractedly, that which they are. Now, the Absolute Quiddity of the sun is not other than the Absolute Quiddity of the moon (since [this] is God Himself, who is the Absolute Being and Absolute Quiddity of all things); but the contracted quiddity of the sun *is* other than the contracted quiddity of the moon (for as the Absolute Quiddity of a thing is not the thing, so the contracted [quiddity of a thing] is none other than the thing). Therefore, [the following] is clear: that since the universe is contracted quiddity, which is contracted in one way in the sun and in another way in the moon, the identity of the universe exists in difference, just as its oneness exists in plurality. Hence, although the universe is neither the sun nor the moon, nevertheless in the sun it is the sun and in the moon it is the moon. However, it is not the case that God is in the sun sun and in the moon moon;[50] rather, He is that which is sun and moon without plurality and difference. *Universe* bespeaks *universality*—i.e., a oneness of many things. Accordingly, just as humanity is neither Socrates nor Plato but in Socrates is Socrates and in Plato is Plato, so is the universe in relation to all things.

116   But since, as was said, the universe is only the contracted first,[51] and in this respect is a maximum, it is evident that the whole universe sprang into existence by a simple emanation[52] of the contracted maximum from the Absolute Maximum. But all the beings which are parts of the universe (and without which the universe, since it is contracted, could not be one and whole and perfect) sprang into existence together with the universe; [there was] not first an intelligence, then a noble soul, and then nature, as Avicenna[53] and other

philosophers maintained. Nevertheless, just as in a craftsman's design the whole (e.g., a house) is prior to a part (e.g., a wall), so because all things sprang into existence from God's design, we say that first there appeared the universe and thereafter all things—without which there could not be either a universe or a perfect [universe]. Hence, just as the abstract is in the concrete, so we consider the Absolute Maximum to be antecedently in the contracted maximum, so that it is subsequently in all particulars because it is present absolutely in that which is contractedly all things [viz., in the universe]. For God is the Absolute Quiddity of the world, or universe. But the universe is contracted quiddity.[54] *Contraction* means contraction to [i.e., restriction by] something, so as to be this or that. Therefore, God, who is one, is in the one universe. But the universe is contractedly in all things. And so, we can understand the following: (1) how it is that God, who is most simple Oneness and exists in the one universe, is in all things as if subsequently and through the mediation of the universe, and (2) [how it is that] through the mediation of the one universe the plurality of things is in God.

117   *Chapter Five*:   Each thing in each thing.

If you pay close attention to what has already been said, you will not have trouble seeing—perhaps more deeply than Anaxagoras—the basis of the Anaxagorean truth "Each thing is in each thing."[55] From Book One it is evident that God is in all things in such way that all things are in Him;[56] and it is now evident [from II, 4] that God is in all things through the mediation of the universe, as it were. Hence, it is evident that all is in all and each in each. For the universe, as being most perfect, preceded all things "in the order of nature," as it were, so that in each thing it could be each thing. For in each created thing the universe is this created thing; and each thing receives all things in such way that in a given thing all things are, contractedly, this thing. Since each thing is contracted, it is not the case that it can be actually all things; hence, it contracts all things, so that they are it. Therefore, if all things are in all things, all things are seen to precede each given thing. Therefore, it is not the case that all things are many things, since it is not the case that plurality precedes each given thing. Hence, in the order of nature all things preceded, without plurality, each thing. Therefore, it is not the case that many things are in each thing actually; rather, all things are, without plurality, each given thing.

118   Now, the universe is in things only contractedly; and every actually existing thing contracts all things, so that they are, actually, that which it is. But everything which exists actually, exists in God, since He is the actuality of all things. Now, actuality is the perfection and the end of possibility. Hence, since the universe is contracted in each actually existing thing: it is evident that God,

who is in the universe, is in each thing and that each actually existing thing is immediately in God, as is also the universe.[57] Therefore, to say that each thing is in each thing is not other than [to say] that through all things God is in all things and that through all things all things are in God.[58] The following very deep [truths] are apprehended clearly by an acute intellect: that God is, without difference, in all things because each thing is in each thing and that all things are in God because all things are in all things. But since the universe is in each thing in such way that each thing is in it: in each thing the universe is, contractedly, that which this thing is contractedly; and in the universe each thing is the universe; nonetheless, the universe is in each thing in one way, and each thing is in the universe in another way.

119   Consider an example: It is evident that an infinite line is a line, a triangle, a circle, and a sphere.[59] Now, every finite line has its being from the infinite line, which is all that which the finite line is.[60] Therefore, in the finite line all that which the infinite line is—viz., line, triangle, and the others—is that which the finite line is. Therefore, in the finite line every figure is the finite line. In the finite line there is not actually either a triangle, a circle, or a sphere; for from what is actually many, there is not made what is actually one. For it is not the case that each thing is in each thing actually; rather, in the line the triangle is the line; and in the line the circle is the line; and so on. In order that you may see more clearly: A line cannot exist actually except in a material object, as will be shown elsewhere.[61] Now, no one doubts that all figures are enfolded in a material object, which has length, width, and depth. Therefore, in an actually existing line all figures are actually the line; and in [an actually existing] triangle [all figures are] the triangle; and so on. In a stone all things are stone; in a vegetative soul, vegetative soul; in life, life; in the senses, the senses; in sight, sight; in hearing, hearing; in imagination, imagination; in reason, reason; in intellect, intellect;[62] in God, God. See, then, how it is that the oneness of things, or the universe, exists in plurality and, conversely, the plurality [of things] exists in oneness.

120   Consider more closely and you will see that each actually existing thing is tranquil because of the fact that in it all things *are* it and that in God it is God. You see that there is a marvelous oneness of things, an admirable equality, and a most wonderful union,[63] so that all things are in all things. You also understand that for this reason there arises a difference and a union of things. For it is not the case that each thing was able to be actually all things (for each would have been God, and consequently all things would [actually] exist in each thing in the way in which they would be possible to exist conformably with that which each thing is); and, as was evident above,[64] [it is] not [the case that] each thing was able to be altogether like the other. This, then, caused all things to exist in different degrees, just as it also caused that being which was unable to exist incorruptibly at once, to exist incorruptibly[65] in temporal succession, so

that all things are that which they are because they were not able to exist in any
121 other way or any better way.[66] Therefore, in each thing all things are tranquil,
since one degree could not exist without another—just as with the members of a
body each contributes [something] to the other, and all are content in all. For
since the eye cannot actually be the hands, the feet, and all the other members,
it is content with being the eye; and the foot [is content with being] the foot.[67]
And all members contribute [something] to one another, so that each is that
which it is in the best way it can be. Neither the hand nor the foot is in the eye;
but in the eye they are the eye insofar as the eye is immediately in the man. And
in like manner, in the foot all the members [are the foot]insofar as the foot is
immediately in the man. Thus, each member through each member is immediately in the man; and the man, or the whole, is in each member through
each member, just as in the parts the whole is in each part through each part.
122   Therefore, suppose you consider humanity as if it were something absolute,
unmixable, and incontractible; and [suppose you] consider a man in whom
absolute humanity exists absolutely and from which humanity[68] there exists the
contracted humanity which the man is. In that case, the absolute humanity is, as
it were, God; and the contracted humanity is, as it were, the universe. The
absolute humanity is in the man principally, or antecedently, and is in each
member or each part subsequently; and the contracted humanity is in the eye
eye, in the heart heart, etc., and so, in each member is contractedly each
member. Thus, in accordance with this supposition, we have found (1) a
likeness of God and the world, and (2) guidance with respect to all the points
touched upon in these two chapters, together with (3) many other points which
follow from this [comparison].

123   *Chapter Six:*   The enfolding, and the degrees of contraction, of the
universe.

In the foregoing we found, beyond all understanding, that the world, or
universe, is one. Its oneness is contracted by plurality, so that it is oneness in
plurality. And because Absolute Oneness is first and the oneness of the
universe is derived from it, the oneness of the universe will be a second
oneness, consisting of a plurality. And since (as I will show in *Conjectures*)[69]
the second oneness is tenfold and unites the ten categories, the one universe
will, by a tenfold contraction, be the unfolding of the first, absolute, and simple
Oneness. Now, all things are enfolded in the number ten, since there is not a
number above it.[70] Therefore, the tenfold oneness of the universe enfolds the
plurality of all contracted things. As ten is the square root of one hundred and
the cube root of one thousand, so—because the oneness of the universe is in all
things as the contracted beginning of all—the oneness of the universe is the root

of all things. From this root there first arises the "square number," so to speak, as a third oneness; and the cubic number [arises thereafter] as a fourth and final oneness. The first unfolding of the oneness of the universe is the third oneness, viz., one hundred; and the last unfolding is the fourth oneness, viz., one thousand.

124   And so, we find three universal onenesses descending by degrees to what is particular, in which they are contracted, so that they are actually the particular. The first and absolute Oneness enfolds all things absolutely; the first contracted [oneness enfolds] all things contractedly. But order requires [the following]: that Absolute Oneness be seen to enfold, as it were, the first contracted [oneness], so that by means of it [it enfolds] all other things; that the first contracted [oneness] be seen to enfold the second contracted [oneness] and, by means of it, the third contracted [oneness]; and that the second contracted [oneness be seen to enfold] the third contracted oneness, which is the last universal oneness, fourth from the first, so that by means of the third contracted oneness the second oneness arrives at what is particular. And so, we see that the universe is contracted in each particular through three grades. Therefore, the universe is, as it were, all of the ten categories [*generalissima*], then the genera, and then the species. And so, these are universal according to their respective degrees; they exist with degrees and prior, by a certain order of nature, to the thing which actually contracts them. And since the universe is contracted, it is not found except as unfolded in genera; and genera are found only in species.[71]

125   But individuals exist actually; in them all things exist contractedly. Through these considerations we see that universals exist actually only in a contracted manner. And in this way the Peripatetics speak the truth [when they say that] universals do not actually exist independently of things. For only what is particular exists actually. In the particular, universals are contractedly the particular. Nevertheless, in the order of nature universals have a certain universal being which is contractible by what is particular. [I do] not [mean] that before contraction they exist actually and in some way other than according to the natural order ([i.e., other than] as a contractible universal which exists not in itself but in that which is actual, just as a point, a line, and a surface precede, in progressive order, the material object in which alone they exist actually). For because the universe exists actually only in a contracted way, so too do all universals. Although universals do not exist as actual apart from particulars, nevertheless they are not mere rational entities.[72] (By comparison, although neither a line nor a surface exists apart from a material object, nevertheless because they exist in material objects—even as universals exist in particulars—they are not mere rational entities.) Nevertheless, by [the process of] abstracting, the intellect makes them exist independently of things. To be sure, the abstraction is a rational entity, since absolute being cannot befit universals. For the altogether absolute universal is God.

126   We shall see in the book *Conjectures* how it is that the universal is in the
intellect as a result of the process of abstracting.[73] Yet, this point can be clearly
enough seen from the preceding, since in the intellect the universal is only the
intellect; and so, it is present there intellectually and contractedly. Since the
intellect's understanding is both loftier and more illustrious being, it
apprehends, both in itself and in other things, the contraction of universals. For
example, dogs and the other animals of the same species are united by virtue of
the common specific nature which is in them. This nature would be contracted
in them even if Plato's intellect had not, from a comparison of likenesses,
formed for itself a species. Therefore, with respect to its own operation,
understanding follows being and living; for [merely] through its own operation
understanding can bestow neither being nor living nor understanding. Now,
with respect to the things understood: the intellect's understanding follows,
through a likeness, being and living and the intelligibility of nature. Therefore,
universals, which it makes from comparison, are a likeness of the universals
contracted in things. Universals exist contractedly in the intellect before the
intellect unfolds them by outward signs for them—unfolds them through
understanding, which is its operation. For it can understand nothing which is
not already contractedly in it as it. Therefore, in understanding, it unfolds, by
resembling signs and characters, a certain resembling world, which is contracted in it.

I have here said enough about the oneness of the universe and about its
contraction in things. Let me add some points about its trinity.

127   *Chapter Seven*:   The trinity of the universe.

Absolute Oneness is necessarily trine—not contractedly but absolutely; for
Absolute Oneness is not other than Trinity, which we grasp more readily by
means of a certain mutual relationship. (I discussed this point adequately in
Book One.)[74] Similarly, just as maximum contracted oneness is oneness, so it
is trine—not absolutely, so that the trinity is oneness, but contractedly, so that
the oneness exists only in trinity, as a whole exists contractedly in its parts. In
God it is not the case that Oneness exists contractedly in Trinity as a whole
exists [contractedly] in its parts or as a universal exists [contractedly] in
particulars; rather, the Oneness is the Trinity. Therefore, each of the persons
[of the Trinity] is the Oneness; and since the Oneness is Trinity, one person is
not another person. But in the case of the universe a similar thing cannot hold
true. Therefore, [in the case of the universe] the three mutual relationships—
which in God are called persons—have actual existence only collectively in
oneness.

128   We must consider the foregoing points carefully. For in God the perfection
of Oneness, which is Trinity, is so great that the Father is actually God, the Son

actually God, and the Holy Spirit actually God; the Son and the Holy Spirit are actually in the Father, the Son and the Father [are actually] in the Holy Spirit, and the Father and the Holy Spirit [are actually] in the Son. But in the case of what is contracted, a similar thing cannot hold true; for the mutual relationships exist per se only conjointly. Therefore, it cannot be the case that each distinct relationship is the universe; rather, all the mutual relationships [are] collectively [the universe]. Nor is the one [of them] actually in the others; rather, they are most perfectly contracted to one another (in the way in which the condition of contraction permits this), so that from them there is one universe,[75] which could not be one without that trinity. For there cannot be contraction without (1) that which is contractible, (2) that which causes contracting, and (3) the union which is effected through the common actuality of these two.

But contractibility bespeaks a certain possibility; and this [possibility] is descendant from the Begetting Oneness in God, just as otherness [is descendant] from Oneness.[76] For [contracted possibility][77] bespeaks mutability and otherness,[78] since [it speaks] with regard to a beginning.[79] For not anything it seems, precedes possibility. For how would anything exist if it had not been possible to exist? Therefore, possibility is descendant from Eternal Oneness.

129 But since that which causes contracting delimits the possibility of that which is contractible, it descends from Equality of Oneness. For Equality of Oneness is Equality of Being. For *being* and *one* are convertible. Hence, since that which causes contracting equalizes the possibility for being one thing or another contractedly, it is rightly said to descend from Equality-of-Being, which, in God, is the Word. And since the Word, which is the Essence (*ratio*) and Idea and Absolute Necessity of things, necessitates and restricts the possibility through such a cause of contracting, some [thinkers] called that which causes contracting "form" or "the world-soul" (and they called possibility "matter"); others [spoke of it as] "fate substantified"; others, e.g., the Platonists, [spoke of it as] a "connecting necessity." For it descends from Absolute Necessity, so that it is a contracted necessity and contracted form, as it were, in which all forms truly exist. This [topic] will be discussed later.[80]

130 Next, there is the union of what is contractible and what causes contracting—i.e., [the union] of matter and form, or of possibility and connecting necessity. This union is actually effected as if by a spirit of love—[a love] which unites the two by means of a certain motion. Certain individuals were accustomed to call this union "determined possibility." For the possibility-to-be is determined toward actually being this or that—[determined] by means of the union of the determining form and the determinable matter. But, clearly, this union descends from the Holy Spirit, who is Infinite Union.

Therefore, the oneness of the universe is three, since it is from possibility, connecting necessity, and union—which can be called possibility, actuality, and union.[81] And herefrom infer four universal modes of being. There is the mode of being which is called Absolute Necessity, according as God is Form of forms, Being of beings, and Essence (*ratio*) or Quiddity of things. With regard to this mode of being: in God all things are Absolute Necessity itself. Another mode [of being] is according as things exist in the connecting necessity; in this necessity, just as in a mind, the forms-of-things, true in themselves, exist with a distinction, and an order, of nature. We shall see later whether this is so.[82] Another mode of being is according as, in determined possibility, things are actually this or that. And the lowest mode of being is according as things are possible to be, and it is absolute possibility.[83]

131   The last three modes of being exist in one universality which is a contracted maximum.[84] From these there is one universal mode of being, since without them not anything can exist. I say *modes of being*. For the universal mode of being is not composed of the three things as parts in the way that a house [is composed] of a roof, a foundation, and a wall. Rather it is from *modes of being*. For a rose which in a rose-garden is in potency in winter and in actuality in the summer has passed from a mode of possible being to something actually determined. Hence, we see that the mode of being of possibility, the mode of being of necessity, and the mode of being of actual determination are distinct. From them there is one universal mode of being, since without them there is nothing; nor does the one mode actually exist without the other.

132   *Chapter Eight*:   The possibility, or matter, of the universe.

To expound here, at least briefly, upon the things which can make our ignorance learned, let me discuss for a moment the previously mentioned three modes of being—beginning with possibility. The ancients made many statements about possibility; the opinion of them all was that from nothing nothing is made. And so, they maintained that there is a certain absolute possibility of being all things and that it is eternal. They believed that in absolute possibility all things are enfolded as possibilities. They conceived this [absolute] matter, or possibility, by reasoning in a reverse way, just as in the case of absolute necessity. For example, they conceived a body incorporeally by abstracting from it the form of corporeity. And so, they attained unto matter only ignorantly. For how can a body be conceived incorporeally and without form? They said that by nature possibility precedes everything, so that the statement "God exists" is never true without the statement "Absolute possibility exists" also being true. Nevertheless, they did not maintain that absolute possibility is coeternal with God, since it is from God. Absolute possibility is neither something nor nothing, neither one nor many, neither this nor that, neither quiddative nor qualitative; rather, it is the possibility for all things and is, actually, nothing of all things.

133   The Platonists called absolute possibility "lack," since it lacks all form. Because it lacks, it desires. And by virtue of the following fact it is aptitude: viz., it obeys necessity, which commands it (i.e., draws it toward actually being), just as wax [obeys] the craftsman who wills to make something from it. But formlessness proceeds from, and unites, lack and aptitude—so that absolute possibility is, as it were, *incompositely* trine. For lack, aptitude, and formlessness cannot be its *parts*; for if they were, something would precede[85] absolute possibility—which is impossible. Hence, [lack, aptitude, and formlessness] are modes in whose absence absolute possibility would not be absolute. For lack exists contingently in possibility. For from the fact that possibility does not have the form it can have, it is said to be lacking. Hence, it is lack. But formlessness is the "form" (so to speak) of possibility, which, as the Platonists maintained, is the "matter" (so to speak) of forms. For the world-soul is united to matter in accordance with formlessness, which they called "the basic power of life," so that when the world-soul is mingled with possibility, the formless power of life is actually brought to the life-giving soul—brought (a) from a motion descending from the world-soul and (b) from the changeableness of possibility, or of power-of-life. Hence, they maintained that formlessness is the matter (so to speak) of forms—which matter is informed through sensitive, rational, and intellectual [form], so that it exists actually.

134   Hence, Hermes[86] said that *hyle* is the nourisher of bodies and that that formlessness is the nourisher of souls. And someone among us said that chaos naturally preceded the world and was the possibility of things—in which chaos that formless power resided, and in which power all souls exist as possibilities. Hence, the ancient Stoics said that all forms are actually in possibility but are hidden and appear as a result of a removal of the covering—just as when a spoon is made from wood only by the removal of portions [of the wood].[87]

135   However, the Peripatetics said that forms are in matter only as possibilities and are educed by an efficient cause. Hence, it is quite true that forms exist not only from possibility but also through an efficient cause. (For example, he who removes portions of a piece of wood, in order that a statue be made from it, adds with respect to form.) This is obvious. For the fact that from stone a chest cannot be made by a craftsman is a defect in the material. But the fact that someone other than the craftsman cannot make a chest from wood is a defect in the agent. Therefore, both matter and an efficient cause are required. Hence, in a certain way, forms are in matter as possibilities, and they are brought to actuality in conformity with an efficient cause. Thus, [the Peripatetics] said that the totality of things is present, as possibility, in absolute possibility. Absolute possibility is boundless and infinite because of its lack of form and because of its aptitude for all forms—just as the possibility of shaping wax into the figure of a lion or a hare or whatever else, is boundless. Now, this infinity contrasts

with the infinity of God because it is due to a lack, whereas [the infinity] of God is due to an abundance, since in God all things are actually God. Thus, the infinity of matter is privative, [but the infinity] of God is negative. This is the position of those who have spoken about absolute possibility.

136   Through learned ignorance we find that it would be impossible for absolute possibility to *exist*. For since among things possible nothing can be less than absolute possibility, which is nearest to not-being (even according to the position of [earlier] writers), we would arrive at a minimum and a maximum with respect to things admitting of greater and lesser degrees; and this is impossible. Therefore, in God absolute possibility is God, but it is not possible outside Him. For we cannot posit anything which exists with absolute potency, since everything except for the First is, necessarily, contracted.[88] For if the different things in the world are found to be so related that more can be from the one than from the other, we do not arrive at the unqualifiedly and absolutely Maximum and Minimum. And because they *are* found to be [such], absolute

137 possibility is obviously not positable. Therefore, every possibility is contracted. But it is contracted through actuality. Therefore, pure possibility—altogether undetermined by any actuality—is not to be found. Nor can the aptitude of the possibility be infinite and absolute, devoid of all contraction. For since God is Infinite Actuality, He is the cause only of actuality.[89] But the possibility of being exists contingently. Therefore, if the possibility were absolute, on what would it be contingent? Now, the possibility results from the fact that being [which derives] from the First cannot be completely, unqualifiedly, and absolutely actuality. Therefore, the actuality is contracted through the possibility, so that it does not at all exist except in the possibility. And the possibility does not at all exist unless it is contracted through the actuality. But there are differences and degrees, so that one thing is more actual, another more potential—without our coming to the unqualifiedly Maximum and Minimum. For maximum and minimum actuality coincide with maximum and minimum possibility and are the aforesaid absolutely Maximum, as was shown in Book One.[90]

138   Furthermore, unless the possibility of things were contracted, there could not be a reason for things but everything would happen by chance, as Epicurus falsely maintained. That this world sprang forth rationally from possibility was necessarily due to the fact that the possibility had an aptitude only for being this world. Therefore, the possibility's aptitude was contracted and not absolute. The same holds true regarding the earth, the sun, and other things: unless they had been latently present in matter—[present] in terms of a certain contracted possibility—there would have been no more reason why they would have been brought forth into actuality than not.

139   Hence, although God is infinite and therefore had the power to create the world as infinite, nevertheless because the possibility was, necessarily, con-

tracted and was not at all absolute or infinite aptitude, the world—in accordance with the possibility of being—was not able to be actually infinite or greater or to exist in any other way [than it does]. Now, the contraction of possibility is from actuality; but the actuality is from Maximum Actuality. Therefore, since the contraction of possibility is from God and the contraction of actuality is the result of contingency, the world—which, necessarily, is contracted—is contingently finite. Hence, from a knowledge of possibility we see how it is that contracted maximality comes from possibility which, of necessity, is contracted. This contraction [of possibility] does not result from contingency, because it occurs through actuality. And so, the universe has a rational and necessary cause of its contraction, so that the world, which is only contracted
140 being, is not contingently from God, who is Absolute Maximality. This [point] must be considered more in detail. Accordingly, since Absolute Possibility is God: if we consider the world as it is in Absolute Possibility, it is as [it is] in God and is Eternity itself.[91] If we consider [the world] as it is in contracted possibility, then possibility, by nature, precedes only the world; and this contracted possibility is neither eternity nor coeternal with God; rather, it falls short of eternity, as what is contracted [falls short] of what is absolute—the two being infinitely different.

What is said about potency or possibility or matter needs to be qualified, in the foregoing manner, according to the rules of learned ignorance. How it is that possibility proceeds by steps to actuality, I leave to be dealt with in the book *Conjectures*.[92]

141 *Chapter Nine*: The soul, or form, of the universe.

All the wise agree that possible being cannot come to be actual except through actual being; for nothing can bring itself into actual being, lest it be the cause of itself; for it would be before it was.[93] Hence, they said that that which actualizes possibility does so intentionally, so that the possibility comes to be actual by
142 rational ordination and not by chance. Some called this excellent [actualizing] nature "mind"; others called it "intelligence," others "world-soul," others "fate substantified," others (e.g., the Platonists) "connecting necessity." The Platonists thought that possibility is necessarily determined through this necessity, so that possibility now actually is that which it was beforehand able to be by nature. For they said that in this mind the forms of things exist actually and intelligibly, just as in matter they exist as possibilities. And [they maintained] that the connecting necessity—which contains in itself the truth of the forms, together with [the truth of] the things which accompany the forms— moves the heavens in accordance with the order of nature, so that by the medium of motion as an instrument [the connecting necessity] brings possibil-

ity into actuality and, as conformably as can be, into congruence with the intelligible concept of truth. The Platonists conceded that form as it is in matter—through this activity of the [world]-mind and by the medium of motion—is the image of true intelligible form and so is not true form but a likeness. Thus, the Platonists said that the true forms are in the world-soul prior—not temporally but naturally—to their presence in things. The Peripatetics do not grant this [point], for they maintain that forms do not have any other existence than in matter and (as a result of abstracting) in the intellect. (Obviously, the abstraction is subsequent to the thing.)

143   However, [the following view] was acceptable to the Platonists: that such a distinct plurality of exemplars in the connecting necessity is—in a natural order—from one infinite Essence, in which all things are one. Nevertheless, they did not believe that the exemplars were created by this [one infinite Essence] but that they descended from it in such way that the statement "God exists" is never true without the statement "The world-soul exists" also being true. And they affirmed that the world-soul is the unfolding of the Divine Mind, so that all things—which in God are one Exemplar—are, in the world-soul, many distinct [exemplars]. They added that God naturally precedes this connecting necessity, that the world-soul naturally precedes motion, and that motion qua instrument [precedes] the temporal unfolding of things, so that those things which exist truly in the [world]-soul and exist in matter as possibilities are temporally unfolded through motion. This temporal unfolding follows the natural order which is in the world-soul and which is called "fate substantified." And the temporal unfolding of substantified fate is a fate (as it is called by many) which descends actually and causally from that [substantified fate].[94]

144   And so, the mode-of-being that is in the world-soul is [the mode] in accordance with which we say that the world is intelligible. The mode of actual being—which results from the actual determination of possibility by way of unfolding—is, as was said, the mode of being according to which the world is perceptible, in the opinion of the Platonists. They did not claim that forms as they exist in matter are other than forms which exist in the world-soul but [claimed] only that forms exist according to different modes of being: in the world-soul [they exist] truly and in themselves; in matter they exist not in their purity but in concealment—as likenesses. [The Platonists] added that the truth of forms is attained only through the intellect; through reason, imagination, and sense, nothing but images [are attained], according as the forms are mixed with possibility. And [they maintained] that therefore they did not attain to anything truly but [only] as a matter of opinion.

145   The Platonists thought that all motion derives from this world-soul, which they said to be present as a whole in the whole world and as a whole in each part of the world. Nevertheless, it does not exercise the same powers in all parts [of

the world]—just as in man the rational soul does not operate in the same way in the hair and in the heart, although it is present as a whole in the whole [man] and in each part. Hence, the Platonists claimed that in the world-soul all souls—whether in bodies or outside [of bodies]—are enfolded. For they asserted that the world-soul is spread throughout the entire universe—[spread] not through parts (because it is simple and indivisible) but as a whole in the earth, where it holds the earth together, as a whole in stone, where it effects the steadfastness of the stone's parts, as a whole in water, as a whole in trees, and so on for each thing. The world-soul is the first circular unfolding (the Divine Mind being the center point, as it were, and the world-soul being the circle which unfolds the center) and is the natural enfolding of the whole temporal order of things. Therefore, because of the world-soul's distinctness and order, the Platonists called it "self-moving number" and asserted that it is from sameness and difference. They also thought that the world-soul differs from the human soul only in number, so that just as the human soul is to man so the world-soul is to the universe. [Moreover,] they believed that all souls are from the world-soul and that ultimately they are resolved into it, provided their moral failures do not prevent this.

146   Many Christians consented to this Platonistic approach. Especially since the essence of stone is distinct from the essence of man[95] and in God there is neither distinction nor otherness, they thought it necessary that these distinct essences (in accordance with which, things are distinct) be subsequent to God but prior to things (for the essence precedes the thing); and [they thought] this [too] with regard to intelligence, the mistress of the orbits. Furthermore, [they believed] that such distinct essences as these are the indestructible notions-of-things in the world-soul. Indeed, they maintained—though they admit that it is difficult to say and think—that the world-soul consists of all the notions of all things, so that in it all notions are its substance.[These Christians] support their view by the authority of divine Scripture: "God said 'Let there be light,' and light was made." If the truth of light had not been naturally antecedent, what sense would it have made for Him to say "Let there be light"? And if the truth of light had not been antecedent, then after the light was temporally unfolded, why would it have been called light rather than something else? Such [Christians] adduce many similar considerations to support this view.

147   The Peripatetics, although admitting that the work of nature is the work of intelligence, do not admit that there are exemplars. I think that they are surely wrong—unless by "intelligence" they mean *God*. For if there is no notion within the intelligence, how does it move according to purpose? [On the other hand,] if there *is* a notion of the thing-to-be-unfolded-temporally (this notion would be the essence), then such a notion could not have been abstracted from a thing which does not yet exist temporally. Therefore, if there exists a notion which has not been abstracted, surely it is the notion about which the Platonists

speak—[a notion] which is not [derived] from things but [is such that] things accord with it. Hence, the Platonists did not affirm that such essences of things are something distinct and different from the intelligence; rather, [they said] that such distinct [essences] jointly constitute a certain simple intelligence which enfolds in itself all essences. Hence, although the essence of man is not the essence of stone but the two are different essences, the humanity from which man derives (as white derives from whiteness) has no other being than—in intelligence—intelligibly and according to the nature of intelligence and—in reality—really.[96] [This does] not [mean] that there is the humanity of Plato and another separate humanity. Rather, according to different modes of being the same humanity exists naturally in the intelligence *before* existing in matter—not temporally before but in the sense that the essence naturally precedes the thing.

148   The Platonists spoke keenly and sensibly enough, being reproached, unreasonably, perhaps, by Aristotle, who endeavored to refute them with a covering of words rather than with deep discernment. But through learned ignorance I shall ascertain what the truer [view] is. I have [already] indicated[97] that we do not attain to the unqualifiedly Maximum and that, likewise, absolute possibility or absolute form (i.e., [absolute] actuality) which is not God cannot exist. And [I indicated] that no being except God is uncontracted[98] and that there is only one Form of forms and Truth of truths[99] and that the maximum truth of the circle is not other than that of the quadrangle.[100] Hence, the forms of things are not distinct except as they exist contractedly; as they exist absolutely they are one, indistinct [Form], which is the Word in God.[101] It follows that [a Platonistic-type] world-soul would exist only in conjunction with possibility, through which it would be contracted.[102] Nor would it be the case that qua mind it is either separated or separable from things; for if we consider mind according as it is separated from possibility, it is the Divine Mind, which alone is completely actual. Therefore, there cannot be many distinct exemplars, for each exemplar would be maximum and most true with respect to the things which are its exemplifications. But it is not possible that there be many maximal and most true things. For only one infinite Exemplar is sufficient and necessary; in it all things exist, as the ordered exists in the order. [This Exemplar] very adequately enfolds all the essences of things, regardless of how different they are, so that Infinite Essence is the most true Essence of the circle and is not greater or lesser or different or other [than the circle]. And Infinite Essence is the Essence of the quadrangle and is not greater or lesser or different [than the quadrangle]. The same holds true for other things, as we can discern from the example of an infinite line.[103]

149   Seeing the differences of things, we marvel that the one most simple Essence of all things is also the different essence of each thing. Yet, we know that this must be the case; [we know it] from learned ignorance, which shows that in

God difference is identity. For in seeing that the difference of the essences of all things exists most truly, we apprehend—since it is most true [that this difference exists most truly]—the one most true Essence-of-all-things, which is Maximum Truth. Therefore, when it is said that God created man by means of one essence and created stone by means of another, this is true with respect to things but not true with respect to the Creator—just as we see with regard to numbers. The number three is a most simple essence, which does not admit of more or less. In itself it is one essence; but as it is related to different things, it is, in accordance therewith, different essences. For example, in a triangle there is one essence of the number three for the three angles; in a substance there is another essence [of the number three] for the matter, the form, and their union; there is another essence [of the number three] for a father, a mother, and their offspring—or for three human beings or three asses. Hence, the connecting necessity is not, as the Platonists maintained, a mind which is inferior to the Begetting Mind; rather, it is the divine Word and Son, equal with the Father. And it is called "Logos" or "Essence," since it is the Essence of all things. Therefore, that which the Platonists said about the images of forms is of no account; for there is only one infinite Form of forms, of which all forms are images, as I stated earlier[104] at a certain point.

150   Therefore, it is necessary to understand clearly the following matters: since [a Platonistic-type] world-soul must be regarded as a certain universal form which enfolds in itself all forms[105] but which has actual existence only contractedly in things and which in each thing is the contracted form of this thing, as was said earlier[106] regarding the universe: then [not such a world-soul but] God—who in one Word creates all things, regardless of how different from one another they are—is the efficient, the formal, and the final Cause of all things; and there can be no created thing which is not diminished from contraction and does not fall infinitely short of the divine work.[107] God alone is absolute; all other things are contracted.[108] Nor is there a medium between the Absolute and the contracted as those imagined who thought that the world-soul is mind existing subsequently to God but prior to the world's contraction. For only God is "world-soul" and "world-mind"—in a manner whereby "soul" is regarded as something absolute in which all the forms of things exist actually. Indeed, the philosophers were not adequately instructed regarding the Divine Word and Absolute Maximum. And so, they envisioned mind and soul and necessity as present uncontractedly in a certain unfolding of Absolute Necessity.

Therefore, forms do not have actual existence except (1) in the Word as Word and (2) contractedly in things.[109] But although the forms which are in the created intellectual nature exist with a greater degree of independence, in accordance with the intellectual nature, nevertheless they are not uncontracted; and so, they are the intellect, whose operation is to understand by means of an abstract likeness, as Aristotle says.[110] In the book *Conjectures* [I will include] certain points regarding this [topic].[111] Let the foregoing points about the world-soul suffice.

151   *Chapter Ten*:   The spirit of all things.

Certain [thinkers] believed that motion, through which there is the union of form and matter, is a spirit—a medium, as it were, between form and matter. They considered it as pervading the firmament, the planets, and things terrestrial. The first [motion] they called "Atropos,"—"without turning," so to speak; for they believed that by a simple motion the firmament is moved from east to west. The second [motion] they called "Clotho," i.e., turning; for the planets are moved counter to the firmament through a turning from west to east. The third [motion they called] "Lachesis," i.e., fate, because chance governs terrestrial things.

The motion of the planets is as an unrolling of the first motion; and the motion of temporal and terrestrial things is the unrolling of the motion of the planets. Certain causes of coming events are latent in terrestrial things, as the produce [is latent] in the seed. Hence, [these thinkers] said that the things enfolded in the world-soul as in a ball are unfolded and extended through such motion. For the wise thought as if [along the following line]:a craftsman [who] wants to chisel a statue in stone and [who] has in himself the form of the statue, as an idea, produces—through certain instruments which he moves—the form of the statue in imitation of the idea; analogously, they thought, the world-mind or world-soul harbors in itself exemplars-of-things, which, through motion it unfolds in matter. And they said that this motion pervades all things, just as does the world-soul. They said that this motion—which, as fate, descends (in the firmament, the planets, and terrestrial things) actually and causally from substantified fate—is the unfolding of substantified fate. For through such motion, or spirit, a thing is actually determined toward being such [as it is].

152   They said that this uniting spirit proceeds from both possibility and the world-soul. For matter has—from its aptitude for receiving form—a certain appetite, just as what is base desires what is good and privation desires possession; furthermore, form desires to exist actually but cannot exist absolutely, since it is not its own being and is not God.[112] Therefore, form descends, so that it exists contractedly in possibility; that is, while possibility ascends toward actual existence, form descends, so that it limits, and perfects, and terminates possibility. And so, from the ascent and the descent motion arises and conjoins the two. This motion is the medium-of-union of possibility and actuality, since from movable possibility and a formal mover, moving arises as a medium.

153   Therefore, this spirit, which is called nature, is spread throughout, and contracted by, the entire universe and each of its parts. Hence, nature is the

enfolding (so to speak) of all things which occur through motion. But the following example shows how this motion is contracted from the universal into the particular and how order is preserved throughout its gradations. When I say "God exists," this sentence proceeds by means of a certain motion but in such an order that I first articulate the letters, then the syllables, then the words, and then, last of all, the sentence—although the sense of hearing does not discern this order by stages. In like manner, motion descends by stages from the universal [*universum*] unto the particular, where it is contracted by the temporal or natural order. But this motion, or spirit, descends from the Divine Spirit, which moves all things by this motion. Hence, just as in an act of speaking there is a certain spirit [or breath] which proceeds from him who speaks— [a spirit] which is contracted into a sentence, as I mentioned—so God, who is Spirit, is the one from whom all motion descends. For Truth says: "It is not you who speak but the Spirit of your Father who speaks in you."[113] A similar thing holds true for all other motions and operations.

154   Therefore, this created spirit[114] is a spirit in whose absence it would not be the case that anything is one or is able to exist. Now, through this spirit, which fills the whole world,[115] the entire world and all things in it are naturally and conjointly that which they are, so that by means of this spirit possibility is present in actuality and actuality is present in possibility. And this [spirit] is the motion of the loving union of all things and oneness, so that there is one universe of all things. For although all things are moved individually so as to be, in the best manner, that which they are and so that none will exist exactly as another,[116] nevertheless each thing in its own way either mediately or immediately contracts, and participates in, the motion of each other thing (just as the elements and the things composed of elemental principles [contract and participate in] the motion of the sky and just as all members [of the body contract and participate in] the motion of the heart), so that there is one universe.[117] And through this motion things exist in the best way they can. They are moved for the following reason: viz., so that they may be preserved in themselves or in species—[preserved] by means of the natural union of the different sexes; these sexes are united in nature, which enfolds motion; but in individuals they are contracted separately.

155   Therefore, it is not the case that any motion is unqualifiedly maximum motion, for this latter coincides with rest. Therefore, no motion is absolute, since absolute motion is rest and is God. And absolute motion enfolds all motions. Therefore, just as all possibility exists in Absolute Possibility, which is the Eternal God, and all form and actuality exist in Absolute Form, which is the Father's divine Word and Son, so all uniting motion and all uniting proportion and harmony exist in the Divine Spirit's Absolute Union, so that God is the one Beginning of all things. In Him and through Him all things exist[118] in a certain oneness of trinity. They are contracted in a like manner in

greater and lesser degree (within [the range between] the unqualifiedly Maximum and the unqualifiedly Minimum) according to their own gradations, so that in intelligent things, where to understand is to move, the gradation of possibility, actuality, and their uniting motion is one gradation, and in corporeal things, where to exist is to move, [the gradation] of matter, form, and their union is another gradation. I will touch upon these points elsewhere.[119] Let the preceding [remarks] about the trinity of the universe suffice for the present.

156   *Chapter Eleven*:   Corollaries regarding motion.

Now that learned ignorance has shown these previously unheard of [doctrines] to be true, perhaps there will be amazement on the part of those who read them. From the foregoing [teachings] we now know [the following]: that the universe is trine;[120] that of all things there is none which is not *one* from possibility, actuality, and uniting motion;[121] and that none of these [three] can at all exist without the other [two], so that of necessity these [three] are present in all things according to very different degrees.[122] [They are present] so differently that no two things in the universe can be altogether equal with respect to them, i.e., with respect to any one of them. However, it is not the case that in any genus—even [the genus] of motion—we come to an unqualifiedly maximum and minimum.[123] Hence, if we consider the various movements of the spheres, [we will see that] it is not possible for the world-machine to have, as a fixed and immovable center, either our perceptible earth or air or fire or any other thing. For, with regard to motion, we do not come to an unqualifiedly minimum— i.e., to a *fixed* center. For the [unqualifiedly] minimum must coincide with the [unqualifiedly] maximum; therefore, the center of the world coincides with the circumference.[124] Hence, the world does not have a [fixed] circumference. For if it had a [fixed] center, it would also have a [fixed] circumference; and hence it would have its own beginning and end within itself, and it would be bounded in relation to something else, and beyond the world there would be both something else and space (*locus*). But all these [consequences] are false. Therefore, since it is not possible for the world to be enclosed between a physical center and [a physical] circumference, the world—of which God is the center and the circumference—is not understood. And although the world is not infinite, it cannot be conceived as finite, because it lacks boundaries within which it is enclosed.

157   Therefore, the earth, which cannot be the center, cannot be devoid of all motion. Indeed, it is even necessary that the earth be moved in such way that it could be moved infinitely less. Therefore, just as the earth is not the center of the world, so the sphere of fixed stars is not its circumference—although when

we compare the earth with the sky, the former *seems* to be nearer to the center, and the latter nearer to the circumference. Therefore, the earth is not the center either of the eighth sphere or of any other sphere. Moreover, the appearance of the six constellations above the horizon does not establish that the earth is at the center of the eighth sphere. For even if the earth were at a distance from the center but were on the axis passing through the [sphere's] poles, so that one side [of the earth] were raised toward the one pole and the other side were lowered toward the other pole, then it is evident that only half the sphere would be visible to men, who would be as distant from the poles as the horizon is extended. Moreover, it is no less false that the center of the world is within the earth than that it is outside the earth; nor does the earth or any other sphere even have a center. For since the center is a point equidistant from the circumference and since there cannot exist a sphere or a circle so completely true that a truer one could not be posited, it is obvious that there cannot be posited a center [which is so true and precise] that a still truer and more precise center could not be posited. Precise equidistance to different things cannot be found except in the case of God, because God alone is Infinite Equality. Therefore, He who is the center of the world, viz., the Blessed God, is also the center of the earth, of all spheres, and of all things in the world. Likewise, He is the infinite circumference of all things.[125]

158   Moreover, in the sky there are not fixed and immovable poles—although the heaven of fixed stars appears to describe by its motion circles of progressively different sizes, colures which are smaller than the equinoctial [colure]. The case is similar for the intermediates. But it is necessary that every part of the sky be moved, even though [the parts are moved] unequally by comparison with the circles described by the motion of the stars. Hence, just as certain stars appear to describe a maximum circle, so certain stars [appear to describe] a minimum [circle]. And there is not a star which fails to describe an [approximate circle]. Therefore, since there is not a fixed pole in the [eighth] sphere, it is evident that we also do not find an exact middle point existing equidistantly, as it were, from the poles. Therefore, in the eighth sphere there is not a star which describes, through its revolution, a maximum circle. (For the star would have to be equidistant from the poles, which do not exist.) And consequently there is

159 not [a star] which describes a minimum circle. Therefore, the poles of the spheres coincide with the center,[126] so that the center is not anything except the pole, because the Blessed God [is the center and the pole]. And since we can discern motion only in relation to something fixed, viz., either poles or centers, and since we presuppose these [poles or centers] when we measure motions, we find that as we go about conjecturing, we err with regard to all [measurements]. And we are surprised when we do not find that the stars are in the right position according to the rules of measurement of the ancients, for we suppose that the ancients rightly conceived of centers and poles and measures.

From these [foregoing considerations] it is evident that the earth is moved. Now, from the motion of a comet, we learn that the elements of air and of fire are moved; furthermore, [we observe] that the moon [is moved] less from east to west than Mercury or Venus or the sun, and so on progressively. Therefore, the earth is moved even less than all [these] others; but, nevertheless, being a star, it does not describe a minimum circle around a center or a pole. Nor does the eighth sphere describe a maximum [circle], as was just proved.

160   Therefore, consider carefully the fact that just as in the eighth sphere the stars are [moved] around conjectural poles, so the earth, the moon, and the planets—as stars—are moved at a distance and with a difference around a pole [which] we conjecture to be where the center is believed to be. Hence, although the earth—as star—is nearer to the central pole, nevertheless it is moved and, in its motion, does not describe a minimum circle, as was indicated. Rather (though the matter appears to us to be otherwise), neither the sun nor the moon nor the earth nor any sphere can by its motion describe a true circle, since none of these are moved about a fixed [point]. Moreover, it is not the case that there can be posited a circle so true that a still truer one cannot be posited. And it is never the case that at two different times [a star or a sphere] is moved in precisely equal ways or that [on these two occasions its motion] describes equal approximate-circles—even if the matter does not seem this way to us.

161   Therefore, if with regard to what has now been said you want truly to understand something about the motion of the universe, you must merge the center and the poles, aiding yourself as best you can by your imagination. For example, if someone were on the earth but beneath the north pole [of the heavens] and someone else were at the north pole [of the heavens], then just as to the one on the earth it would appear that the pole is at the zenith, so to the one at the pole it would appear that the center is at the zenith.[127] And just as antipodes have the sky above, as do we, so to those [persons] who are at either pole [of the heavens] the earth would appear to be at the zenith. And wherever anyone would be, he would believe himself to be at the center. Therefore, merge these different imaginative pictures so that the center is the zenith and vice versa.[128] Thereupon you will see—through the intellect, to which only learned ignorance is of help—that the world and its motion and shape cannot be apprehended.[129] For [the world] will appear as a wheel in a wheel and a sphere in a sphere—having its center and circumference nowhere, as was stated.

162   *Chapter Twelve:*   The conditions of the earth.

The ancients did not attain unto the points already made, for they lacked learned ignorance. It has already[130] become evident to us that the earth is indeed moved, even though we do not perceive this to be the case. For we apprehend motion only through a certain comparison with something fixed. For example, if someone did not know that a body of water was flowing and did not see the shore while he was on a ship in the middle of the water, how would he recognize that the ship was being moved? And because of the fact that it would always seem to each person (whether he were on the earth, the sun, or another star) that he was at the "immovable" center, so to speak, and that all other things were moved: assuredly, it would always be the case that if he were on the sun, he would fix a set of poles in relation to himself; if on the earth, another set; on the moon, another; on Mars, another; and so on. Hence, the world-machine will have its center everywhere and its circumference nowhere, so to speak; for God, who is everywhere and nowhere, is its circumference and center.[131]

163   Moreover, the earth is not spherical, as some have said; yet, it tends toward sphericity, for the shape of the world is contracted in the world's parts, just as is the world's motion. Now, when an infinite line is considered as contracted in such way that, as contracted, it cannot be more perfect and more capable, it is [seen to be] circular; for in a circle the beginning coincides with the end. Therefore, the most nearly perfect motion is circular; and the most nearly perfect corporeal shape is therefore spherical. Hence, for the sake of the perfection, the entire motion of a part is toward the whole. For example, heavy things [are moved] toward the earth and light things upwards; earth [is moved] toward earth, water toward water, air toward air, fire toward fire. And the motion of the whole tends toward circular motion as best it can, and all shape [tends toward] spherical shape—as we experience with regard to the parts of animals, to trees, and to the sky. Hence, one motion is more circular and more perfect than another. Similarly, shapes, too, are different.

164   Therefore, the shape of the earth is noble and spherical, and the motion of the earth is circular; but there could be a more perfect [shape or motion]. And because in the world there is no maximum or minimum with regard to perfections, motions, and shapes (as is evident from what was just said), it is not true that the earth is the lowliest and the lowest. For although [the earth] seems more central with respect to the world, it is also for this same reason nearer to the pole, as was said.[132] Moreover, the earth is not a proportional part, or an aliquot part, of the world. For since the world does not have either a maximum or a minimum, it also does not have a middle point or aliquot parts, just as a man or an animal does not either. For example, a hand is not an aliquot part of a man, although its weight does seem to bear a comparative relation to the body—and likewise regarding its size and shape.[133] Moreover, [the earth's] blackness is not evidence of its lowliness. For if someone were on the sun, the brightness which is visible to us would not be visible [to him]. For when the body of the sun is considered, [it is seen to] have a certain more central "earth," as it were,

and a certain "fiery and circumferential" brightness, as it were, and in its middle a "watery cloud and brighter air," so to speak—just as our earth [has]

165 its own elements. Hence, if someone were outside the region of fire, then through the medium of the fire our earth, which is on the circumference of [this] region, would appear to be a bright star—just as to us, who are on the circumference of the region of the sun, the sun appears to be very bright. Now, the moon does not appear to be so bright, perhaps because we are within its circumference and are facing the more central parts—i.e., are in the moon's "watery region," so to speak. Hence, its light is not visible [to us], although the moon does have its own light, which is visible to those who are at the most outward points of its circumference; but only the light of the reflection of the sun is visible to us. On this account, too, the moon's heat—which it no doubt produces as a result of its motion and in greater degree on the circumference, where the motion is greater—is not communicated to us, unlike what happens with regard to the sun. Hence, our earth seems to be situated between the region of the sun and the region of the moon; and through the medium of the sun and the moon it partakes of the influence of other stars which—because of the fact that we are outside their regions—we do not see. For we see only the regions of those stars which gleam.

166 Therefore, the earth is a noble star which has a light and a heat and an influence that are distinct and different from [that of] all other stars, just as each star differs from each other star with respect to its light, its nature, and its influence. And each star communicates its light and influence to the others, though it does not aim to do so, since all stars gleam and are moved only in order to exist in the best way [they can]; as a consequence thereof a sharing arises (just as light shines of its own nature and not in order that I may see; yet, as a consequence, a sharing occurs when I use light for the purpose of seeing). Similarly, Blessed God created all things in such way that when each thing desires to conserve its own existence as a divine work, it conserves it in communion with others. Accordingly, just as by virtue of the fact that the foot exists merely for walking, it serves not only itself but also the eye, the hands, the body, and the entire human being (and similarly for the eye and the other members), so a similar thing holds true regarding the parts of the world. For Plato referred to the world as an animal.[134] If you take God to be its soul, without intermingling, then many of the points I have been making will be clear to you.

167 Moreover, we ought not to say that because the earth is smaller than the sun and is influenced by the sun, it is more lowly [than the sun]. For the entire region-of-the-earth, which extends to the circumference of fire, is large. And although the earth is smaller than the sun—as we know from the earth's shadow and from eclipses—we do not know to what extent the *region* of the sun is

larger or smaller than the region of the earth. However, the sun's region cannot
be precisely equal to the earth's, for no star can be equal to another star.
Moreover, the earth is not the smallest star, because the earth is larger than the
moon, as our experience of eclipses has taught us. And [the earth is larger] than
Mercury, too, as certain [people] maintain; and perhaps [it is also larger] than
other stars. Hence, the evidence from size does not establish [the earth's]
lowliness.

168   Furthermore, the influence which [the earth] receives is not evidence estab-
lishing its imperfection. For being a star, perhaps the earth, too, influences the
sun and the solar region, as I said.[135] And since we do not experience ourselves
in any other way than as being in the center where influences converge, we
experience nothing of this counter-influence. For suppose the earth is possibility; and suppose the sun is the soul, or formal actuality, with respect to the
possibility; and suppose the moon is the middle link, so that these [three] stars,
which are situated within one region, unite their mutual influences (the other
stars—viz., Mercury, Venus, and the others—being above, as the ancients and
even some moderns said). Then, it is evident that the mutual relationship of
influence is such that one influence cannot exist without the other. Therefore,
in each alike [viz., earth, sun, moon] the influence will be both one and three in
accordance with its [i.e., the influence's] own degrees. Therefore, it is evident
that human beings cannot know whether with respect to these things [viz., the
influences] the region of the earth exists in a less perfect and less noble degree
in relation to the regions of the other stars (viz., the sun, the moon, and the
169 others). Nor [can we know this] with respect to space, either. For example, [we
cannot rightly claim to know] that our portion of the world is the habitation of
men and animals and vegetables which are proportionally less noble [than] in
the region of the inhabitants of the sun and of the other stars. For although God
is the center and circumference of all stellar regions and although natures of
different nobility proceed from Him and inhabit each region (lest so many
places in the heavens and on the stars be empty and lest only the earth—
presumably among the lesser things—be inhabited), nevertheless with regard
to the intellectual natures a nobler and more perfect nature cannot, it seems, be
given (even if there are inhabitants of another kind on other stars) than the
intellectual nature which dwells both here on earth and in its own region. For
man does not desire a different nature but only to be perfected in his own nature.
170   Therefore, the inhabitants of other stars—of whatever sort these inhabitants
might be—bear no comparative relationship to the inhabitants of the earth
(*istius mundi*). [This is true] even if, with respect to the goal of the universe,
that entire region bears to this entire region a certain comparative relationship
which is hidden to us—so that in this way the inhabitants of this earth or region
bear, here and there, through the medium of the whole region, a certain mutual

relationship to those other inhabitants. (By comparison, the particular parts of the fingers of a hand bear, through the medium of the hand, a comparative relationship to a foot; and the particular parts of the foot [bear], through the medium of the foot, [a comparative relationship] to a hand—so that all [members] are comparatively related to the whole animal.)[136]

171   Hence, since that entire region is unknown to us, those inhabitants remain altogether unknown. By comparison, here on earth it happens that animals of one species—[animals] which constitute one specific region, so to speak—are united together; and because of the common specific region, they mutually share those things which belong to their region; they neither concern themselves about other [regions] nor apprehend truly anything regarding them.[137] For example, an animal of one species cannot grasp the thought which [an animal] of another [species] expresses through vocal signs—except for a superficial grasping in the case of a very few signs, and even then [only] after long experience and only conjecturally. But we are able to know disproportionally less about the inhabitants of another region. We surmise that in the solar region there are inhabitants which are more solar, brilliant, illustrious, and intellectual—being even more spiritlike than [those] on the moon, where [the inhabitants] are more moonlike, and than [those] on the earth, [where they are] more material and more solidified. Thus, [we surmise], these intellectual solar natures are mostly in a state of actuality and scarcely in a state of potentiality; but the terrestrial [natures] are mostly in potentiality and scarcely

172   in actuality; lunar [natures] fluctuate between [solar and terrestrial natures]. We believe this on the basis of the fiery influence of the sun and on the basis of the watery and aerial influence of the moon and the weighty material influence of the earth. In like manner, we surmise that none of the other regions of the stars are empty of inhabitants—as if there were as many particular mondial parts of the one universe as there are stars, of which there is no number.[138] Resultantly, the one universal world is contracted—in a threefold way and in terms of its own fourfold descending progression—in so many particular [parts] that they are without number except to Him who created all things in a [definite] number.[139]

Moreover, the earthly destruction-of-things which we experience is not strong evidence of [the earth's] lowliness. For since there is one universal world and since there are causal relations between all the individual stars, it cannot be evident to us that anything is altogether corruptible;[140] rather [a thing is corruptible only] according to one or another mode of being, for the causal influences—being contracted, as it were, in one individual—are separated, so that the mode of being such and such perishes. Thus, death does not occupy any space, as Virgil says.[141] For death seems to be nothing except a composite thing's being resolved into its components. And who can know whether such dissolution occurs only in regard to terrestrial inhabitants?

173   Certain [people] have said that on earth there are as many species of things as there are stars. Therefore, if in this way the earth contracts to distinct species the influence of all the stars, why is there not a similar occurrence in the regions of other stars which receive stellar influences? And who can know whether all the influences which at first are contracted at the time of composition revert at the time of dissolution, so that an animal which is now a contracted individual of a certain species in the region of the earth is freed from all influence of the stars, so that it returns to its origins? Or [who can know] whether only the form reverts to the exemplar or world-soul, as the Platonists say, or whether only the form reverts to its own star (from which the species received actual existence on mother earth) and the matter [reverts] to possibility, while the uniting spirit remains in the motion of the stars?—[whether, i.e.,] when this spirit ceases to unite and when it withdraws because of the indisposition of the [animal's] organs or for some other reason, so that by its difference of motion it induces a separation, then it returns as if to the stars, and its form ascends above the influence of the stars, whereas its matter descends beneath [their influence]. Or [who can know] whether the forms of each region come to rest in a higher form—e.g., an intellectual form—and through this higher form attain the end

174   which is the goal of the world? And how is this end in God attained by the lower forms through this higher form? And how does the higher form ascend to the circumference, which is God, while the body descends toward the center, where God is also present, so that the motion of all [the components] is toward God? For just as the center and the circumference are one in God, so some day the body (although it seemed to descend as if to the center) and the soul ([although it seemed to ascend as if] to the circumference) will be united again in God, at the time when not all motion will cease but [only] that which relates to generation. So to speak: the essential parts of the world (without which the world could not exist) will, necessarily, come together again when there ceases to be successive generation and when the uniting spirit returns and unites possibility to its [i.e., spirit's] own form.

Of himself a man cannot know these matters; [he can know them] only if he has [this knowledge] from God in a quite special way. Although no one doubts that the Perfect God created all things for Himself and that He does not will the destruction of any of the things He created, and although everyone knows that God is a very generous rewarder of all who worship Him, nevertheless only God Himself, who is His own Activity, knows the manner of Divine Activity's present and future remuneration. Nevertheless, I will say a few things about this later,[142] according to the divinely inspired truth. At the moment, it suffices that I have, in ignorance, touched upon these matters in the foregoing way.

175   *Chapter Thirteen*:   The admirable divine art in the creation of the
world and of the elements.

Since it is the unanimous opinion of the wise that visible things—in particular,
the size, beauty, and order of things—lead us to an admiration for the divine art
and the divine excellence, and since I have dealt with some of the products of
God's admirable knowledge, let me (with regard to the creation of the universe
and by way of admiration) very briefly add a few points about the place and the
order of the elements.

   In creating the world, God used arithmetic, geometry, music, and likewise
astronomy.[143] (We ourselves also use these arts when we investigate the
comparative relationships of objects, of elements, and of motions.) For through
arithmetic God united things. Through geometry He shaped them, in order that
they would thereby attain firmness, stability, and mobility in accordance with
their conditions. Through music He proportioned things in such way that there
is not more earth in earth than water in water, air in air, and fire in fire, so that
no one element is altogether reducible to another. As a result, it happens that the
world-machine cannot perish. Although part of one [element] can be reduced to
another, it is not the case that all the air which is mixed with water can ever be
transformed into water; for the surrounding air would prevent this; thus, there is
ever a mingling of the elements. Hence, God brought it about that *parts* of the
elements would be resolved into one another. And since this occurs with a
delay, a thing is generated from the harmony of elements in relation to the
generable thing itself; and this thing exists as long as the harmony of elements
continues; when the harmony is destroyed, what was generated is destroyed
and dissolved.

176   And so, God, who created all things in number, weight, and measure,[144]
arranged the elements in an admirable order. (Number pertains to arithmetic,
weight to music, measure to geometry.) For example, heaviness is dependent
upon lightness, which restricts it (for example, earth, which is heavy, is
dependent upon fire in its "center," so to speak); and lightness depends upon
heaviness (e.g., fire depends upon earth). And when Eternal Wisdom ordained
the elements, He used an inexpressible proportion, so that He foreknew to what
extent each element should precede the other and so that He weighted the
elements in such way that proportionally to water's being lighter than earth, air
is lighter than water, and fire lighter than air—with the result that weight
corresponds to size and, likewise, a container occupies more space than what is
contained [by it]. Moreover, He combined the elements with one another in
such a relationship that, necessarily, the one element is present in the other.
With regard to this combination, the earth is an animal, so to speak, according
to Plato.[145] It has stones in place of bones, rivers in place of veins, trees in place

of hair; and there are animals which are fostered within its hair, just as worms are fostered in the hair of animals.

177   And, so to speak: earth is to fire as the world is to God. For fire, in its relation to earth, has many resemblances to God. [For example,] there is no limit to fire's power; and fire acts upon, penetrates, illumines, distinguishes, and forms all earthly things through the medium of air and of water, so that, as it were, in all the things which are begotten from earth there is nothing except fire's distinct activities. Hence, the forms of things are different as a result of a difference in fire's brightness. But fire is intermingled with things; it does not exist without them; and terrestrial things do not exist [without it]. Now, God is only absolute.[146] Hence, God, who is light and in whom there is no darkness,[147] is spoken of by the ancients as absolute consuming fire[148] and as absolute brightness. All existing things endeavor, as best they can, to participate in His "brightness and blazing splendor," so to speak—as we notice with regard to all the stars, in which participated brightness is found materially contracted. Indeed, this distinguishing and penetrating participated brightness is contracted "immaterially," so to speak, in the life of things which are alive with an intellective life.

178   Who would not admire this Artisan, who with regard to the spheres, the stars, and the regions of the stars used such skill that there is—though without complete precision—both a harmony of all things and a diversity of all things? [This Artisan] considered in advance the sizes, the placing, and the motion of the stars in the one world; and He ordained the distances of the stars in such way that unless each region were as it is, it could neither exist nor exist in such a place and with such an order—nor could the universe exist. Morever, He bestowed on all stars a differing brightness, influence, shape, color, and heat. (Heat causally accompanies the brightness.) And He established the interrelationship of parts so proportionally that in each thing the motion of the parts is in relation to the whole. With heavy things [the motion is] downward toward the center, and with light things it is upward from the center and around the center (e.g., we perceive the motion of the stars as circular).

179   With regard to these objects, which are so worthy of admiration, so varied, and so different, we recognize—through learned ignorance and in accordance with the preceding points—that we cannot know the rationale for any of God's works but can only marvel; for the Lord is great, whose greatness is without end.[149] Since He is Absolute Maximality: as He is the Author and Knower of all His works, so He is also the End [of them all]; thus, all things are in Him and nothing is outside Him. He is the Beginning, the Middle, and the End of all things, the Center and the Circumference of all things—so that He alone is sought in all things; for without Him all things are nothing. When He alone is possessed, all things are possessed, because He is all things. When He is

known, all things are known, because He is the Truth of all things. He even wills for us to be brought to the point of admiring so marvelous a world-machine. Nevertheless, the more we admire it, the more He conceals it from us; for it is Himself alone whom[150] He wills to be sought with our whole heart and affection. And since He dwells in inaccessible light,[151] which all things seek, He alone can open to those who knock and can give to those who ask.[152] Of all created things none has the power to open itself to him who knocks and to show what it is; for without God, who is present in all things, each thing is nothing.

180　　　But all things reply to him who in learned ignorance asks them what they are or in what manner they exist or for what purpose they exist: "Of ourselves [we are] nothing, and of our own ability we cannot tell you anything other than nothing. For we do not even know ourselves; rather, God alone—through whose understanding we are that which He wills, commands, and knows in us—[has knowledge of us]. Indeed, all of us are mute things. He is the one who speaks in [us] all. He has made us; He alone knows what we are, in what manner we exist, and for what purpose. If you wish to know something about us, seek it in our Cause and Reason, not in us. *There* you will find all things, while seeking one thing. And only in Him will you be able to discover yourself."

See to it, says our learned ignorance, that you discover yourself in Him. Since in Him all things are Him, it will not be possible that you lack anything. Yet, our approaching Him who is inaccessible is not our prerogative; rather, it is the prerogative of Him who gave us both a face which is turned toward Him and a consuming desire to seek [Him]. When we do [seek Him], He is most gracious and will not abandon us. Instead, having disclosed Himself to us, He will satisfy us eternally "when His glory shall appear."[153]

May He be blessed forever.

BOOK III

Prologue

Having set forth the few preceding points about how the universe exists in contraction, I will very briefly expound for Your most admirable Diligence[1] the concept of Jesus. [I will do so] to the end that—as regards Him who is both Absolute Maximum and contracted maximum, viz., the ever-blessed Jesus Christ—I may learnedly in ignorance investigate several points, in order to increase our faith and perfection. I will call upon Christ, in order that He may be the way unto Himself, who is the Truth.[2] By this Truth we are made alive—at present by faith and in the future by actual attainment—in Him and throughHim who is Everlasting Life.

182   *Chapter One*:   A maximum which is contracted to this or that and than which there cannot be a greater cannot exist apart from the Absolute [Maximum].

Book One shows that the one absolutely Maximum—which is incommunicable, unfathomable, incontractible to this or that—exists in itself as eternally, equally, and unchangeably the same. Book Two thereafter exhibits the contraction of the universe, for the universe exists only as contractedly this and that. Thus, the Oneness of the Maximum exists absolutely in itself; the oneness of the universe exists contractedly in plurality. Now, the many things in which the universe is actually contracted cannot at all agree in supreme equality; for then they would cease being many. Therefore, it is necessary that all things differ from one another—either (1) in genus, species, and number or (2) in species and number or (3) in number—so that each thing exists in its own number, weight, and measure.[3] Hence, all things are distinguished from one another by

183 degrees, so that no thing coincides with another. Accordingly, no contracted thing can participate precisely in the degree of contraction of another thing, so that, necessarily, any given thing is comparatively greater or lesser than any other given thing. Therefore, all contracted things exist between a maximum and a minimum, so that there can be posited a greater and a lesser degree of contraction than [that of] any given thing. Yet, this process does not continue

actually unto infinity, because an infinity of degrees is impossible,[4] since to say that infinite degrees actually exist is nothing other than to say that no degree exists—as I stated about number in Book One.[5] Therefore, with regard to contracted things, there cannot be an ascent or a descent to an absolutely maximum or an absolutely minimum. Hence, just as the Divine Nature, which is absolutely maximal, cannot be diminished so that it becomes finite and contracted, so neither can the contracted nature become diminished in contraction to the point that it becomes altogether absolute [i.e., altogether free of contraction.][6]

184   Therefore, it is not the case that any contracted thing attains to the limit either of the universe or of genus or of species; for there can exist a less greatly contracted thing or a more greatly contracted thing [than it]. The first general contraction of the universe is through a plurality of genera, which must differ by degrees. However, genera exist only contractedly in species; and species exist only in individuals, which alone exist actually.[7] Therefore, just as in accordance with the nature of contracted things the individual is positable only within the limit of its species, so too no individual can attain to the limit of its genus and of the universe. Indeed, among many individual things of the same species, there must be a difference of degrees of perfection. Hence, with respect to a given species, there will be no maximally perfect [individual thing], than which a more perfect [individual thing] could not be posited; nor is there positable [an individual thing] so imperfect that a more imperfect is not positable. Therefore, no [individual thing] reaches the limit of its species.

185   Therefore, there is only one Limit of species, of genera, or of the universe. This Limit is the Center, the Circumference, and the Union of all things. And it is not the case that the universe exhausts the infinite, absolutely maximum power of God so that the universe is an unqualifiedly maximum, delimiting the power of God. Hence, it is not the case that the universe reaches the limit of Absolute Maximality; genera do not reach the limit of the universe; species [do not reach] the limit of their genera; and individual things [do not reach] the limit of their species. Thus, all things are that-which-they-are in the best way [possible for them][8] and between a maximum and a minimum; and God is the Beginning, the Middle, and the End of the universe and of each thing, so that all things—whether they ascend, descend, or tend toward the middle—approach God.[9] However, the union of all things is through God, so that although all things are different, they are united. Accordingly, among genera, which contract the one universe, there is such a union of a lower [genus] and a higher [genus] that the two coincide in a third [genus] in between. And among the different species there is such an order of combination that the highest species of the one genus coincides with the lowest [species] of the immediately higher 186   [genus], so that there is one continuous and perfect universe. However, every union is by degrees; and we do not arrive at a maximum union, because that is

God. Therefore, the different species of a lower and a higher genus are not united in something indivisible which does not admit of greater and lesser degree; rather, [they are united] in a third species, whose individuals differ by degrees, so that no one [of them] participates equally in both [the higher and the lower species], as if this individual were a composite of these [two species]. Instead, [the individual of the third species] contracts, in its own degree, the one nature of its own species. As related to the other species this [third] species is seen to be composed of the lower and of the higher [species], though not equally, since no thing can be composed of precise equals; and this third species, which falls between the other two, necessarily has a preponderant conformity to one of them—i.e., to the higher or to the lower. In the books of the philosophers examples of this are found with regard to oysters, sea mussels, and other things.

187   Therefore, no species descends to the point that it is the minimum species of some genus, for before it reaches the minimum it is changed into another species; and a similar thing holds true of the [would-be] maximum species, which is changed into another species before it becomes a maximum species. When in the genus *animal* the human species endeavors to reach a higher gradation among perceptible things, it is caught up into a mingling with the intellectual nature; nevertheless, the lower part, in accordance with which man is called an animal, prevails. Now, presumably, there are other spirits. ([I will discuss] these in *Conjectures*).[10] And because of a certain nature which is capable of perception they are said, in an extended sense, to be of the genus *animal*. But since the intellectual nature in them prevails over the other nature, they are called spirits rather than animals, although the Platonists believe that they are intellectual animals. Accordingly, it is evident that species are like a number series which progresses sequentially and which, necessarily, is finite, so that there is order, harmony, and proportion in diversity, as I indicated in Book One.[11]

188   It is necessary that, without proceeding to infinity, we reach (1) the lowest species of the lowest genus, than which there is not actually a lesser, and (2) the highest [species] of the highest [genus], than which, likewise, there is not actually a greater and higher—even though a lesser than the former and a greater than the latter could be respectively posited. Thus, whether we number upwards or downwards we take our beginning from Absolute Oneness (which is God)—i.e., from the Beginning of all things. Hence, species are as numbers that come together from two opposite directions—[numbers] that proceed from a minimum which is maximum and from a maximum to which a minimum is not opposed.[12] Hence, there is nothing in the universe which does not enjoy a certain singularity that cannot be found in any other thing, so that no thing excels all others in all respects or [excels] different things in equal measure. By comparison, there can never in any respect be something equal to another;[13]

even if at one time one thing is less than another and at another [time] is greater than this other, it makes this transition with a certain singularity, so that it never attains precise equality [with the other]. Similarly, a square inscribed in a circle passes—with respect to its size—from being a square which is smaller than the circle to being a square larger than the circle, without ever arriving at its equal. And an angle of incidence increases from being lesser than a right [angle] to being greater [than a right angle] without the medium of equality. (Many of these points will be brought out in the book *Conjectures*.)[14]

189   Individuating principles cannot come together in one individual in such harmonious comparative relation as in another [individual]; thus, through itself each thing is one and is perfect in the way it can be. And in each species—e.g., the human species—we find that at a given time some individuals are more perfect and more excellent than others in certain respects. (For example, Solomon excelled others in wisdom, Absalom in beauty, Sampson in strength; and those who excelled others more with regard to the intellective part deserved to be honored above the others.) Nevertheless, a difference of opinions—in accordance with the difference of religions, sects, and regions—gives rise to different judgments of comparison (so that what is praiseworthy according to one [religion, sect, or region] is reprehensible according to another); and scattered throughout the world are people unknown to us.[15] Hence, we do not know who is more excellent than the others in the world;[16] for of all [individuals] we cannot know even one perfectly. God produced this state of affairs in order that each individual, although admiring the others, would be content with himself, with his native land (so that his birthplace alone would seem most pleasant to him), with the customs of his domain, with his language, and so on, so that to the extent possible there would be unity and peace, without envy.[17] For there can be [peace] in every respect only for those who reign with God, who is our peace which surpasses all understanding.[18]

190   *Chapter Two*:   The maximum contracted [to a species] is also the Absolute [Maximum; it is both] Creator and creature.

It is thoroughly clear that the universe is only contractedly-many-things; these are actually such that no one of them attains to the unqualifiedly Maximum. I will add something more: if a maximum which is contracted to a species could be posited as actually existing, then, in accordance with the given species of contraction, this maximum would be actually all the things which are able to be in the possibility of that genus or species. For the absolutely Maximum is actually and absolutely all possible things, and for this reason it is absolutely and maximally infinite; similarly, a maximum which is contracted to a genus and a species is *actually* [all] possible perfection in accordance with the given contraction; in this [contraction] the maximum is (since a greater cannot be posited) infinite and encompasses the entire nature of the given contraction. And just as the [Absolute] Minimum coincides with the Absolute Maximum, so also the contractedly minimum coincides with the contracted maximum.[19] A

191   very clear illustration of this [truth] occurs with regard to a maximum line, which admits of no opposition, and which is both every figure and the equal measure of all figures, and with which a point coincides—as I showed in Book One.[20] Hence, if any positable thing were the contracted maximum individual of some species, such an individual thing would have to be the fulness of that genus and species, so that in fulness of perfection it would be the means, form, essence, and trugh of all the things which are possible in species. This contracted maximum individual would exist above the whole nature of that [given] contraction—[exist] as its final goal.[21] It would enfold in itself the entire perfection of the [given contraction]. And it would be—above all comparative relation—perfectly equal to each given thing [of that species], so that it would not be too great [a measure] for anything nor too small [a measure] for anything but would enfold in its own fulness the perfections of all the things [of that species].[22]

192   And herefrom it is evident—in conformity with the points I exhibited a bit earlier—that the contracted maximum [individual] cannot exist as purely contracted. For no such [purely contracted thing] could attain the fulness of perfection in the genus of its contraction. Nor would such a thing qua contracted be God, who is most absolute.[23] But, necessarily, the contracted maximum [individual]—i.e., God and creature—would be both absolute and contracted, by virtue of a contraction which would be able to exist in itself[24] only if it existed in Absolute Maximality. (For as I indicated in Book One,[25] there is only one Maximality through which what is contracted could be called maximum.) Suppose Maximum Power united to itself this contracted [maximum individual thing—united it] in such way that it could not be more united and the respective natures still be preserved. [And suppose that] as a result [Maximum Power] would be this contracted thing, whose contracted nature would be preserved. [And suppose that] this contracted thing—its contracted nature being preserved (in accordance with which nature it is the contracted and created fulness of its species)—were, on account of a hypostatic union, both God and all things. [In that case,] this admirable union would transcend our

193   entire understanding. For if this union were conceived as [analogous to the way in which] different things are united, then [this conception] would be mistaken; for Absolute Maximality is not other or different, since it is all things. If it were conceived as are two things which previously were separate but now are conjoined, [then this conception] would be mistaken. For Divinity does not exist in different ways according to an earlier and a later time, nor is it *this*

rather than *that*; nor was this contracted [maximum] able—before the union— to be this or that as is an individual person existing in himself; nor are [the Divinity and the contracted maximum] conjoined as parts in a whole, for God cannot be a part.

194   Who, then, could conceive of so admirable a union, which is not as [the union] of form to matter, since the Absolute God cannot be commingled with matter and does not inform [it]. Assuredly, this [union] would be greater than all intelligible unions; for what is contracted would (since it is maximum) exist there only in Absolute Maximality—neither adding anything to Maximality (since Maximality is absolute) nor passing over into its nature (since it itself is contracted). Therefore, what is contracted would exist in what is absolute in such way that (1) if we were to conceive of this [being] as [only] God, we would be mistaken, since what is contracted does not change its nature, and (2) if we were to imagine it as [merely] a creature, we would be wrong, since Absolute Maximality, which is God, does not relinquish its nature, but (3) if we were to think of [it] as a composite of the two, we would err, since a composition of God and creature, of what is maximally contracted and of what is maximally Absolute, is impossible. For such a [being] would have to be conceived by us as (1) in such way God that it is also a creature, (2) in such way a creature that it is also Creator, and (3) Creator and creature without confusion and without composition. Who, then, could be lifted to such a height that in oneness he would conceive diversity and in diversity oneness? Therefore, this union would transcend all understanding.

195   *Chapter Three*:   Only in the case of the nature of humanity can there be such a maximum [individual].

With regard to these matters, then, we can readily ask: Of what nature should this contracted maximum be? For since it must be the case that this maximum is one (just as Absolute Maximality is Absolute Oneness) and since, in addition, [this maximum] is contracted to this or that: it is first of all evident that the order of things necessarily requires that some things be of a lower nature in comparison with others (as natures devoid of life and intelligence are), that some things be of a higher nature (viz., intelligences), and that some things be of an in-between [nature]. Therefore, if Absolute Maximality is in the most universal way the Being of all things, so that it is not more of one thing than of another: clearly, that being which is more common to the totality of beings is more unitable with the [Absolute] Maximum.

196   Now, if the nature of lower things is considered and if one of these lower beings were elevated unto [Absolute] Maximality, such a being would be both God and itself. An example is furnished with regard to a maximum line. Since

the maximum line would be infinite through Absolute Infinity and maximal through [Absolute] Maximality (to which, necessarily, it is united if it is maximal): through [Absolute] Maximality it would be God;[26] and through contraction it would remain a line. And so, it would be, actually, everything which a line can become. But a line does not include [the possibility of] life or intellect. Therefore, if the line would not attain to the fulness of [all] natures, how could it be elevated to the maximum gradation? For it would be a maximum which could be greater and which would lack [some] perfections.

197   We must say something similar with regard to the Supreme Nature, which does not embrace a lower [nature] in such way that the union of the lower [nature] and the higher [nature] is greater than their separation. Now, it befits the Maximum—with which the Minimum coincides—to embrace one thing in such way that it does not repel another thing but is all things together. Therefore, a middle nature, which is the means of the union of the lower [nature] and the higher [nature], is alone that [nature] which can be suitably elevated unto the Maximum by the power of the maximal, infinite God. For since this middle nature—as being what is highest of the lower [nature] and what is lowest of the higher [nature]—enfolds within itself all natures: if it ascends wholly to a union of itself with Maximality, then—as is evident—all natures and the entire universe have, in this nature, wholly reached the supreme gradation.

198   Now, human nature is that [nature] which, though created a little lower than the angels, is elevated above all the works of God;[27] it enfolds intellectual and sensible nature and encloses all things within itself, so that the ancients were right in calling it a microcosm, or a small world. Hence, human nature is that [nature] which, if it were elevated unto a union with Maximality, would be the fulness of all the perfections of each and every thing, so that in humanity all
199 things would attain the supreme gradation. Now, humanity is present only contractedly in this or that. Therefore, it would not be possible that more than one true human being [*homo*] could ascend to union with Maximality.[28] And, assuredly, this being would be a man in such way that He was also God and would be God in such way that He was also a man. [He would be] the perfection of the universe and would hold preeminence in all respects. In Him the least, the greatest, and the in-between things of the nature that is united to Absolute Maximality would so coincide that He would be the perfection of all things; and all things, qua contracted, would find rest in Him as in their own perfection. The measure of this man would also be the measure of an angel (as John says in the Book of Revelation)[29] and of each thing; for through union with Absolute [Maximality], which is the Absolute Being of all things, He would be the universal contracted being of each creature. Through Him all things would receive the beginning and the end of their contraction, so that through Him who is the contracted maximum [individual] all things would go forth from the

Absolute Maximum into contracted being and would return unto the Absolute [Maximum] through this same Medium—[in other words,] through [Him who is] the Beginning of their emanation and the End [i.e., the Goal] of their return, as it were.

200   But as the Equality of being all things, God is the Creator of the universe, since the universe was created in consequence of Him. Therefore, supreme and maximum Equality-of-being-all-things-absolutely would be that to which the nature of humanity would be united, so that through the assumed humanity God Himself would, in the humanity, be all things contractedly, just as He is the Equality of being all things absolutely. Therefore, since that man would, through the union, exist in maximum Equality of Being, He would be the Son of God—just as [He would also be] the Word [of God], in whom all things were created.[30] That is, [He would be] Equality-of-Being, which is called Son of God, according to what was previously indicated.[31] Nevertheless, He would not cease being the son of man, just as He would not cease being a man—as will be explained later.[32]

201   The things which can be done by God without any variation, diminuation, or diminishment of Himself are not repugnant to our most excellent and most perfect God; instead, they besuit His immense goodness, so that all things were created by Him and in consequence of Him in a most excellently and most perfectly congruent order. Therefore, since it is not[33] the case that anything could be more perfect if this order were removed,[34] no one—unless he denied either God or that God is most excellent—could reasonably find fault with these [created objects]. For all envy is far removed from God, who is supremely good and whose work cannot be defective; on the contrary, just as He is maximal, so too His work approaches as closely as possible to the maximum. But Maximum Power is not limited except with respect to itself; for there is not anything beyond it, and it is infinite. Therefore, [Maximum Power] is not limited with respect to any creature; rather, Infinite Power can create a better and more perfect [creature] than any given one.[35]

202   But if a human nature (*homo*)[36] is elevated unto a oneness with this Power—so that the human nature is a creature existing not in itself but in oneness with Infinite Power—then, this Power is limited not with respect to the creature but with respect to itself. Now, this [work, viz., such an elevated nature] is the most perfect work[37] of the maximum, infinite, and unlimitable power of God; in it there can be no deficiency; otherwise it would not be either Creator or creature. How would it be a creature [existing] contractedly from the Divine Absolute Being if contraction could not be united with it? Through it all things, qua existing,[38] would be from Him who exists absolutely; and, qua contracted, they would be from Him to whom contraction is supremely united. Thus, God exists first of all as Creator. Secondly, [He exists as] God-and-man (a created humanity having been supremely assumed into oneness with God);

the universal-contraction-of-all-things [i.e., the humanity] is, so to speak, "personally" and "hypostatically" united with the Equality-of-being-all-things).[39] Thus, in the third place, all things—through most absolute God and by the mediation of the universal contraction, viz., the humanity—go forth into contracted being so that they may be that-which-they-are in the best order and manner possible.[40] But this order should not be considered temporally—as if God temporally preceded the Firstborn of creation.[41] And [we ought not to believe] that the Firstborn—viz., God and man—preceded the world temporally but [should believe that He preceded it] in nature and in the order of perfection and above all time. Hence, by existing with God above time and prior to all things, He could appear to the world in the fulness of time,[42] after many cycles had passed.

203   *Chapter Four*:   Blessed Jesus, who is God and man, is the [contracted maximum individual].

In sure faith and by such considerations as the foregoing, we have now been led to the place that without any hesitancy at all we firmly hold the aforesaid to be most true. Accordingly, I say by way of addition that the fulness of time has passed and that ever-blessed Jesus is the Firstborn of all creation.

On the basis of what Jesus, who was a man, divinely and suprahumanly wrought and on the basis of other things which He, who is found to be true in all respects, affirmed about Himself—[things to which] those who lived with Him bore witness with their own blood and with an unalterable steadfastness that was formerly attested to by countless infallible considerations—we justifiably assert that Jesus is the one (1) whom the whole creation, from the beginning, expected to appear at the appointed time and (2) who through the prophets had foretold that He would appear in the world. For He came "in order to fill all things,"[43] because He willingly restored all [human beings] to health. Being powerful over all things, He disclosed all the secrets and mysteries of wisdom. As God, He forgave sins, raised the dead, transformed nature, commanded spirits, the sea, and the winds. He walked on water and established a law in fulness of supply for all laws.[44] According to the testimony of that most unique preacher of truth, Paul, who in a rapture was illuminated from on high,[45] we have in Him complete perfection, as well as redemption and remission of sins. "He is the Image of the Invisible God, the Firstborn of all creation because in Him all things were created, in heaven and on earth, visible and invisible, whether thrones or dominions or principalities or powers; all things were created through Him and in Him; and He is prior to all things, and in Him all things exist. And He is the head of the body, the church; He is the Beginning, the Firstborn from the dead, so that He holds the primacy in all respects. For it was pleasing that all fulness dwell in Him and that through Him all things be reconciled unto Him."[46]

204 Such testimonies, together with more elsewhere, are exhibited by the saints regarding the fact that He is God and man. In Him the humanity was united to the Word of God, so that the humanity existed not in itself but in the Word;[47] for the humanity could not have existed in the supreme degree and in complete fulness otherwise than in the divine person of the Son.

To the end that we may conceive—above all our intellectual comprehension and in learned ignorance, as it were—this person who united a human nature to Himself, let us ascend in our understanding and consider [the following]: Through all things God is in all things, and through all things all things are in God—as I indicated earlier at a certain place.[48] Therefore, since these [statements] must be considered conjointly as "God is in all things in such way that all things are in God" and since the Divine Being is of supreme equality and simplicity: God, qua present in all things, is not in them according to degrees—as if communicating Himself by degrees and by parts. However, none of these things can exist without [its respective] difference of degree; hence, all things are in God according to themselves with a [respective] difference of degree.[49] Therefore, since God is in all things in such way that all things are in Him, it is evident that God—in equality of being all things and without any change in Himself—exists in oneness with the maximum humanity of Jesus; for the maximum human nature can exist in God only maximally.[50] And so, in Jesus, who is the Equality of being all things, the Eternal Father and the Eternal Holy Spirit exist (just as they exist in God-the-Son, who is the middle person); and [in Jesus], just as in the Word, all things [exist]; and every creature [exists] in the supreme and most perfect humanity, which completely enfolds all creatable things. Thus, all fulness dwells in Jesus.

205 Let us somehow be directed to these [points] by the following example: Perceptual knowledge is a certain contracted knowledge because the senses attain only to particulars; intellectual knowledge is universal knowledge because in comparison with the perceptual it is free (*absoluta atque abstracta*) from contraction to the particular. But perception is contracted to various gradations in various ways. Through these contractions various species of animals arise according to grades of nobility and perfection. And although there is no ascent to the unqualifiedly maximum gradation (as I indicated earlier),[51] nevertheless in that species which is actually supreme within the genus *animal*, viz., the human species, the senses give rise to an animal such that it is so animal that it is also intellect. For a man is his own intellect. In the intellect the perceptual contractedness is somehow subsumed in (*suppositatur*) the intellectual nature, which exists as a certain divine, separate, abstract being, while the perceptual remains temporal and corruptible in accordance with its own nature.

206   Therefore, by means of a certain similarity (howbeit a remote one) we must reason in a similar way regarding Jesus, in whom the humanity—since otherwise it could not be maximal in its own fulness—is subsumed in the divinity. For since the intellect of Jesus is most perfect and exists in complete actuality, it can be personally subsumed only in the divine intellect, which alone is actually all things. For in all human beings the [respective] intellect is potentially all things; it gradually progresses from potentiality to actuality, so that the greater it [actually] is, the lesser it is in potentiality. But the maximum intellect, since it is the limit of the potentiality of every intellectual nature and exists in complete actuality, cannot at all exist without being intellect in such way that it is also God, who is all in all. By way of illustration: Assume that a polygon inscribed in a circle were the human nature and the circle were the divine nature. Then, if the polygon were to be a maximum polygon, than which there cannot be a greater polygon, it would exist not through itself with finite angles but in the circular shape. Thus, it would not have its own shape for existing—[i.e., it would not have a shape which was] even conceivably separable from the circular and eternal shape.[52]

207   Now, the maximality of human nature's perfection is seen in what is substantial and essential [about it]—i.e., with respect to the intellect, which is served by human nature's corporeal features. Hence, the maximally perfect man is not supposed to be prominent with regard to accidental features but with regard to His intellect. For example, it is not required that He be a giant or a dwarf or [that He be] of this or that size, color, figure—and so on for other accidents. Rather, it is only necessary that His body so avoid the extremes that it be a most suitable instrument for His intellectual nature, to which it be obedient and submissive without recalcitrance, complaint, and fatigue. Our Jesus—in whom were hidden (even while He appeared in the world) all the treasures of knowledge and wisdom,[53] as if a light were hidden in darkness—is believed to have had, for the sake of His most excellent intellectual nature, a most suitable and most perfect body (as also is reported by the most holy witnesses of His life).

208   *Chapter Five*:   Christ, conceived through the Holy Spirit, was born of the Virgin Mary.

Furthermore, we must consider that since the most perfect humanity, which is subsumed upwards, is the terminal contracted precision, it does not altogether exceed [the limits of] the species of human nature. Now, like is begotten from like; and, hence, the begotten proceeds from the begetter according to a natural comparative relation. But since what is terminal is free of termination, it is free of limitation and comparative relation. Hence, the maximum human being is not begettable by natural means; and yet, He cannot be altogether free of origin from that species whose terminal perfection He is. Therefore, because He is a human being, He proceeds partly according to human nature. And since He is the highest originated [being], most immediately united to the Beginning: the Beginning, from which He most immediately exists, is as a creating or begetting [Beginning], i.e., as a father; and the human beginning is as a passive [beginning] which affords a receiving material. Hence, [He comes] from a

209 mother apart from a male seed. But every operation proceeds from a spirit and a love which unite the active with the passive, as I earlier indicated in a certain passage.[54] Hence, necessarily, the maximum operation (which is beyond all natural comparative relation and through which the Creator is united to the creation and which proceeds from a maximum uniting Love) is, without doubt, from the Holy Spirit, who is absolutely Love. Through the Holy Spirit alone and without the assistance of a contracted agent, the mother was able to conceive—within the scope of her species—the Son of God the Father. Thus, just as God the Father formed by His own Spirit all the things which by Him came forth from not-being into being, so by the same most holy Spirit He did this more excellently when He worked most perfectly [i.e., when He formed Jesus].

210 To instruct our ignorance by an example: When some very excellent teacher wants to disclose to his students his intellectual, mental word (in order that they may feed spiritually upon the conceived truth once it has been shown to them), he causes his mental word to be indued with sound, since it is not disclosable to his students unless he indues it with a perceptible figure. But this cannot be done in any other way than through the natural spirit [i.e., breath] of the teacher. From the forced air he adapts a vocal figure that befits the mental word. To this figure he unites the word in such way that the sound exists with the word, so that those listening attain to the word by means of the sound.

211 By means of this admittedly very remote likeness we are momentarily elevated in our reflection—[elevated] beyond that which we can understand. For through the Holy Spirit (who is consubstantial with the Father) the Eternal Father of immense goodness (who willed to show us the richness of His glory and all the fulness of His knowledge and wisdom) indued with human nature the Eternal Word, His Son (who is the richness and the fulness of all things). Tolerating our weaknesses— since we were unable to perceive [the Word] in any other way than in visible form and in a form similar to ourselves—the Father manifested the Word in accordance with our capability. As a sound [is formed] from forced air, so, as it were, this Spirit, through an outbreathing,[55] formed from the fertile purity of the virginal blood the animal body. He added reason[56] so that it would be a human nature. [To it] He so inwardly united the Word of God the Father that the Word would be human nature's center of existence. And all these things were done not serially (as a concept is temporal-

ly expressed by us) but by an instantaneous operation—beyond all time and in accordance with a willing that befits Infinite Power.[57]

212 No one should doubt that this mother, who was so full of virtue and who furnished the material, excelled all virgins in the complete perfection of virtue and had a more excellent blessing than all other fertile women. For this [virgin-mother], who was in all respects foreordained to such a unique and most excellent virginal birth, ought rightfully to have been free of whatever could have hindered the purity or the vigor, and likewise the uniqueness, of such a most excellent birth. For if the Virgin had not been preelected, how would she have been suited for a virginal birth without a male seed? If she had not been superblessed of the Lord and most holy, how could she have been made the Holy Spirit's sacristy, in which the Holy Spirit would fashion a body for the Son of God. If she had not remained a virgin after the birth, she would beforehand have imparted to the most excellent birth the center of maternal fertility not in her supreme perfection of brightness but dividedly and diminishedly—not as would have befit [this] unique, supreme, and so great son. Therefore, if the most holy Virgin offered her whole self to God, for whom she also wholly partook of the complete nature of fertility by the operation of the Holy Spirit, then in her the virginity remained—before the birth, during the birth, and after the birth—immaculate and uncorrupted, beyond all natural and ordinary begetting.

213 Therefore, Jesus Christ—God and man—was born from the Eternal Father and from a temporal mother, viz., the most glorious Virgin Mary. [He was born] from the maximum and absolutely most abundant Father and from a mother most filled with virginal fertility—filled, in the fulness of time, with a heavenly blessing. For from the virgin-mother [Jesus] was able to exist as a human being only temporally—and from God the Father only eternally. But the temporal birth required a fulness of perfection in time—just as [it required] in
214 the mother a fulness of fertility. Therefore, when the fulness of time arrived: since [Jesus] could not be born as a human being apart from time, He was born at the time and place most fitting thereto and yet most concealed from all creatures. For the supreme bounties (*plenitudines*) are incomparable with our daily experiences. Hence, no reasoning was able to grasp them by any sign, even though by a certain very hidden prophetic inspiration certain obscure signs, darkened by human likenesses, transmitted them; and from these signs the wise could reasonably have foreseen that the Word would be incarnated in the fulness of time. But the precise place, time, or manner was known only to the Eternal Begetter, who ordained that when all things were in a state of moderate silence, the Son would in the course of the night[58] descend from the Heavenly Citadel into the virginal womb and would at the ordained and fitting time manifest Himself to the world in the form of a servant.

215   *Chapter Six*:   The mystery of the death of Jesus Christ.

It accords with the expression of my intent [in the chapter title] that a short digression first be made—in order to attain more clearly unto the mystery of the Cross. There is no doubt that a human being consists of senses, intellect, and reason (which is in between and which connects the other two).[59] Now, order subordinates the senses to reason and reason to intellect. The intellect is not temporal and mundane but is free of time and of the world. The senses are temporally subject to the motions of the world. With respect to the intellect, reason is on the horizon, so to speak; but with respect to the senses, it is at the zenith, as it were; thus, things that are within time and things that are beyond time coincide in reason.

216   The senses, which belong to the animal [nature], are incapable [of attaining unto] supratemporal and spiritual things. Therefore, what is animal does not perceive the things which are of God,[60] for God is spirit and more than spirit.[61] Accordingly, perceptual knowledge occurs in the darkness of the ignorance of eternal things; and in accordance with the flesh it is moved, through the power of concupiscence, toward carnal desires and, through the power of anger, toward warding off what hinders it. But supraexcellent reason contains—in its own nature and as a result of its capability of participating in the intellectual nature—certain laws through which, as ruler over desire's passions,[62] it tempers and calms the passions, in order that a human being will not make a goal of perceptible things and be deprived of his intellect's spiritual desire. And the most important of [these] laws are that no one do to another what he would not want done to himself,[63] that eternal things be preferred to temporal things, and clean and holy things to unclean and base things. The laws which are elicited from reason by the most holy lawgivers and are taught (according to the difference of place and time) as remedies for those who sin against reason work

217 together to the foregoing end. Even if the senses were subject to reason in every respect and did not follow after the passions which are natural to them, the intellect—soaring higher [than reason]—sees that nonetheless man cannot of himself attain to the goal of his intellectual and eternal desires. For since from the seed of Adam man is begotten with carnal delight[64] (in whom, in accordance with propagation, the animality prevails over the spirituality): his nature—which in its basis of origin is immersed in the carnal delights through which the man springs forth into existence by way of a father—remains altogether unable to transcend temporal things in order to embrace spiritual things. Accordingly, if the weight of carnal delights draws reason and intellect downward, so that they consent to these motions and do not resist them, it is clear that a man so drawn downward and so turned away from God, is altogether deprived of the enjoyment of the most excellent good, which, in the manner of the intellectual, is upward and eternal. But if reason governs the senses, still it is necessary that

the intellect govern reason in order that the intellect may adhere—by formed faith[65] and above reason—to the Mediator, so that it can be drawn unto glory by God the Father.

218   Except for Christ Jesus who descended from Heaven, there was never anyone who had [enough] power over himself and over his own nature (which in its origin is so subject to the sins of carnal desire) to be able, of himself, to ascend beyond his own origin to eternal and heavenly things. Jesus is the one who ascended by His own power and in whom human nature (begotten not from the will of the flesh but from God)[66] was not hindered from returning, of its own power, to God the Father. Therefore, through its union [with the divine nature] the human nature in Christ was exalted to the Supreme Power and was delivered from the weight of temporal and burdensome desires. But Christ the Lord willed to mortify completely—and in mortifying to purge—by means of His own human body all the sins of human nature which draw us toward earthly things. [He did this] not for His own sake (since He had committed no sin) but for our sakes, so that all men, of the same humanity with Him, would find in Him the complete purgation of their sins. The man Christ's voluntary and most innocent, most shameful, and most cruel death on the Cross was the deletion and purgation of, and the satisfaction for, all the carnal desires of human nature. Whatever humanly can be done counter to the love for a neighbor is abundantly made up for in the fulness of Christ's love, by which He delivered

219 Himself unto death even on behalf of His enemies. Therefore, the humanity in Christ Jesus made up for all the defects of all men. For since it is maximum [humanity], it encompasses the complete possibility of the species, so that it is such equality-of-being for each man that it is united to each man much more closely than is a brother or a very special friend. For the maximality of human nature brings it about that in the case of each man who cleaves to Christ through formed faith Christ is this very man[67] by means of a most perfect union—each's numerical distinctness being preserved. Because of this union the following statement of Christ is true: "Whatever you have done to one of the least of my [brethren], you have done to me."[68] And, conversely, whatever Christ Jesus merited by His suffering, those who are one with Him also merited—different degrees of merit being preserved in accordance with the different degree of each [man's] union with Christ through faith formed by love. Hence, in Christ the faithful are circumcised; in Him they are baptized; in Him they die; in Him they are made alive again through resurrection; in Him they are united to God and are glorified.[69]

220   Therefore, our justification is not from ourselves but from Christ. Since He is complete fulness, in Him we obtain all things, if we possess Him. Since in this life we attain unto Him by formed faith, we can be justified only by faith, as I will explain more fully in a later section.[70]

This is that ineffable mystery of the Cross of our redemption. In this mystery

Christ showed (in addition to the things already touched upon) that truth, justice, and the divine virtues ought to be preferred to temporal life—just as eternal things ought to be preferred to transitory things. And [herein He also showed] that in the most perfect man supreme constancy, strength, love, and humility ought to be present—just as the death of Christ on the Cross showed that these and all other virtues were maximally present in Jesus, the maximum [individual]. Therefore, the higher a man ascends in the immortal virtues, the more Christlike he becomes. For minimum things coincide with maximum things. For example, maximum humiliation [coincides] with exaltation; the most shameful death of a virtuous man [coincides] with his glorious life, and so on—as Christ's life, suffering, and crucifixion manifest all these [points] to us.

221 *Chapter Seven*: The mystery of the Resurrection.

The man Christ, being passible and mortal, could attain unto the glory of the Father (who is Immortality itself, since He is Absolute Life) by no other way than [the following]: that what was mortal put on immortality.[71] And this was not at all possible apart from death. For how could what is mortal have put on immortality otherwise than by being stripped of mortality? How would it be free of mortality except by having paid the debt of death? Therefore, Truth itself says that those who do not understand that Christ had to die and in this way enter into glory are foolish and of slow mind.[72] But since I have already indicated[73] that for our sakes Christ died a most cruel death, I must now say the following: since it was not fitting for human nature to be led to the triumph of immortality otherwise than through victory over death, [Christ] underwent death in order that human nature would rise again with Him to eternal life and that the animal, mortal body would become spiritual and incorruptible. [Christ] was able to be a true man only if He was mortal; and He was able to lead mortal [human] nature to immortality only if through death human nature became stripped of mortality.

222 Hear how beautifully Truth itself, speaking about this [matter], instructs us when it says: "Except a grain of wheat falling into the ground die it remains alone; but if it die it brings forth much fruit."[74] Therefore, if Christ had always remained mortal (even if He had never died), how would He, as a mortal man, have bestowed immortality on human nature? Although He would not have died, He would have remained a mere deathless mortal. Therefore, through death, He had to be freed from the possibility of dying, if He was to bear much fruit—so that, when exalted, He would draw all things unto Himself,[75] since His power would be present not only in this corruptible[76] world and on this corruptible earth but also in incorruptible Heaven. Now, if we keep in mind the

points that have already been frequently made, we will be able in our ignorance to apprehend the present point to some extent.

223   In what precedes I indicated that the maximum man, Jesus, was not able to have in Himself a person that existed separately from the divinity. For He is the maximum [human being]. And, accordingly, there is a sharing of the respective modes of speaking [about the human nature and the divine nature], so that the human things coincide with the divine things; for His humanity—which on account of the supreme union is inseparable from His divinity (as if it were put on and assumed by the divinity)—cannot exist as separate in person.[77] But a man is a union of a body and a soul—the separation of which is death. Therefore, because the maximum humanity is subsumed in the divine person: at the time of [Jesus's] death neither the soul nor the body could have been separated (not even with respect to spatial separation) from the divine person, without which the man [Jesus] did not exist.

224   Therefore, Christ did not die as if His person had forsaken Him; rather He remained hypostatically united with the divinity—there not being even spatial separation with regard to the [personal] center, in which the humanity was subsumed. (But in accordance with the lower nature—which in conformity with the truth of its own nature was able to undergo a separation of the soul from the body— a separation was made temporally and spatially, so that at the hour of death the soul and the body were not together at the same place and at the same time.) Therefore, in His body and soul no corruptibility was possible, since they were united with eternity. But the temporal birth was subject to death and temporal separation, so that when the circle of return (from temporal composition to dissolution) was completed and when, furthermore, the body was freed from these temporal motions, the truth of the humanity that is beyond time and that, as united to the divinity, remained undestroyed united (as its truth required) the truth of the body with the truth of the soul. Thus, when the shadowy image of the truth of the man who appeared in time departed, the true man arose, free from all temporal passion. Hence, the same Jesus most truly arose above all temporal motions (through a union of soul to body—[a union] beyond all temporal motion) and was never again going to die. Without this union the truth of the incorruptible humanity would not have been unconfusedly and most truly united hypostatically with the nature of the divine person.

225   Assist your smallness of intellect and your ignorance by Christ's example about the grain of wheat.[78] In this example the numerical distinctness of the grain is destroyed, while the specific essence remains intact; by this means nature raises up many grains. But if the grain were maximum and most perfect, then when it died in very good and very fertile soil, it could bring forth fruit not only one hundredfold or one thousandfold but as manifold as the nature of the species encompassed in its possibility. This is what Truth means [when it says]

that [the grain] would bring forth much fruit; for a multitude is a limitedness without number.

Therefore, discern keenly: with respect to the fact that the humanity of Jesus is considered as contracted to the man Christ, it is likewise understood to be united also with His divinity. As united with the divinity, [the humanity] is fully absolute; [but] as it is considered to be that true man Christ, [the humanity] is contracted, so that Christ is a man through the humanity. And so, Jesus's humanity is as a medium between what is purely absolute and what is purely contracted. Accordingly, then, it was corruptible only in a given respect; but absolutely it was incorruptible. Therefore, it was corruptible according to temporality, to which it was contracted; but in accordance with the fact that it was free from time, beyond time, and united with the divinity, it was incorruptible.

226   But truth, as temporally contracted, is a "sign" and an "image," so to speak, of supratemporal truth. Thus, the temporally contracted truth of the body is a "shadow," so to speak, of the supratemporal truth of the body. So too, the [temporally] contracted truth of the soul is, as it were, a "shadow" of the soul which is free from time. For when the soul is in time, where it does not apprehend without images, it seems to be the senses or reason rather than the intellect; and when it is elevated above time, it is the intellect, which is free from images. And since the humanity was inseparably rooted on high in the divine incorruptibility: when the temporal, corruptible motion was completed, the dissolution could occur only in the direction of the root of its incorruptibility. Therefore, after the end of temporal motion ([an end] which was death) and after the destruction of all the things which temporally befell the truth of human nature, the same Jesus arose—not with a body which was burdensome, corruptible, shadowy, passible (and so on for the other things which follow upon temporal composition) but with a true body which was glorious, impassible, unbehindered, and immortal (as the truth which was free from temporal conditions required). Moreover, the truth of the hypostatic union of the human nature with the divine nature necessarily required this union [of body and soul]. Hence, Blessed Jesus had to arise from the dead, as He Himself says when He states: "Christ had to suffer in this way and to arise from the dead on the third day."[79]

227   *Chapter Eight*:   Christ, the Firstfruits of those who sleep,[80] ascended to Heaven.

Now that the foregoing points have been exhibited, it is easy to see that Christ is the Firstborn from the dead.[81] For before Him no one was able to arise [from the dead]—since human nature had not yet, in the course of time, reached a maximum and was not yet united with incorruptibility and immortality, as it was in Christ. For all human beings were powerless until the coming of Him who said: "I have the power to lay down my life and the power to take it up again."[82] Therefore, in Christ, who is the Firstfruits of those who sleep,[83] human nature put on immortality. But there is only one indivisible humanity and specific essence of all human beings. Through *it* all individual human beings are numerically distinct human beings, so that Christ and all human beings have the same humanity, though the numerical distinctness of the individuals remains unconfused. Hence, it is evident that the humanity of all the human beings who—whether temporally before or after Christ—either have existed or will exist has, in Christ, put on immortality. Therefore, it is evident that the following inference holds: the man Christ arose; hence, after [the cessation of] all motion of temporal corruptibility, all men will arise through Him, so that they will be eternally incorruptible.

228   And although there is a single humanity of all human beings, there are various individuating principles which contract it to this or that person (*suppositum*)—so that in Jesus Christ there were only the most perfect and powerful principles and those nearest to the essence of the humanity that was united with the divinity. Through the power of His divinity Christ was able to arise by His own power, which came to Him from His divinity; hence, God is said to have raised Him from the dead. Since Jesus was God and man, He arose by His own power; and—except in the power of Christ, who is God—no man besides Christ can arise as Christ.[84] Therefore, Christ is the one through whom, according to the nature of His humanity, our human nature has contracted immortality and through whom, as well, we (who were born altogether subject to motion) will (when motion ceases) rise beyond time and unto a likeness to Him. This will occur at the end of time. But Christ, who was born temporally only insofar as He issued forth from a mother, did not, as regards His resurrection, wait for the whole course of time [to end], for time did not wholly affect His birth. Remember that in Christ human nature put on immortality. Therefore, all of us, whether good or evil, shall arise; but not all of us shall be changed through a glory which transforms us—through Christ, the Son of God—into adopted sons. Therefore, all shall arise through Christ, but not all shall arise as Christ and in Christ through union; rather, only those who are Christ's through faith, hope, and love [shall so arise].[85]

229   If I am not mistaken, you see that [a religion] which does not embrace Christ as mediator and savior, as God and man, as the way, the truth, and the life[86] is not a perfect religion, leading men to the final and most coveted goal of peace. Think of how discordant is the belief of the Saracens, who (1) affirm that Christ is the maximum and most perfect man, born of a virgin and translated alive into Heaven but (2) deny that He is God. Surely they have been blinded, because they assert what is impossible. But even from the points stated in the foregoing

manner one who has understanding can see, clearer than day, that a man who is not also God cannot be maximum and in all respects most perfect, supernaturally born of a virgin. These [Saracens] are mindless persecutors of the Cross of Christ, being ignorant of His mysteries. They will not taste the divine fruit of His redemption, nor are they led to expect it by their law of Mohammed, which promises only to satisfy their cravings for pleasure.[87] In the hope that these cravings are extinguished in us by the death of Christ, we yearn to apprehend an incorruptible glory.

230   The Jews likewise confess with the Saracens that Messiah is the maximum, most perfect, and immortal man; but, held back by the same diabolical blindness, they deny that He is God. They also do not hope (as do we servants of Christ) to obtain the supreme happiness of enjoying God—even as they also shall not obtain it. And what I deem to be even more remarkable is that the Jews, as well as the Saracens, believe that there will be a general resurrection but do not admit its possibility through the man who is also God. For suppose [the following] be granted: that if the motion of generation and corruption ceases, the perfection of the universe cannot occur apart from resurrection, since human nature (which is an intermediate nature) is an essential part of the universe; and without human nature not only would the universe [not] be perfect but it would not even be a universe. And [suppose it also be granted] that therefore the following is necessary: that if motion ever ceases, either the entire universe will cease or men will rise to incorruptibility. (In these men the nature of all intermediate things is complete, so that the other animals will not have to arise, since man is their perfection.) Or [suppose] the resurrection be said to be going to occur in order that the whole man will receive, from a just God, retribution according to his merits. [Even if all of the foregoing be said], still, above all, Christ—through whom alone human nature can attain unto incorruptibility—must be believed to be God and man.

231   And so, all those who believe that there is resurrection and who deny that Christ is the medium of its possibility have been blinded, since faith in resurrection is the affirmation of the divinity and the humanity of Christ and of the death and the resurrection of Christ, who, according to the aforesaid, is the Firstborn from the dead. For He arose in order thereby to enter into glory through ascending to Heaven. I think that this ascent must be understood to have been above all motion of corruptibility and all influence of the heavens. For although in accordance with His divinity Christ is everywhere, nevertheless His place is more properly said to be where there never is change, emotion, sadness, and other [accidents] which befall temporality. And we say that this place of eternal joy and peace is beyond the heavens, although it is not apprehensible, describable, or definable in respect to space.

232   Christ is the center and the circumference of intellectual nature;[88] and since the intellect encompasses all things, Christ is above all things. Nevertheless, as

if in His own temple, He dwells in the holy rational souls and in the holy intellectual spirits, which are the heavens, declaring His glory. So, then, we understand that Christ—in that He "ascended above all the heavens, in order to fill all things"—ascended above all space and time unto an incorruptible mansion, beyond everything which can be spoken of.[89] Since He is God, He is all in all. Since He is Truth, He reigns in the intellectual heavens. And since as the life of all rational spirits He is their center, it is not the case that, with respect to location, He is seated on the circumference rather than at the center. And, therefore, He who is the "Fount of life"[90] for souls, as well as their goal, affirms that the Kingdom of Heaven is also within men.[91]

233   *Chapter Nine*:   Christ is judge of the living and the dead.

Who is a judge more just than He who is Justice itself? For Christ, the head and the source of every rational creature, is Maximal Reason, from which all reason derives. But reason[92] judges discriminatively. Hence, Christ—who (while remaining God, who is the rewarder of all) assumed rational human nature with all rational creatures—is rightfully the judge of the living and the dead. But through Himself and in Himself Christ judges—above all time—all things. For He embraces all creatures, since He is the maximum human being, in whom, because He is God, all things exist. As God He is infinite light in which there is no darkness.[93] This light illumines all things, so that in it all things are most manifest to it. For this infinite, intellectual light enfolds, beyond all time, what is present as well as what is past, what is living as well as what is dead—just as corporeal light is the basis (*hypostasis*) of all colors. But Christ is as purest fire, which is inseparable from light and which exists not in itself but in light. And He is that spiritual fire of life and understanding which—as consuming[94] all things and taking all things into itself—tests and judges all things, as does the judgment of material fire, which examines all things.

234   All rational spirits are judged in Christ, as what is heatable by fire [is judged] in fire.[95] Of these [heatable things] the one, if it remains in the fire for a long time, is transformed into the likeness of fire (e.g., most excellent and most perfect gold is so gold and so intensely fire-hot that it appears to be no more gold than fire); but some other thing does not participate in the intensity of the fire to such a degree (e.g., purified silver, bronze, or iron); nevertheless, they all seem to be transformed into fire, although each [is transformed] in its own degree. And this judgment belongs only to the fire, not to the things heated by fire, since each thing heated by fire apprehends in each other such thing only that very radiant fire and not the differences between each such thing. By comparison, if we were to see gold, silver, and copper fused in a maximum fire, we would not apprehend the differences of the metals after they had been

transformed into the form of fire. However, if the fire were an intellectual [being], it would know the degrees of perfection of each [metal] and to what extent (according to these degrees) the fire's capability for intensity would be
235 differently present in each thing. Hence, there are certain things—things heatable by fire, continuing incorruptibly in fire, and capable of receiving light and heat—which on account of their purity are transformable into the likeness of fire; and this occurs differently, according to greater and lesser degrees. But there are other things which, because of their impurity, are not transformable into light, even if they are heatable. In a similar manner, Christ, who is judge, according to one and the same most simple judgment, imparts most justly and without envy, at one instant and to all [rational spirits] (imparts not in the order of time but in the order of nature) the "warmth," so to speak, of created reason—in order to bestow, by the heat which is received, a divine, intellectual light from on high. Thus, God is all things in all things;[96] and all things are in God through the Mediator; and [every rational spirit] is equal to God to the extent that this is possible in accordance with each's capability.

But some things, because of the fact that they are more unified and pure, are able to receive not only heat but also light; other things are barely [able to receive] heat and are not [at all able to receive] light. This results from [the
236 disposition or] indisposition of the [receiving] objects. Hence, since that Infinite Light is Eternity itself and Truth itself, it is necessary that a rational creature desiring to be illuminated by that Light turn to true and eternal things, which are above these mundane and corruptible things. Corporeal and spiritual things are related to each other as contraries. For example, vegetative power is corporeal; it converts nourishment which is received from without into the nature of that which is nourished; an animal is not converted into bread but conversely. However, when an intellectual spirit—whose operation is supratemporal and, as it were, on the horizon of eternity—turns toward eternal things, it cannot convert these things into itself, since they are eternal and incorruptible. But since it itself is incorruptible, it also is not converted into these things in such way that it ceases to be an intellectual substance. Instead, it is converted into these [in such way] that it is absorbed into a likeness to the eternal things—[absorbed], however, according to degrees, so that the more fervently it is turned toward these things, the more fully it is perfected by them and the more deeply its being is hidden in the Eternal Being. But since Christ is immortal and still lives and is still life and truth, whoever turns to Him turns to life and truth. And the more ardently [he does] this, the more he is elevated from mundane and corruptible things unto eternal things, so that his life is hidden in Christ.[97] For the virtues are eternal: justice remains forever, and so too does truth.
237   Whoever turns to the virtues walks in Christ's ways, which are the ways of purity and immortality. Now, the virtues are divine illuminations. Therefore, if

during this life someone turns by faith to Christ, who is virtue, then when he is freed from this temporal life, he will exist in purity of spirit, so that he can enter into the joy of eternal possession. But the turning of our spirit occurs when in accordance with all its intellectual powers our spirit turns by faith to the eternal and most pure truth (which it places before all else) and when it chooses and loves such truth as being alone worthy to be loved. For to turn by most assured faith to the truth which is Christ is to forsake this world and to tread on it in victory. But to love Christ most ardently is to attain unto Him through spiritual motion, for He is not only lovable but is Love itself. For when through the grades of love the spirit attains unto Love itself, it is plunged into Love itself—not temporally but above all time and mundane motion.

238   Therefore, just as everyone who loves is within love, so all who love truth are in Christ. And just as everyone-who-loves loves through love, so all who love truth love it through Christ. Hence, no one knows the truth unless the spirit of Christ is in him. And just as it is impossible that there be a lover without love, so it is impossible that someone have God without [having] the spirit of Christ; only in this spirit can we worship God. Accordingly, unbelievers—who are unconverted to Christ and who are incapable of receiving the light of transforming glory—have already been condemned to darkness and to the shadow of death, since they have turned from the life which is Christ.[98] Through union [with Christ] all [who love Christ] are gloriously filled with His fulness alone.[99] Later, when I shall speak about the church, I will add—on the same foundation and for the sake of our consolation—some more points regarding this union.[100]

239   *Chapter Ten:*   The Judge's sentence.

It is evident that no one among mortals comprehends the judgment and sentence of this judge. For since it is beyond all time and motion, it is not disclosed by comparative or inferential investigation or by vocal utterance or by such signs as indicate a delay or a protraction. But just as all things were created in[101] the Word (for He spoke and they were created),[102] so in the same Word, which is also called Reason, all things are judged. And there is no interval between the sentence and its execution, but what happens at an instant is the following: the resurrection and the securing of the respective end (viz., glorification with regard to the translation of the sons of God and damnation with regard to the exclusion of the unconverted) are not separated by a moment of time—[not] even by an indivisible [moment].

240   The intellectual nature, which is beyond time and is not subject to temporal corruption,[103] contains, in accordance with its nature, incorruptible forms—e.g., mathematical forms, which in their own way are abstract, and also natural forms,[104] which are easily abstracted (*transformantur*) and are stored away in

the intellectual nature. These [incorruptible forms] are, for us, guiding signs of the intellectual nature's incorruptibility; for [the intellect is] the incorruptible locus of incorruptible [forms]. Now, by its natural movement [the intellectual nature] is moved toward most abstract truth—as if toward the goal of its own desires and toward the ultimate and most delectable object. And since such an object as this is all things, because it is God, the intellect—insatiable until it attains thereunto—is immortal and incorruptible, for it is not satisfied except by an eternal object.

241   But suppose that an intellect, upon being freed from this body in which it is subject to temporal thoughts, does not attain the desired goal but rather falls into ignorance when it should be seeking the truth and when with utmost desire it should be desiring nothing other than to apprehend the truth, not by a symbolism or signs but assuredly and "face to face."[105] In that case, since (because of its turning away from truth at the hour of separation and because of its turning to what is corruptible) it falls toward corruptible objects of desire, toward uncertainty and confusion, and into the dark chaos of pure possibility (where there is no actual certainty): the intellect is rightly said to have descended unto intellectual death. Indeed, for the intellectual soul to understand is for it to be; and for it to understand the object of desire is for it to live. Hence, just as, for it, eternal life is finally to apprehend the unchanging, eternal object of its desire, so, for it, eternal death is to be separated from this unchanging object of desire and to be hurled into the chaos of confusion, where in its own manner it is eternally tormented by fire. [This manner is] graspable by us only analogously to the torment of someone who is deprived of vital nourishment and health—and [deprived] not only of these but also of the hope of ever obtaining them, so that he is ever dying an agonizing death, without extinction and termination.

242   The foregoing is a life wretched beyond what can be conceived. It is life in such way that it is death; it is existence in such way that it is not-existence; it is understanding in such way that it is lack of understanding. Now, earlier[106] I proved [all of the following]: The resurrection of men occurs above all motion and time and quantity and other [determinations] which are subject to time, so that the corruptible is resolved into the incorruptible and the animal is resolved into the spiritual. Accordingly, a whole [resurrected] man *is* his intellect, which is spirit; and a true body is engulfed by his spirit. Thus, the body does not exist in itself (i.e., in its corporeal, quantitative, and temporal relations) but exists as translated into the spirit (i.e., exists in a manner contrary to our present body). *Here* [in this lifetime] not the intellect but the body is seen, and in the body the intellect seems to be imprisoned, as it were; but *there* [in the resurrected life] the body exists in the spirit, just as here the spirit exists in the body. Accordingly, as here the soul is weighed down by the body, so there the body is lightened by the spirit. Therefore, [in accordance with the foregoing proven points]: as

the spiritual joys of the intellectual life are the greatest (which joys are participated in by even the body, which is glorified within the spirit), so the infernal sorrows of spiritual death are the greatest (which sorrows are experienced even by the body, which is in the spirit). And since our God (who is understood to be eternal life) is comprehensible [only] above all understanding,[107] these eternal joys which exceed our entire understanding are
243 greater than can be conveyed by any sign; likewise, the punishments of the damned occur beyond all conceivable and describable punishments. Therefore, with regard to all the musical and harmonic signs of joy, delight, and glory which, as signs for thinking what is known to us, are found to be indicators-of-eternal-life handed down by the Fathers: they are very remote perceptible signs—infinitely distant from the intellectual [realities], which are not perceivable by any imaging. Similarly, with regard to the punishments of Hell, which are likened to a fire of the element sulphur, to a fire from pitch, and to other perceptible torments: these latter do not admit of any comparison with those fiery intellectual miseries from which Jesus Christ, our life and our salvation, deigns to save us. He is blessed forever. Amen.

244   *Chapter Eleven*:   The mysteries of faith.

All our forefathers unanimously maintain that faith is the beginning of understanding. For in every branch of study certain things are presupposed as first principles.[108] They are grasped by faith alone, and from them is elicited an understanding of the matters to be treated. For everyone who wills to ascend to learning must believe those things without which he cannot ascend. For Isaiah says "Unless you believe, you will not understand."[109] Therefore, faith enfolds within itself everything which is understandable. But understanding is the unfolding of faith. Therefore, understanding is guided by faith, and faith is increased by understanding. Hence, where there is no sound faith, there is no true understanding. Thus, it is evident what kind of conclusion erroneous beginnings and a weakness of foundation imply. But there is no more perfect faith than Truth itself, which is Jesus.[110]
     Who does not understand that right faith is a most excellent gift of God?[111] The Apostle John states that faith in the incarnation of the Word of God leads us unto the truth in order that we may be made sons of God.[112] At the outset John plainly discloses this [faith]; then in accordance with it he expounds the many works of Christ, in order that the intellect may be illumined in faith; finally, he draws the conclusion when he says, "These things were written in order that you would believe that Jesus is the Son of God."[113]
245   But soundest faith-in-Christ, made steadfastly firm in simplicity, can, in accordance with previously given instruction in ignorance, be increased and

unfolded in ascending degrees. For although hidden from the wise, the very great and very deep mysteries of God are revealed, through faith in Jesus, to the small and humble inhabitants of the world.[114] For Jesus is the one in whom all the treasures of wisdom and knowledge are hidden,[115] and without Him no one can do anything.[116] For He is the Word and the Power through which God (who as the Most High, having power over all things in heaven and on earth) created even the aeons. Since God is not knowable in this world[117] (where by reason and by opinion or by doctrine we are led, with symbols, through the more known to the unknown), He is apprehended only where persuasive considerations cease and faith appears. Through faith we are caught up, in simplicity, so that being in a body incorporeally (because in spirit) and in the world not mundanely but celestially we may incomprehensibly contemplate Christ above all reason and intelligence, in the third heaven of most simple intellectuality. Thus, we see even the following: viz., that because of the immensity of His excellence God cannot be comprehended. And this is that learned ignorance through which most blessed Paul, in ascending, saw that when he was being elevated more highly to Christ, he did not know Christ, though at one time he had known only Christ.[118]

246   Therefore, we who are believers in Christ are led in learned ignorance unto the Mountain that is Christ and that we are forbidden to touch with the nature of our animality.[119] And when we attempt to view this Mountain with our intellectual eye, we fall into an obscuring mist, knowing that within this mist is the Mountain on which, alone, all living beings possessed of an intellect are well pleased to dwell. If we approach this Mountain with greater steadfastness of faith, we will be snatched from the eyes of those who live sensually, so that with an inward hearing we will perceive the sounds and thunderings and frightening signs of its majesty. [And thus too] we will easily perceive that Christ alone is Lord, whom all things obey, and we will progressively come to certain of His incorruptible footprints (as if [coming to] certain most divine marks). At this point we [shall] hear, in the holy instruments and signs of the prophets and the saints, the voice not of mortal creatures but of God Himself; and we [shall] see God more clearly, as if through a more rarefied cloud.

247   Thereupon the believers, who continue to ascend with more ardent desire, are caught up unto simple intellectuality; and leaping beyond all perceptible things, they pass as if from sleeping to waking, from hearing to seeing. There they see things which, because they are things beyond all hearing and all vocal instruction, cannot be revealed. But should it be claimed that they are there revealed, then the unsayable would [there] be said and the unhearable would [there] be heard—even as the invisible is there seen. For Jesus—who is blessed forever,[120] who is the goal not only of all understanding (because He is Truth) but also of all sensing (because He is Life), and who, further, is both the goal of all being (because He is Being itself) and the perfection of every creature

(because He is God and man)—is, as the goal of every utterance, *there* heard incomprehensibly. For every utterance has come forth from Him and terminates in Him. Whatever truth is in an utterance is from Him. Every utterance has as its goal instruction; therefore, [every utterance] has as its goal Him who is Wisdom itself. "Whatever things were written were written for our instruction."[121] Utterances are befigured in written characters. "By the Word of the Lord the heavens were established."[122] Therefore, all created things are signs of the Word of God. Every corporeal utterance is a sign of a mental word. The cause of every corruptible mental word is an incorruptible word, viz., a concept. Christ is the incarnated Concept of all concepts,[123] for He is the Word made flesh.[124] Therefore, Jesus is the goal of all things.

248   Such things are progressively manifested to one who ascends to Christ by faith. The divine efficacy of this faith is inexplicable. For if this faith is great, it unites the believer with Jesus in order that he may be above all things which do not exist in oneness with Jesus Himself. If the [believer's] faith is whole, then with the power of Jesus, with whom he is united, he commands even the evil spirits and has power over nature and motion. And it is not he himself but rather Jesus who—in him and through him—works wondrous things, as the deeds of the saints bear witness.

It is necessary that perfect faith in Christ be—to the extent that this is really possible—most pure, maximum, and formed by love. For this faith does not allow anything to be mixed with it, since it is faith in the purest Truth's power for all things. In the preceding [sections] there can very frequently be found repeated [the doctrine] that the minimum coincides with the maximum. This doctrine applies to the faith which is unqualifiedly maximum in actuality and in power. [This maximum faith] cannot be in a pilgrim, who is still not a full attainer [of his goal], as was Jesus. However, the pilgrim must will actually to have for himself maximum faith in Christ—[to have it] to such an extent that his faith will be elevated to such a level of indubitable certainty that it will also be not at all faith but supreme certainty devoid of all doubt in any respect

249 whatsoever. This is the mighty faith which is so maximal that it is also minimal,[125] so that it embraces all the things which are believable with regard to Him who is Truth. Even if, perhaps, one man's faith does not reach the level of another man's,[126] because of the impossibility of there being equality (just as one visible object cannot be seen in equal measure by many [different perceivers]), nevertheless it is necessary that each [person], as best he can, actually believe maximally. And thus, [as regards] him who in relation to others would attain a faith scarcely [the size of] a grain of mustard: his faith would be of such immense power that he would find obedience even on the part of the mountains.[127] For he would command with the power of the Word of God, with whom he would be (as much as he could) maximally united by faith and whom nothing could resist.

250   Notice how great your intellectual spirit's power is in the power of Christ, provided [your spirit] cling to Him above all else, so that it be nourished by Him—being, through union, subsumed in Him (its numerical distinctness being preserved) as in its own life. But since this occurs only through the conversion of the intellect (which the senses obey) to Christ by maximum faith, this [faith] must be formed by uniting love. For without love faith cannot be maximum. For if every living thing loves to live and if every understanding thing loves to understand, how can Jesus be believed to be immortal life and infinite truth if He is not loved supremely? For life per se is lovable; and if Jesus is most greatly believed to be eternal life, He cannot fail to be loved. For without love faith is not living but dead and is not faith at all. But love is the form of faith, giving to faith true being; indeed, love is the sign of most steadfast faith. Therefore, if for the sake of Christ all things are set aside, and if in relation to Christ the body and the soul are counted as nothing: this is a sign of maximum faith.

251   Moreover, faith cannot be great apart from the holy hope of enjoying Jesus. For how would anyone have assured faith if he did not hope for what was promised him by Christ? If he does not believe that he will have the eternal life promised by Christ to believers, in what sense does he believe Christ? Or how is it that he believes that Christ is truth if he does not have assured hope in His promises? How would he choose death for Christ's sake if he did not hope for immortality? Because the believer believes that [Christ] does not forsake those who hope in Him but rather bestows on them eternal happiness: on account of such a great reward of recompense he counts it as a small matter to endure all things for Christ.[128]

252   Assuredly, the power of faith is great: it makes a man Christlike, so that he abandons perceptible things, divests himself of the contaminating things of the flesh, walks in the ways of God with reverence, follows the steps of Christ with joy, willingly bears a cross with exaltation—so that he exists in the flesh as a spirit for whom (on account of Christ) this world is death and for whom removal from this world (in order to be with Christ) is life. Who, in your opinion, is this spirit in which Christ dwells by faith? What is this admirable gift of God which is such that we, who on this pilgrimage are constituted with frail flesh, can by the power of faith be elevated to this power over[129] all the things which are not Christ through union? Be aware that as someone's flesh is progressively and gradually mortified by faith, he progressively ascends to oneness with Christ, so that he is absorbed into Christ by a deep union—to the extent that this is possible on [this pilgrim's] pathway. Leaping beyond all things which are

253 visible and mundane, he obtains the full perfection of his nature. This is the perfect nature which we who have been transformed into Christ's image can obtain in Christ after the flesh and sin have been mortified. It is not that fantastic [nature] of the magicians, who allege that by faith and through certain practices

a man ascends to a nature of influential spirits who are akin to himself—so that by the power of such spirits, with which the magicians themselves are united by faith, they perform many special wonders as regards fire or water or musical knowledge, visible transformations, the revealing of hidden matters, and the like. For it is evident that with regard to all these [wonders] there is deception as well as a departure from real life and from truth. Accordingly, such [magicians] are bound to alliances, and to pacts of unity, with evil spirits. [They are bound] in such way that that which they believe by faith they display by deed in incense-offerings and acts of worship due only to God. These they devote (with great observance and veneration) to spirits [whom they regard] as able to grant their requests and as able to be summoned forth by these means. United in this way with a spirit to whom they will also cling while eternally separated from Christ and in torment, they sometimes do obtain, by faith, these transitory objects of desire.

Blessed is God, who by His own son has redeemed us from the darkness of such great ignorance[130] in order that we may discern to be false and deceptive all the things which are somehow done by a mediator other than Christ, who is truth, and by a faith other than [faith] in Jesus. For there is only one Lord—Jesus—who is powerful over all things, who fills us with every blessing, and who alone causes our every deprivation to be filled to overflowing.

254   *Chapter Twelve*:   The church.

Although an understanding of the church of Christ can be obtained from what has already been said, I will add a word or two in order that nothing will be missing from my work.

Since it is necessary that the faith in different men be of unequal degree and therefore admit of greater and lesser degree,[131] no one can attain to maximum faith, than which there can be no greater power. (Similarly, no one [can attain] to maximum love either.) For if maximum faith, which could not be a greater power, were present in a pilgrim, he would also have to be an attainer [of his pilgrim's goal].[132] For just as the maximum in a genus is the supreme goal of the genus, so it is the beginning of a higher [genus]. Accordingly, unqualifiedly maximum faith cannot be present in anyone who is not also an attainer [of his pilgrim's goal]. Similarly, unqualifiedly maximum love cannot be present in a lover who is not also the beloved. Accordingly, neither unqualifiedly maximum faith nor unqualifiedly maximum love befit anyone other than Jesus Christ, who was both pilgrim and attainer, both loving man and beloved God. But all things are included in the maximum, since the maximum encompasses all things. Hence, all true faith is included in Christ Jesus's faith,[133] and all true love is included in Christ's love—though distinctions of degree always remain.

255 And since these distinct degrees are below the maximum and above the minimum, no one—even if he actually has maximum faith in Christ [in the sense of having] as much as he can—can attain unto that [unqualifiedly] maximum faith in Christ through which he would understand Christ as God and man. And no one can love Christ so much that Christ could not be loved even more; for Christ *is* love (*amor et caritas*) and is therefore infinitely lovable. Hence, no one either in this life or the next can so love Christ that he would therefore be Christ and man. For all who are united with Christ (differences of degree remaining) either in this life through faith and love or in the next life through attainment and enjoyment are united in the following way: they could not be more greatly united and still have their respective difference of degree remain. Thus, none [of them] exist in themselves and apart from that union, and yet none [of them] lose their respective degree on account of the union.

256 Therefore, this union is a church, or congregation, of many in one—just as many members are in one body, each member existing with its own role. (In the body, one member is not the other member; but each member is in the one body, and by the mediation of the body it is united with each other member.[134] No member of the body can have life and existence apart from the body, even though in the body one member is all the others only by the mediation of the body.) Therefore, as we journey here below, the truth of our faith can exist only in the spirit of Christ—the order of believers remaining, so that in one Jesus there is diversity in harmony. And once we are freed from this church militant: when we arise, we can arise only in Christ, so that in this way there will also be *one* church of those who are triumphant, each existing in his own order. And at that time the truth of our flesh will exist not in itself but in the truth of Christ's flesh; and the truth of our body will exist in the truth of Christ's body; and the truth of our spirit will exist in the truth of Christ Jesus's spirit—as branches exist in the vine.[135] Thus, Christ's one humanity will be in all men, and Christ's one spirit will be in all spirits—so that each [believing individual] will be in Christ, so that from all [members] there will be one Christ. And then whoever in this life receives any one of those who are Christ's receives Christ; and what is done to one of the least of these is done to Christ.[136] (By comparison, whoever injures Plato's hand injures Plato; and whoever harms the smallest toe harms the whole man.) And whoever rejoices in Heaven over the least one rejoices over Christ and sees in each one Jesus, through whom [he sees] Blessed God. Thus, through His son, our God will be all things in all things;[137] and in His son and through Him each [believer] will be with God and with all things, so that [each's] joy will be full, free of all envy and deprivation.

257   And since faith can be continually increased in us while we journey here below, so also [can] love. Although each [believer] can actually have such a degree [of faith and love] that of himself, as he then is, he cannot actually have a greater degree, nevertheless when he has one degree, he has a potency for

another. Yet, no such progression can be made—through a common basis [of comparison]—unto infinity. Hence, we ought to endeavor to have our capability actualized by the grace of our Lord Jesus Christ, so that in this way we may, through Him who is faith and love, progress from virtue to virtue and from degree [of intensity] to degree [of intensity]. Without Him we can do nothing of ourselves qua of ourselves.[138] Rather, all that we can do we can do in Him who alone is able to supply what we lack in order that on the day of resurrection we may be found to be a whole and noble member of Him. And believing and loving with all our might, we can no doubt by constant prayer obtain this gracious increase of faith and love and ascend confidently to His throne. For He is most gracious and lets no one be deceived by his holy desire.

258   If you will reflect upon these indeed lofty [matters], you will be overwhelmed with an admirable sweetness of spirit. For with an inner relishing you will scent, as in the case of a very fragrant incense, God's inexpressible goodness. God, passing over to you, will supply you with this goodness; you will be filled with Him when His glory shall appear.[139] You will be filled, that is, without surfeit; for this immortal food is life itself. And just as the desire-for-living always increases, so the food of life is always consumed without being transformed into the nature of the consumer. For otherwise it would be loathsome food which would weigh down and which could not bestow immortal life because it would be deficient in itself and would be transformed into the one who is nourished. Now, our intellectual desire is [the desire] to live intellectually—i.e., to enter further and further into life and joy. And since that life is infinite: the blessed, still desirous, are brought further and further into it. And so, they are filled—being, so to speak, thirsty ones drinking from the fount of life. And because this drinking does not pass away into a past (since it is within eternity), the blessed are ever drinking and ever filled; and yet, they have never drunk and have never been filled.

259   Blessed is God, who has given us an intellect which cannot be filled in the course of time. Since the intellect's desire does not attain its end, the intellect—on the basis of its temporally insatiable desire—apprehends itself as beyond corruptible time and as immortal. And the intellect recognizes that it cannot be satisfied by the intellectual-life-it-desires except during the enjoyment of the maximum, most excellent, and never-failing good. This enjoyment does not pass away into a past, because the appetite does not fade away during the enjoyment. [The situation is] as if—to use an illustration from the body—someone hungry were seated at the table of a great king, where he was supplied with the food he desired, so that he did not seek any other food. The nature of this food would be [such] that in filling him up it would also whet his appetite. If this food were never deplenished, it is obvious that the perpetual consumer would always be filled, would always desire this same food, and would always willingly be brought to the food. And so, he would always be able to eat; and,

after having eaten, he would still be able to be led to the food with whetted appetite. Such, then, is the capability of the intellectual nature, so that in receiving into itself life, it is transformed into life in accordance with its own transformable nature—just as air, in receiving into itself the sun's ray, is transformed into light. Accordingly, since the intellect is of a nature which is turnable toward the intelligible, it understands only universal, incorruptible, abiding things.[140] For the incorruptible truth is the object of the intellect—unto which object the intellect is brought intellectually. Indeed, in quiet tranquility it apprehends this truth in eternity and in Christ Jesus.

260   This is the church of the triumphant,[141] in which our God, who is blessed forever, is present. Here the true man Christ Jesus is united, in supreme union, with the Son of God—in so great a union that the humanity exists only in the divinity; it is present in the divinity by means of an ineffable hypostatic union—[present] in such way that it cannot be more highly and more simply united if the truth [i.e., the reality] of the nature of the humanity is to remain. Then every rational nature—provided that in this life it turn to Christ with supreme faith, hope, and love—is united with Christ the Lord (though the personal truth of each nature remains) to the following extent: (1) that all the angels and all the men (each [man] having the truth of his body absorbed and attracted through his spirit) exist only in Christ, through whom they exist in God, so that each of the blessed, having the truth-of-his-own-being preserved, exists in Christ Jesus as Christ and—through Christ—in God as God; and (2) that God, while remaining the Absolute Maximum, exists in Christ Jesus as
261 Jesus and, through Jesus, in all things as all things. The church cannot in some other way be more one. For "church" bespeaks a oneness of many [members]—each of whom has his personal truth preserved without confusion of natures or of degrees; but the more *one* the church is, the greater it is; hence, this church—[viz.,] the church of the eternally triumphant—is maximal, since no greater union of the church is possible.

Therefore, consider now how great is the following union: [viz.,] where there is found (1) the divine, absolute maximum Union, (2) the union, in Jesus, of the deity and the humanity, and (3) the union of the church of the triumphant [i.e., the union] of Jesus's deity and the blessed. The Absolute Union is neither a greater nor a lesser [union] than the union of the natures in Jesus or [the union] of the blessed in Heaven. For it is the maximum Union which is (a) the Union of all unions and (b) that which is complete union. It does not admit of degrees of more or less, and it proceeds from Oneness and Equality—as is indicated in Book One. And the union of the natures in Christ is neither a greater nor a lesser [union] than the oneness of the church of the triumphant; for since it is the maximum union of the natures, it therefore does not admit of degrees of more
262 and less; hence, all the different things which are united receive their oneness from the maximum union of the natures of Christ,[142] through which union the

union of the church is that which it is. But the union of the church is the maximum ecclesiastical union. Therefore, since it is maximal, it coincides on high with the hypostatic union of the natures in Christ. And since the union of the natures of Jesus is maximal, it coincides with the Absolute Union, which is God. And so, the union of the church, which is [a union] of individuals, [coincides] with the [Absolute Union].[143] Although the union of the church does not seem to be as *one* as is the hypostatic [union], which is [a union] only of the natures, or as is the first, divine, most simple [Union], in which there can be no otherness or diversity, nevertheless, it is, through Jesus, resolved into the Divine Union, from which it also has its origin. And, assuredly, this [point] is seen quite clearly if attention is paid to what is repeatedly found earlier on. For the Absolute Union is the Holy Spirit. Now, the maximum hypostatic union coincides with the Absolute Union. Hence, necessarily, the union of the natures in Christ exists through and in the Absolute Union, which is the Holy Spirit. But the ecclesiastical union coincides with the hypostatic union, as was said. Hence, the union of the triumphant is in the spirit of Jesus, which is in the Holy Spirit. Truth itself makes such a statement in John: "I have given them the glory which You have given me, in order that they may be one, as we also are one, I in them and You in me, so that they may be perfected in oneness"[144]—so that the church may be so perfect in eternal rest that it could not be more perfect and may exist in so inexpressible a transformation of the light of glory that in all [the triumphant] only God appears.

With very great affection we triumphantly aspire to this [glory]. And with humble heart we entreat God the Father that because of His immense graciousness He will to give—through His son, our Lord Jesus Christ, and in Him through the Holy Spirit—this [glory] to us in order that we may eternally enjoy Him who is blessed forever.

The Author's Letter to Lord Cardinal Julian.

Receive now, Reverend Father,[145] the things which I have long desired to attain by various doctrinal approaches but could not—until, while I was at sea en route back from Greece,[146] I was led (by, as I believe, a heavenly gift from the Father of lights, from whom comes every excellent gift)[147] to embrace—in learned ignorance and through a transcending of the incorruptible truths which are humanly knowable—incomprehensible things incomprehensibly.[148] Thanks to Him who is Truth, I have now expounded this [learned ignorance] in these books, which, [since they proceed] from [one and] the same principle, can be condensed or expanded.

264   But the whole effort of our human intelligence ought to center on those lofty [matters], so that the intellect[149] may raise itself to that Simplicity where contradictories coincide. The conception of Book One labors with this [task]. From this [conception] Book Two elicits a few [teachings] about the universe— [teachings which go] beyond the usual approach of the philosophers and [which will seem] unusual to many. Always proceeding from [one and] the same foundation, I have now at last completed Book Three, which deals with superblessed Jesus. And through the increase of my faith the Lord Jesus is continually magnified in my understanding and affection. For no one who has faith in Christ can deny that on this [pilgrim's] pathway he would like to be more highly inflamed with desire, so that after long meditations and ascensions he would see most sweet Jesus as alone to be loved and, abandoning all, would joyously embrace Him as his true life and eternal joy. All things work favorably for one who enters into Jesus in such a way. And neither this world nor any writings can cause [him] any difficulty; for he is transformed into Jesus on account of the spirit of Christ which dwells in him. Christ is the end of intellectual desires. May you, Most Devout Father, humbly and continually entreat Him for me, a most wretched sinner, so that we may both deserve to enjoy Him eternally.[150]

CORRIGENDA
ABBREVIATIONS
BIBLIOGRAPHY
PRAENOTANDA
NOTES
INDEX

CORRIGENDA FOR THE LATIN TEXT OF
DE DOCTA IGNORANTIA

IN THE LATIN-GERMAN SERIES PUBLISHED BY F. MEINER VERLAG

The following revisions have been taken account of in the English translation. (The Latin text is fully cited in the *Praenotanda*.)

4:15:	Change 'doctissimus' to 'doctissimum'.
24:13:	Change 'unitas' to 'unitatis' *coni*.
29:6:	Put colon after 'esse maximum'.
29:8:	Change punctuation to: 'unio, hinc'.
29:16:	Change 'acuetur' to 'acuatur'.
37:10:	Move '10' down one line.
41:10:	Add '10'.
61:1:	Correct '1' to '61'.
68:15:	Change 'si' to 'etsi' *coni*.
71:6:	Change to read: 'et in ea curvitas' *p*.
91:2:	Change 'corrolaria' to 'correlaria'.
99:13:	Change 'contingenti' to 'contingenter'.
107:4:	Change 'explicata' to 'complicata'.
108:14:	Change to read: 'explicare omnia, scilicet' *p*.
111:17–19:	Change punctuation to: 'multiplicationem (non dico . . . non possit): in ipsis'.
112:13:	Change 'absoluta absoluto' to 'absoluto absolute'.
113:6:	Change 'quo' to 'qua' *p*.
114:8:	Change punctuation to: 'maximum:'.
122:3:	Change 'a quo' to 'a qua' *p*.
128:18–19:	Delete 'nihil prius sit unitate. Sed tamen nihil in esse producitur, quod prius non possit'.
152:5	Delete 'et subsistere'.
156:2:	Change 'Corrolaria' to 'Correlaria'.
156:27:	Delete 'licet'.
171:6:	Delete 'non'.
173:9:	Change punctuation to: 'redeat?'.
173:16:	Change 'rediet' to 'rediens'.
179:14:	Change 'qui vult' to 'quem vult' *coni*.
201:6:	Change to read: 'non possent' *coni*.
202:9:	Add comma after first 'sunt'.
206:	Move note for line 15 to preceding Latin page.
230:12:	Change note to read: 'Cusanus, subsequentis'.
243:10:	Change note to read: 'illos).'.
262:8:	Change punctuation to: 'illa. Quae'.

ABBREVIATIONS

Ap.	*Apologia Doctae Ignorantiae*
DI	*De Docta Ignorantia*
DP	*De Possest* (reprinted in *PNC*)
IL	*De Ignota Litteratura*
MFCG	*Mitteilungen und Forschungsbeiträge der Cusanus-Gesellschaft* (ed. Rudolf Haubst)
NA	*De Li Non Aliud* (reprinted in J. Hopkins. *Nicholas of Cusa on God as Not-other: A Translation and an Appraisal of De Li Non Aliud.* Minneapolis: University of Minnesota Press, 1979)
NC	*Nicolò da Cusa.* Florence: Sansoni, 1962. (Pubblicazioni della Facoltà di Magisterio dell'Università di Padova)
NK	*Nikolaus von Kues. Einführung in sein philosophisches Denken.* Ed. Klaus Jacobi. Munich: K. Alber, 1979
PL	*Patrologia Latina,* ed. J. P. Migne
PNC	J. Hopkins. *A Concise Introduction to the Philosophy of Nicholas of Cusa.* Minneapolis: University of Minnesota Press, 1978; 2nd ed. 1980
SHAW	*Sitzungsberichte der Heidelberger Akademie der Wissenschaften. Philosophisch-historische Klasse.* Heidelberg: C. Winter

BIBLIOGRAPHY

(Supplementary to that found in *PNC*)

Heidelberg Academy Edition of *Nicolai de Cusa Opera Omnia* (Leipzig/Hamburg: F. Meiner Verlag).

I. *De Docta Ignorantia*, ed. Ernst Hoffmann and Raymond Klibansky, 1932.

II. *Apologia Doctae Ignorantiae*, ed. Raymond Klibansky, 1932.

III. *De Coniecturis*, ed. Josef Koch, Karl Bormann, and Hans G. Senger, 1972.

IV. *Opuscula I: De Deo Abscondito, De Quaerendo Deum, De Filiatione Dei, De Dato Patris Luminum, Coniectura de Ultimis Diebus, De Genesi*, ed. Paul Wilpert, 1959.

V. *Idiota: De Sapientia, De Mente, De Staticis Experimentis*, ed. Ludwig Baur, 1937 (new edition in press).

VI. *De Visione Dei* (in preparation; publication uncertain).

VII. *De Pace Fidei* (also includes a letter to John of Segovia), ed. Raymond Klibansky and Hildebrand Bascour, 1959; 2nd ed. 1970.

VIII. *Cribratio Alchoran* (in preparation).

IX. *De Ludo Globi* (in preparation).

X. *Opuscula II: De Theologicis Complementis, De Principio, De Aequalitate, Epistulae ad Bohemos* (in preparation).

XI/1. *De Beryllo*, ed. Ludwig Baur, 1940 (new edition in preparation).

2. *Trialogus de Possest*, ed. Renate Steiger, 1973.

3. *Compendium*, ed. Bruno Decker and Karl Bormann, 1964.

XII. *De Venatione Sapientiae, De Apice Theoriae*, ed. Raymond Klibanksy and Hans G. Senger (in press).

XIII. *Directio Speculantis seu De Non Aliud*, ed. Ludwig Baur and Paul Wilpert, 1944; reissued 1950 with a list of *addenda* and *corrigenda*.

XIV. *De Concordantia Catholica*.

1. Book I, ed. Gerhard Kallen, 1939; 2nd ed. 1964.

2. Book II, ed. G. Kallen, 1941; 2nd ed. 1965.

3. Book III, ed. G. Kallen, 1959.

4. Indices, ed. G. Kallen and Anna Berger, 1968.

XV. *Scripta Mathematica* (in preparation).

XVI. *Sermones I* (1430–1441).

1. *Sermones I–IV*, ed. Rudolf Haubst, Martin Bodewig, and Werner Krämer, 1970.

2. *Sermones V–X*, ed. R. Haubst, M. Bodewig, and W. Krämer, 1973.

3. *Sermones XI–XXI*, ed. R. Haubst and M. Bodewig 1977.

4. *Sermones XXII–XXVI*, ed. R. Haubst and M. Bodewig (in press).

Bibliography

XVII. *Sermones II (1442–1452).*
  1. *Sermones XXVII–XLVI* (in preparation).

Sermons (editions in *SHAW*)

"Dies Sanctificatus" vom Jahre 1439. ed. and trans. Ernst Hoffmann and Raymond Klibansky. *SHAW*, 1929.
Vier Predigten im Geiste Eckharts, ed. and trans. Josef Koch. *SHAW*, 1937.
Die Auslegung des Vaterunsers in vier Predigten, ed. and trans. Josef Koch and Hans Teske. *SHAW*, 1940.

Letters

Collection I. ed. Josef Koch. *SHAW*, 1944 (Jahrgang 1942/43).
  II. *Das Brixner Briefbuch des Kardinals Nikolaus von Kues*. ed. Friedrich Hausmann. *Shaw*, 1952
  III. *Das Vermächtnis des Nikolaus von Kues. Der Brief an Nikolaus Albergati nebst der Predigt in Montoliveto (1463)*, ed. and trans. Gerda von Bredow. *SHAW*, 1955.
  IV. *Nikolaus von Kues und der Deutsche Orden. Der Briefwechsel des Kardinals Nikolaus von Kues mit dem Hochmeister des Deutschen Ordens*, ed. Erich Maschke. *SHAW*, 1956.

Acta and Miscellanea.

De Auctoritate Presidendi in Concilio Generali (presented to the Council of Basel in 1434), ed. and trans. Gerhard Kallen. *SHAW*, 1935.
De Reparatione Kalendarii (presented to the Council of Basel in 1436). See Paris edition of *Nicolai Cusae Opera Omnia*.
Akten zur Reform des Bistums Brixen, ed. Heinz Hürten. *SHAW*, 1960.
Acta Cusana. Quellen zur Lebensgeschichte des Nikolaus von Kues, ed. Erich Meuthen and Hermann Hallauer. Hamburg: F. Meiner, 1976 (Vol. I).

Selected Books and Articles.

Alvarez-Gómez, Mariano. "Der Mensch als Schöpfer seiner Welt. Überlegungen zu *De coniecturis*," *MFCG*, 13 (1978), 160 –166.
Bantle, Franz X. "Nikolaus Magni de Jawor und Johannes Wenk im Lichte des Codex Mc. 31 der Universitätsbibliothek Tübingen," *Scholastik*, 38 (1963), 536–574.
Beck, Lewis W. "Nicholas of Cusa," pp. 57–71 of his *Early German Philosophy: Kant and His Predecessors*. Cambridge, Mass.: Harvard University Press, 1967.

Bibliography

Beierwaltes, Werner. "Deus Oppositio Oppositorum (Nicolaus Cusanus De visione dei XIII)." *Salzburger Jahrbuch für Philosophie.* 8 (1964), 175–185.

———. "Identität und Differenz. Zum Prinzip cusanischen Denkens." *Rheinisch-Westfälische Akademie der Wissenschaften.* Opladen: Westdeutscher Verlag, 1977 (*Vorträge/Rheinisch-Westfälische Akademie der Wissenschaften: Geisteswissenschaften; G 220*).

———. "Visio Absoluta. Reflexion als Grundzug des göttlichen Prinzips bei Nicolaus Cusanus." *SHAW* 1978, 5–33.

Boehm, Gottfried. "Die Perspektivität in der Metaphysik des Nicolaus Cusanus." pp. 137–171 of his *Studien zur Perspektivität. Philosophie und Kunst in der Frühen Neuzeit.* Heidelberg: C. Winter, 1969.

Boethius, Anicius. *De Institutione Arithmetica.* Ed. G. Friedlein. Leipzig: B. G. Teubner, 1867.

Bohnenstädt, Elisabeth. "Kirche und Reich im Schrifttum des Nikolaus von Cues." *SHAW,* 1939.

Bormann, Karl. "Zur Lehre des Nikolaus von Kues von der 'Andersheit' und deren Quellen." *MFCG,* 10 (1973), 130–137.

———. " 'Übereinstimmung und Verschiedenheit der Menschen' (De coni. II, 15).]" *MFCG,* 13 (1978), 88–104.

Bredow, Gerda von. "Der Sinn der Formel 'meliori modo quo' . . .," *MFCG,* 6 (1967), 21–30.

———. "Der Geist als lebendiges Bild Gottes (Mens viva dei imago)." *MFCG,* 13 (1978), 58–67.

Breidert, Wolfgang von. "Mathematik und symbolische Erkenntnis bei Nikolaus von Kues," *MFCG,* 12 (1977), 116–126.

Caminiti, Francis N. "Nikolaus von Kues und Bonaventura." *MFCG,* 4 (1964), 129–144.

Cassirer, Ernst. "Nikolaus Cusanus." pp. 21–61 in Vol. I of his *Das Erkenntnisproblem in der Philosophie und Wissenschaft der neueren Zeit.* Berlin: Verlag Bruno Cassirer, 1911 (2nd ed.).

Colomer, Eusebius. "Nikolaus von Kues und Heimeric van den Velde." *MFCG,* 4 (1964), 198–213.

———. "Das Menschenbild des Nikolaus von Kues in der Geschichte der christlichen Humanismus," *MFCG,* 13 (1978), 117–143.

Coreth, Emerich. "Nikolaus von Kues, ein Denker an der Zeitwende." pp. 3–16 of *Cusanus Gedächtnisschrift,* ed. Nikolaus Grass. Innsbruck: Universitätsverlag, 1970.

Cousins, Ewert H. "Bonaventure, the Coincidence of Opposites and Nicholas of Cusa," pp. 177–197 of *Studies Honoring Ignatius Charles Brady, Friar Minor,* ed. Romano Stephen Almagno and Conrad L. Harkins. St. Bonaventure, N.Y.: Franciscan Institute, 1976.

Cranz, F. Edward. "Cusanus, Luther, and the Mystical Tradition," pp. 93–102 of *The Pursuit of Holiness in Late Medieval and Renaissance Religion.* Papers from the

Bibliography

University of Michigan Conference. Ed. Charles Trinkaus and Heiko Oberman. Leiden: E. J. Brill, 1974.

Duclow, Donald F. "The Analogy of the Word: Nicholas of Cusa's Theory of Language," *Bijdragen*, 38 (1977), 282–299.

Dupré, Wilhelm. "Der Mensch als Mikrokosmos im Denken des Nikolaus von Kues," *MFCG*, 13 (1978), 68–87.

Fuehrer, Mark L. "Wisdom and Eloquence in Nicholas of Cusa's Idiota de sapientia and de mente," *Vivarium*, 16 (November 1978), 142–155.

Gandillac, Maurice de. "Nikolaus von Kues zwischen Platon und Hegel," *MFCG*, 11 (1975), 21–38.

Gane, Erwin R. "The Intellect-Will Problem in the Thought of Some Northern Renaissance Humanists: Nicholas of Cusa." *Andrews University Seminary Studies* (Michigan), 12 (July 1974), 83–93.

Garin, Eugenio. "Cusano e i platonici italiani del Quattrocento," pp. 75–100 of *NC.*

Glossner, Michael. *Nikolaus von Cusa und Marius Nizolius als Vorläufer der neueren Philosophie*, Münster: Theissing, 1891.

Gutwenger, Engelbert. "Das 'Nichtandere' bei Nikolaus von Kues," pp. 17–22 of *Cusanus Gedächtnisschrift*, ed. Nikolaus Grass. Innsbruck: Universitätsverlag, 1970.

Haubst, Rudolf. "Johannes Wenck aus Herrenberg als Albertist," *Recherches de théologie ancienne et médiévale*, 18 (1951), 308–323.

———. "Zum Fortleben Alberts des Grossen bei Heymerich von Kamp und Nikolaus von Kues," *Beiträge zur Geschichte der Philosophie und Theologie des Mittelalters*, Supplementary Vol. 4 (1952), 420–447.

———. *Studien zu Nikolaus von Kues und Johannes Wenck* (Vol. 38 [1955] of *Beiträge zur Geschichte der Philosophie des Mittelalters*).

———. "Das christologische Schrifttum des Johannes Wenck in Codex Mainz 372 und die von ihm benutzte ps.-albertinische 'Litania de sanctis.' " *Römische Quartalschrift für christliche Altertumskunde und Kirchengeschichte*, 52 (1957), 211–228.

———. "Johannes von Franckfurt als der mutmassliche Verfasser von 'Eyn deutsch Theologia,' " *Scholastik*, 33 (1958), 375–398.

———. 'Nikolaus von Kues und Johannes Wenck. Neue Erörterungen und Nachträge," *Römische Quartalschrift für christliche Altertumskunde und Kirchengeschichte*, 53 (1958), 81–88.

———. "Nikolaus von Kues und die heutige Christologie," pp. 165–175, Vol. I of *Universitas. Dienst an Wahrheit und Leben* (Festschrift for Albert Stohr). Mainz: Matthias-Grünewald, 1960 (2 vols.).

———. "Zu Erich Meuthen, Bemerkungen zu Rudolf Haubst: 'Nikolaus von Kues und Johannes Wenck. Neue Erörterungen und Nachträge.' " *Römische Quartalschrift für christliche Altertumskunde und Kirchengeschichte*, 56 (1961), 75–76.

———. "Nikolaus von Kues auf den Spuren des Thomas von Aquin," *MFCG*, 5 (1965), 15–62.

———. "Welcher 'Frankfurter' schrieb die 'Theologia deutsch'?" *Theologie und Philosophie*, 48 (1973), 218–239.

———. "Die Rezeption und Wirkungsgeschichte des Thomas von Aquin im 15.

Bibliography

Jahrhundert, besonders im Umkreis des Nikolaus von Kues.'' *Theologie und Philosophie*, 49 (1974), 252–273.

Hopkins, Jasper. *Nicholas of Cusa on God as Not-other: A Translation and an Appraisal of De Li Non Aliud*. Minneapolis: University of Minnesota Press, 1979.

Jacob, E. F. *Cusanus the Theologian* (reprinted from the ''Bulletin of the John Rylands Library,'' Vol. 21, no. 2, October, 1937). Manchester: Manchester University Press, 1937.

————. 'Nicolas of Cusa,'' pp. 32-60 of *The Social & Political Ideas of Some Great Thinkers of the Renaissance and Reformation*, ed. F. J. C. Hearnshaw. New York: Barnes & Noble, 1949 (reprint of 1925 edition).

Jacobi, Klaus. ''Ontologie aus dem Geist 'belehrten Nichtwissens,' '' *NK*, pp. 27–55.

Kallen, Gerhard. ''Die politische Theorie im philosophischen System des Nikolaus von Cues,'' *Historische Zeitschrift*, 165 (1941–42), 246–277.

Kampits, Peter. ''Substanz und Relation bei Nicolaus Cusanus,'' *Zeitschrift für philosophische Forschung*, 30 (January-March 1976), 31–50.

Kandler, Karl-Hermann. ''Die Einheit von Endlichem und Unendlichem. Zum Verhältnis von Paul Tillich zu Nikolaus von Kues,'' *Kerygma und Dogma*, 25 (April-June 1979), 106–122.

Koch, Josef. ''Nikolaus von Kues 1401–1464,'' pp. 275–287 in Vol. I of *Die Grossen Deutschen. Deutsche Biographie*, ed. Hermann Heimpel *et al.* (Gütersloh: Prisma Verlag, 1978; reprinted from the 1966 edition published by Ullstein Verlag [Berlin], 1956).

————. ''Nikolaus von Kues und Meister Eckhart. Randbemerkungen zu zwei in der Schrift *De coniecturis* gegebenen Problemen,'' *MFCG*, 4 (1964), 164–173.

Kremer, Klaus. ''Erkennen bei Nikolaus von Kues. Apriorismus-Assimilation-Abstraktion,'' *MFCG*, 13 (1978), 23–57.

Kuhnekath, Klaus D. *Die Philosophie des Johannes Wenck von Herrenberg im Vergleich zu den Lehren des Nikolaus von Kues*. Ph.D. dissertation, University of Cologne, 1975.

Lorenz, Siegfried. *Das Unendliche bei Nicolaus von Cues*. Ph.D. dissertation, University of Leipzig, 1926.

Meinhardt, Helmut. ''Der christologische Impuls im Menschenbild des Nikolaus von Kues. Erwägungen eines Philosophen über den christologischen Humanismus im dritten Buch von *De docta ignorantia*,'' *MFCG*, 13 (1978), 105–116.

————. ''Exaktheit und Mutmassungscharakter der Erkenntnis,'' *NK*, pp. 101–120.

Meurer, Karl. *Die Gotteslehre des Nikolaus von Kues in ihren philosophischen Konsequenzen*. Ph.D. dissertation, University of Bonn, 1970.

Meuthen, Erich. ''Leben in der Zeit'' *NK*, pp. 7–26.

Miller, Clyde Lee. ''Aristotelian *Natura* and Nicholas of Cusa,'' *Downside Review*, 96 (January 1978), 13–20.

Morin, Frédéric. ''Nicolas de Cusa,'' *Dictionnaire de philosophie et de théologie scolastiques*, Vol. 2, columns 292–390 (Vol. 22 of *Encyclopédie théologique*, ed. J.-P. Migne). Paris: J.-P. Migne, 1857.

Nicholas of Cusa. *Idiota de Mente. The Layman: About Mind*. Translation and introduction by Clyde Lee Miller. New York: Abaris Books, 1979.

Bibliography

————. *Concordance Catholique*. Translated by Roland Galibois; revised by Maurice de Gandillac. Sherbrooke, Canada: Centre d'Etudes de la Renaissance, University of Sherbrooke, 1977.

Oide, Satoshi. "Über die Grundlagen der cusanischen Konjekturenlehre," *MFCG*, 8 (1970), 147–178.

Peukert, Kurt W. "Die Entsprachlichung der Metaphysik durch den Unendlichkeitsbegriff des Cusaners," *Philosophisches Jahrbuch*, 72 (1964), 49–65.

Platzeck, Erhard W. "Von der lullschen zur cusanischen Denkform," *MFCG*, 4 (1964), 145–163.

Rigobello, Armando. "Contributo del dialogo cusaniano 'Idiota de mente' alla precisazione di un problema teoretico," pp. 243–251 of *NC*.

Ritter, Gerhard. *Studien zur Spätscholastik. II. Via Antiqua und Via Moderna auf den deutschen Universitäten des XV. Jahrhunderts*. SHAW, 1922.

————. *Die Heidelberger Universität. Ein Stück deutscher Geschichte*. Vol. I: *Das Mittelalter (1386–1508)*. Heidelberg: C. Winter, 1936.

Rombach, Heinrich. *Substanz, System, Struktur*. Vol. I: *Die Ontologie des Funktionalismus und der philosophische Hintergrund der modernen Wissenschaft*. Freiburg: Karl Alber, 1965. (Chap. 2).

Sakamoto, Peter T. "Die theologische und anthropologische Fundierung der Ethik bei Nikolaus von Kues," *MFCG*, 10 (1973), 138–151.

Santinello, Giovanni. "Das Leib-Seele-Verhältnis nach Nikolaus von Kues. Zwischen Platon und Pomponazzi," *MFCG*, 13 (1978), 3–22.

Schaefer, Jacob. *Des Nicolaus von Kues Lehre vom Kosmos*. Ph.D. dissertation, University of Giessen. Published in Mainz: Kupferberg, 1887.

Schnarr, Hermann. "Das Wort Idea bei Nikolaus von Kues," *MFCG*, 13 (1978), 182–197.

Schönborn, Christoph. " 'De docta ignorantia' als christozentrischer Entwurf," *NK*, pp. 138–156.

Schramm, Michael-Angelo. "Zur Lehre vom Zeichen innerhalb des Compendiums des Nikolaus von Kues," *Zeitschrift für philosophische Forschung*, 33 (October-December 1979), 616–620.

Schulz, Walter. "Cusanus und die Geschichte der neuzeitlichen Metaphysik," pp. 11–30 of his *Der Gott der neuzeitlichen Metaphysik*. Pfullingen: G. Neske, 1957.

Schulze, Werner. *Zahl, Proportion, Analogie. Eine Untersuchung zur Metaphysik und Wissenschaftshaltung des Nikolaus von Kues*. Münster: Aschendorff, 1978.

Senger, Hans G. "Die Sprache der Metaphysik," *NK*, pp. 74–100.

Spamer, Adolf. "Zur Überlieferung der Pfeiffer'schen Eckeharttexte," *Beiträge zur Geschichte der deutschen Sprache und Literatur*, 34 (1909), 307–420.

Stallmach, Josef. "Ansätze neuzeitlichen Philosophierens bei Cusanus," *MFCG*, 4 (1964), 339–356.

————. "Die cusanische Erkenntnisauffassung zwischen Realismus und Idealismus," *MFCG*, 6 (1967), 50–54.

————. "Zusammenfall der Gegensätze und die Philosophie des Nichtwissens," pp. 95–104 of *Gegenwart und Tradition. Strukturen des Denkens* (Festschrift for Bernhard Lakebrink), ed. Cornelio Fabro. Freiburg: Rombach, 1969.

Bibliography

———. "Geist als Einheit und Andersheit. Die Noologie des Cusanus in *De coniecturis* und *De quaerendo deum*," *MFCG*, 11 (1975), 86–124.

———. "Der Mensch zwischen Wissen und Nichtwissen. Beitrag zum Motiv der docta ignorantia im Denken des Nikolaus von Kues," *MFCG*, 13 (1978), 147–159.

———. "Der 'Zusammenfall der Gegensätze' und der unendliche Gott," *NK*, pp. 56–73.

Steiger, Renate. "Die Lebendigkeit des erkennenden Geistes," *MFCG*, 13 (1978), 167–181.

Teltscher, Helga–Beate. "Verwandte Strukturen im Systemdenken von Cusanus und Leibniz," *Studia Leibnitiana Supplementa*, 12 (1973), 149–164.

Uebinger, Johannes. *Philosophie des Nicolaus Cusanus*. Ph.D. dissertation, University of Würzburg. Published in Würzburg: Fleischmann, 1880.

Volkmann-Schluck, Karl-Heinz. "Die Philosophie des Nicolaus von Cues. Eine Vorform der neuzeitlichen Metaphysik," *Archiv für Philosophie*, 3 (1949), 379–399.

Weier, Reinhold. "Der Einfluss des Nicolaus Cusanus auf das Denken Martin Luthers," *MFCG*, 4 (1964), 214–229.

Wenck, Johannes. *Das Büchlein von der Seele*. Ed. Georg Steer. Munich: W. Fink, 1967.

Zimmermann, Albert. " 'Belehrte Unwissenheit' als Ziel der Naturforschung," *NK*, pp. 121–137.

PRAENOTANDA

1. The English translation of *De Docta Ignorantia* was made from the Latin texts in the following critical editions:

DI I: *De docta ignorantia. Die belehrte Unwissenheit,* Book I (Hamburg: Felix Meiner, 1970, 2nd edition), text edited by Paul Wilpert; revised by Hans G. Senger.

DI II: *De docta ignorantia. Die belehrte Unwissenheit,* Book II (Hamburg: Felix Meiner, 1967), text edited by Paul Wilpert.

DI III: *Nicolai de Cusa Opera Omnia,* Vol. I: *De Docta Ignorantia* (Leipzig: Felix Meiner, 1932), text edited by Ernst Hoffman and Raymond Klibansky. For purposes of standardization the margin numbers in the English translation are taken from *De docta ignorantia. Die belehrte Unwissenheit,* Book III (Hamburg: Felix Meiner, 1977), text edited by Raymond Klibansky. The list of *corrigenda* (on p. 159 above) is for this 1977 text, as well as for the texts of 1967 and 1970.

2. All references to Nicholas's works are to the Latin texts—specifically to the following texts in the following editions:

   A. Heidelberg Academy edition: *De Coniecturis, De Deo Abscondito, De Quaerendo Deum, De Filiatione Dei, De Dato Patris Luminum, Apologia Doctae Ignorantiae, Idiota de Sapientia, Idiota de Mente, Idiota de Staticis Experimentis, De Pace Fidei, De Li Non Aliud* (Minnesota reprint).

   B. Heidelberg Academy editions as found in the Latin-German edition of Felix Meiner Verlag's Philosophische Bibliothek: *De Docta Ignorantia, De Possest* (Minnesota reprint), *De Venatione Sapientiae.*

   C. Strasburg edition as reprinted by W. de Gruyter: All remaining Cusanus works, unless otherwise specified explicitly as Paris edition.

   For some treatises the reference indicates book and chapter; for others, margin number and line; for still others, page and line. Readers should have no difficulty determining which is which when they consult the particular Latin text. For example, "*DI* II, 6 (125:19–20)" indicates *De Docta Ignorantia,* Book II, chap. 6, margin number 125, lines 19 and 20.

3. A number of references in the Notes have been adapted from Vol. I of the Heidelberg Academy edition of *Nicolai de Cusa Opera Omnia.*

4. To reduce publication costs, extensive references to the writings of Anicius Boethius, Meister Eckhart, and Thierry of Chartres have not been incorporated into the

170

Notes. Readers are advised to consult the works of Joseph E. Hofmann, Hans G. Senger, Herbert Wackerzapp, and Pierre Duhem as listed in *PNC*.

5. The margin numbers in the English translation of *DI* correspond to those found in the Latin-German editions, cited in n. 1 above.

6. Any Latin words inserted into the English translations for purposes of clarification are placed in parentheses—except that nouns whose case has been changed to the nominative are bracketed. All expansions of the translations are bracketed.

7. References to the Psalms are to the Douay version (and, in parentheses, to the King James' version).

8. References to *IL* are given in terms of the new critical edition published in *Nicholas of Cusa's Debate with John Wenck: A Translation and an Appraisal of De Ignota Litteratura and Apologia Doctae Ignorantiae* (Minnneapolis: The Arthur J. Banning Press, 1981).

NOTES

NOTES TO THE PREFACE

1. I opt for the transcription *"cursorie"* (rather than *"cursoriae"*); and I take it to mean "cursorily," rather than to be an allusion to the cursory lessons at the University of Heidelberg. Cf. Nicholas of Cusa *Idiota de Mente* 7 (79:8): *"Haec autem nunc sic dixerim cursorie et rustice."* Cf. *ibid.*, 15 (114:23): *"Haec sic cursim dicta ab idiota grate recipito!"*

2. Nicholas often uses Latin words—even the more common ones—in a special way, with a special sense. For example, in *DI* I, 7 (20:3) *"vel . . . vel"* means "both . . . and"; and in *DI* II, 1 (95:5) *"aut"* can be translated as "i.e. "A Latinist who compares my translation with Nicholas's texts should not be too quick to judge that something is amiss simply because I have not translated various words and phrases in accordance with, say, Lewis and Short's *A Latin Dictionary*.

I have regularly consulted Paul Wilpert's fine German translation of *DI* I and II and Hans G. Senger's equally fine translation of *DI* III; yet, my translation is my own, for it is a translation of Nicholas, not of Wilpert and of Senger. Where I am at variance with the latter two, as often enough occurs, I am so intentionally. Like these German translations, my own work, though painstakingly done, is nonetheless bound to fall short of perfection. Indeed, translations of lengthy and difficult philosophical works must necessarily be refined, over time, in accordance with the scrutinizing judgment of the larger community of scholars, who, after surveying the published translation, will offer their own insightful suggestions for its subsequent improvement. I ask only that the scholarly community, in the course of formulating these valuable suggestions, guard against entertaining, a priori, the following presumption: viz., that wherever there appears to be a discrepancy between the Latin text and the English translation, the apparent discrepancy must be a sign of the translator's deviation from the Latin, rather than being a sign that the syntax and usage of Nicholas's Latin expressions, which have been rightly translated, deviate from Cicero's. Let it also be noted that I have not always signaled, by a footnote, the various places where I regard the editors' punctuation of the Latin text as in need of revision; nonetheless, this revision has been taken account of, and it is reflected in the English sentence structure.

3. See chap. 6 ("What Is a Translation?") of my book *Anselm of Canterbury: Vol. IV: Hermeneutical and Textual Problems in the Complete Treatises of St. Anselm* (New York: The Edwin Mellen Press, 1976).

4. The following is a summary of Nicholas's views in *DI* (spoken as if by Nicholas himself):

"Learned ignorance" means, primarily, an ignorance which someone has come to learn of and, secondarily, an ignorance which renders its possessor wise. The root of such learned ignorance is the recognition that God cannot be known as He is. *DI* does not attempt to prove the existence of God but proceeds by working out the implications of the conviction that God is the Absolute Maximum, i.e., is that than which there cannot be anything greater, is all that which can be. By a sequence of assorted considerations *DI* demonstrates both that the Absolute Maximum coincides with the Absolute Minimum and that it is Oneness which is trine, or Trinity which is one. Yet, there is no composition in God, whose trinity is not *numerical*. As undifferentiated Oneness, God is also undifferentiated Being itself, which is beyond all human conception. Therefore, we can only conceive of what He is not. Even though we affirm that God is the Absolute Maximum, we cannot conceive of what it is like to be Absolute Maximum. Moreover, though we call the Maximum *Goodness, Love, Justice*, etc., these names—as indeed even the names "Being" and "Oneness"—cannot, insofar as we comprehend their significations, succeed in signifying God's infinite Being. Insofar as we grasp all these points about God, we will be possessors of learned ignorance.

God is the Being of things in the sense that He is the Being of all beings. And He is the latter in the sense that (1) He is the Creator of these beings, imparting to them their respective being, and that (2) they would not now exist if He did not exist (though He would exist even if they did not). Similarly, God is the Essence of things in the sense that He is the Essence of all essences. And He is the latter in the sense that (1) He is the Creator of these essences, imparting to them their respective essence, and that (2) each thing would not be what it is if God were not what He is (though His self-identity would remain unimpaired even if all else perished). We may speak of things as *enfolded* in God—i.e., as existing in God prior to their creation—as long as we realize that this priority is ontological rather than chronological and that as things exist in God they are God and not their distinct, finite selves. (By comparison: in a chronological sense we sometimes say that what is going to be caused is already enfolded in its cause.) We may even correctly say that God *is* all things—if what we mean is that He is these things insofar as they are enfolded in Him. Moreover, things are *unfolded* from Him in the sense that from Him every created thing derives, ultimately, its entire being and essence.

The world cannot be identical with God because the world is originated from God, and what is originated cannot be its own originator; otherwise it would have existed *before* it existed—an impossibility. Moreover, the world (also called the universe) and each thing in it are contracted and finite, whereas God is Absolute and Infinite. So the world falls as far short of God as the contracted falls short of the Absolute and as the finite falls short of the Infinite. The word "contracted" has a number of different meanings; but as used in *DI* "contraction" means contraction to (i.e., restriction by) something, so as to be *this* or *that*. God, who alone is uncontracted, is neither *this* nor *that*, because He is altogether undifferentiated, as was said earlier.

The universe is composed of genera, species, and individual things. Genera exist in, and are contracted by (i.e., are received in a restricted way by), species; species exist in, and are contracted by, individual things. Moreover, genera are universal, because the same genus may be contracted differently by a plurality of individuals. Species are less universal and more contracted than are genera; and individuals are not at all universal and are the most contracted things in the universe. Individuals are the only *actually* existing things in the universe, in the sense that genera and species do not actually exist apart from individual things. We may call these individuals things *substances*, as did Aristotle; and with him we may distinguish them from their accidents. Accidents too are present only in substances. Insofar as accidents are considered purely as categories, they are more universal than are even genera. Though the universe as well as each thing in it is contracted, no one thing in the universe is contracted to the same extent as another: no two substances or accidents, no two genera or species, are exactly alike in their degree of contraction. Human nature, for example, which is a species, is contracted to a different extent than is canine nature, which is also a species. And both of these differ in degree of contraction from animality, their genus. Two dogs have the same canine nature (and two human beings the same human nature); in *DI* this statement is construed to mean that two dogs have numerically distinct natures, which are, however, identical in species. The dogs differ from each other in their degree of contraction and as they more perfectly and less perfectly individuate the species. The species qua individuated is the respective dog; if the species qua species existed independently, it would be unindividuated. But the species never exists unindividuated; it exists only in the different dogs.

Though the universe is contracted, it is not God contracted, i.e., God in a state of contraction. For, as was already indicated, God is the Absolute, i.e., the Uncontracted. And what is uncontracted cannot also be contracted. Similarly, although the universe is unfolded from God, it is not God unfolded. For God enfolds and unfolds, but He Himself is neither enfolded nor unfolded—just as, likewise, He encompasses but is not encompassed. He may be said to be in all things, as the original is in the reflection of itself. Similarly, all actually existing things may be said to be immediately in God (in a sense other than their being enfolded in Him); for they exist in actuality, and God is actuality. Since all things exist in God and God exists in all things, everything exists in everything else *(quodlibet in quolibet est)*.

Though the universe is a reflection of God, it bears no resemblance to God, for between the Infinite and the finite there is no comparative relation. The universe is a reflection of God in that it conforms to what God wills for it to be; but such conformity is not resemblance. Moreover, the universe reflects God insofar as it helps us to recognize that the Creator of the universe cannot be less excellent than the most excellent created things. Thus, the universe points us toward inconceivable Divine Excellence. In creating, God willed that each thing be perfect. No created thing, however, can be maximally and absolutely perfect; for if it were, it would not be a created thing but would be God. Accordingly, God created each thing to be as perfect as it could be and still be that thing. Therefore, each thing qua created exists in the best way it can. Insofar as it cannot actually be more perfect—i.e., insofar as it is as perfect as it can be—it may be called a created god or a god manqué. But a created god falls as short of being God as the contracted falls short of the uncontracted. Moreover, Adam's sinning resulted in the marring of the entire creation (and not just of human nature), so that now many things are subject to even greater defect and corruptibility. Though every thing qua created and unfallen was created to be as perfect as it could be, nonetheless with respect to any given thing, God can always create something else which is more perfect. But there cannot actually exist an infinite number of finite things; for if there could, then the Infinite would be of the nature of the finite—something impossible. Indeed, anything which admits of being comparatively greater or lesser can neither be, nor become, infinite. So the universe—whose finite parts are comparatively greater and lesser—is not infinite. Yet, it is also not finite; for since it is everything other than God, it has no physical bounds: there is nothing outside it which physically limits it. Accordingly, the universe is neither infinite nor finite—though in different respects (i.e., the signification of "finite" is not simply the contradictory of the signification of "infinite"). We may, if we like, refer to the universe as both infinite and finite. It is privatively infinite insofar as it is "deprived" of bounds; and it is finite insofar as it has a definite measure, known only to God. God could have created a greater universe (though not an actually infinite one); but the present universe with its present matter, or contracted possibility, cannot be greater. For the matter cannot extend itself farther. Of course, if the universe's matter could keep extending itself ever farther, without limit, then the universe could become actually infinite. But the universe cannot so extend itself, because it cannot both have finite parts qua universe and not have finite parts qua actually infinite—and also because matter, which is contracted possibility, cannot through itself become infinite actuality.

There are many things about God's creating which we cannot understand; for example, we cannot understand how a contracted plurality could have arisen from Absolute Oneness. Similarly, there are many things about the universe itself which we cannot comprehend; for instance, we cannot comprehend either the shape or the motion of the universe. We do know, however, that the universe cannot have a fixed, immovable physical center, since this immovable center would be unqualifiedly minimum motion (i.e., would be rest), than which there could not be a lesser motion. But the unqualifiedly minimum coincides with the maximum. Hence, the physical center would be the physical circumference; i.e., the smallest physical point would also be the largest physical circle—an impossibility. Only God, who is equally close to all things and who is unqualifiedly Minimum and unqualifiedly Maximum, is the center and circumference of the universe, of the earth, and of all spheres. Since God is the universe's center and circumference and since God is everywhere and nowhere, we may say that the universe has its center everywhere and its circumference nowhere.

If the universe has no center other than God, then the earth is not its center, though to us the earth *seems* more central than do any of the other planets or than does the sphere of fixed stars. The earth is spherical but is not an exact sphere. For, like the universe, the earth has no fixed physical center—i.e., no point equidistant from every point on its circumference. Therefore, it is only approximately spherical. It has a motion, a light, a heat, and an influence of its own. Its motion is approximately circular and is from east to west around a conjectural pole in the heavens—i.e., around a pole which we conjecture to be where we believe the center to be. From our point of view on earth the moon, in its motion from east to west, does not appear to describe as large an approximate circle as does Mercury; Mercury does not appear to describe as large an approximate circle as does Venus; and so on, progressively, with the sun, Mars, Jupiter, and Saturn—the Ptolemaic ordering of the spheres. The earth is not the lowliest of all the planets; it is, for example, larger than the moon, as our experience of eclipses teaches. Finally, the movement of the spheres is detectable only in comparative terms; wherever anyone would be (whether he were on the earth or the sun or another "star") he would perceive himself as at the "immovable" center, as it were. Thus, someone on earth regards himself as motionless and the sun as moving; similarly, if he were on the sun, he would regard the sun as motionless and the earth as moving. In fact, however, both the earth and the sun move, with an approximately circular motion, from east to west, around a conjectural pole, as was said.

Between the universe and God there is no intermediate being—not even a world-soul, which various of the Platonists posited as existing ontologically posterior to God but ontologically prior to the world's contraction. The Platonists also thought that all souls are enfolded in the world-soul, as are also all motions. Indeed, they maintained that the world-soul is the source of all motion and that it is the repository of the true forms of things. In God, these forms are, they said, one uncreated Exemplar; but in the world-soul, which is the unfolding of the Divine Mind, they are an uncreated plurality. (The Exemplar in the Divine Mind exists ontologically prior to the exemplars in the world-soul, or world-mind.) The world-soul is related to the world analogously to the human soul's relation to a human body, according to the Platonists. Many Christians consented to these doctrines. But they ought not to have, for there is no such Platonistic world-soul. There is only one infinite Form of forms, viz., God. In particular, God the Son—through whom all things were created—is the Form of all creation.

In itself no created thing can be a maximum or a minimum, for maximum and minimum do not exist in the domain of the purely contracted. Than any individual created thing or any species or any genus God can always create a greater and a lesser individual or species or genus. But what if there were a maximum individual thing contracted to some species? Well, in that case it would be actually everything that is in the possibility of that species; it would be the entire perfection of the species; it would be the maximum and the minimum of the species and thus would be beyond all comparative relation. But, of course, no purely contracted thing could be this maximum individual. The contracted maximum individual thing would be maximum because it existed in Absolute Maximality. Because of this union it would be not only a contracted creature but also the uncontracted God. This union would not be a composite of the Absolute and the contracted. Rather, the created nature would be subsumed in the divine person (and, therefore, in the divine nature), as what is perceptual is subsumed in what is intellectual. Yet, the contracted nature, though maximum, would not become the divine, absolute nature; nor would the latter become the former. In the union of the two natures neither nature would be changed into the other.

But within what species would the Absolute Maximum unite itself to what is contracted? Well, since the Maximum is in a most universal way the being of all things, it would unite with that species which has more in common with the totality of contracted beings. Thus, it would unite with a human nature, because human nature is a medium nature between lower natures, which perceive, and higher natures, which understand. Human nature is the highest of the lower natures and the lowest of the higher natures. By enfolding them, human nature also enfolds all the things which they enfold. It is therefore a microcosm, as the ancients were accustomed to call it.

From Scripture and from the testimony of the church we know that the human nature of Jesus is the contracted maximum individual, which is elevated into union with the divine nature. For Jesus became incarnate as a man by assuming a human nature, being born into this world through the Virgin Mary, who was ever sinless and ever a virgin.

Accordingly, Jesus, as the maximum human being, is the perfection not only of human nature but also of all creatable things, which are enfolded in His maximum humanity. Through His death and resurrection, He reunites the creation with the Creator. All human beings are resurrected through Christ; but only those who are Christ's through faith, hope, and love shall arise as Christ and in Christ through union. In this union believers shall still retain their individuality; but they shall be so one with Christ that His merit will be theirs, in proportion to their love. They shall be filled with His goodness and joy, when His glory will appear. Until that resurrection day believers should seek, through ever increased faith, to attain unto the mystical vision of Christ—a vision which it is God's prerogative to grant or to withhold. Blessed be God. Amen.

NOTES TO THE INTRODUCTION

1. Throughout the Introduction the title *"De Docta Ignorantia"* will be abbreviated by *"DI"*.

2. In *Ap*. 12:19–22 Nicholas denies that he received the idea of learned ignorance from (Pseudo-) Dionysius or "any of the true theologians." But he acknowledges that after his voyage to Greece he began to examine these teachers. In *DI* he several times cites the opinions of Dionysius, though the main influences came subsequently to the writing of *DI* and to his having been presented with the translations made by Ambrose Traversari. Nicholas seems to have received these translations in 1443. See p. 187 of Paul Wilpert's translation *Vom Nichtanderen* (Hamburg: Felix Meiner, 1976, 2nd edition).

3. Ernst Cassirer, *The Individual and the Cosmos in Renaissance Philosophy*, trans. Mario Domandi (Oxford: Blackwell, 1963), p. 38.

4. Erich Meuthen, *Nikolaus von Kues 1401-1464. Skizze einer Biographie* (Münster: Aschendorff, 1976, 3rd ed.), p. 53.

5. Also see I, 2 (5:3) and I, 3 (10:20–22). Note the use of *"ad indoctorum manus"* in *Ap*. 5:20.

6. The entire passage (4:13–17) reads: "For a man—even one very well versed in learning—will attain unto nothing more perfect than to be found to be most learned in the ignorance which is distinctively his. The more he knows that he is unknowing, the more learned he will be." To translate this last sentence even Wilpert has recourse to the word *"gelehrt"*!

7. Cf. *DP* 41:15: "Therefore, the one who knows that he is unable to know is the more learned."

8. *Idiota de Sapientia, Idiota de Mente, Idiota de Staticis Experimentis*.

9. Provided the latter point were not denied, I myself would not find anything objectionable in translating the title as "On a Knowledge of Our Ignorance" (though some purists might object). Even Wenck takes *"docta"* in the sense of *"notum"* (*IL* 23:4) and takes *"doctrina"* in the sense of *"scientia"* (*IL* 34:2).

10 Cf. *DI* III, 11 (245:20–23).

11. *DI* II, 1 elaborates and illustrates this point.

12. In *DP* 43 the Abbot (John Andrea) protests that our knowledge of mathematical truths *is* exact knowledge. Nicholas does not deny this but instead makes the following

distinction: "Regarding mathematical [entities], which proceed from our reason and which we experience to be in us as in their source [*principium*]: they are known by us as our entities and as rational entities; [and they are known] precisely, by our reason's precision, from which they proceed. . . . Without these notional entities reason could not proceed with its work, e.g., with building, measuring, and so on. But the divine works, which proceed from the divine intellect, remain unknown to us precisely as they are. If we know something about them, we surmise it by likening a figure to a form. Hence there is no precise knowledge of any of God's works, except on the part of God, who does all these works. If *we* have any knowledge of them, we derive it from the symbolism and the mirror of [our] mathematical knowledge."

13. *DI* I, 26 (88:16–20). Cf. *De Visione Dei* 13 (51:4–8); 16 (67:7–8). *Cribratio Alkoran* II, 1 (88:6–19).

14. Note the frequent appearance of the verb "*convenire*" in *DI* I, 24.

15. Cf. *DI* III, 11 (e.g., 252). Notice that in III, 12 (257:9–10) Christ is called faith and love.

16. *DI* II, 2 (100:12–15). Cf. II, 13 (180:1–11). *Idiota de Mente* 10 (91:18–21); *De Deo Abscondito* 2:9–4:9; *VS* 12 (31:14–16); *DP* 38:12–15.

17. In *DI* I, 4 Nicholas does not present a tightly sequential line of reasoning. In fact, the order of his steps there differs from the order in which they are sketched in I, 2, his "preliminary clarification." In discussing the intent of his thought, I do not fully adhere to the actual order of his presentation in I, 4, since there is no special need—whether philosophical or hermeneutical—for doing so. In slightly rearranging what Nicholas says, I am not thereby transforming or in any important sense *reconstructing* his argument, which is more of a conglomeration than a set of deductive steps. N.B. Nicholas also uses "unqualifiedly minimum" and "unqualifiedly maximum" in contexts in which they do not refer to God [e.g., in I, 20 (60:7-8) and II, 11 (156:12, 16)]. The role of "unqualifiedly" ("*simpliciter*") is to indicate that there are no degrees of comparatively more and less.

18. Just as the faster the top spins the more it seems to be at rest, so if it could spin with infinite speed it would *be* at rest. (See *DP* 18–20).

19. *DI* II, 10 (155:2–3); II,11 (156:11–12). *DP* 10:19–21.

20. *DI* I, 21 (65:7–8).

21. *IL* 21:20–25. *Ap.* 14:5–9.

22. *Ap.* 15:14–15; 9:6. See *PNC*, pp. 12 and 21.

23. In *DI* II, 1 (96:15) Nicholas alludes didactically to the infinite number, which he does not however posit. See the entire discussion in section 96 of *DI*.

24. *IL* 32:7–8.

25. *DI* I, 16 (45:4). Cf. *NA* 10 (37:13–14).

26. *DI* I, 23 (70:23–24); II, 7 (130:14–15); I, 17 (51:8); I, 8 (22:8).

27. *IL* 23:27 and 33:3.

28. Wenck associates Nicholas with the Beghards, whom he refers to as teaching "that God is, formally, whatever is" (*IL* 25:19–20).

29. See Wenck's first thesis.

30. *IL* 26:20–21.

31. See the entire passage at *Ap.* 26:4–25; also note 33:19–25. Cf. *NA* 10 (39). Also see Giovanni Santinello, *Il pensiero di Nicolò Cusano nella sua prospettiva*

estetica (Padova: Liviana, 1958), p. 95, and Maria T. Liaci, "Accenti spinoziani nel 'De dato patris luminum' del Cusano?" *NC*, pp. 217-242.

32. This theme is a central theme of *NA*, where Nicholas teaches that God, who is Not-other, is the definition of all things. Not-other is definable solely in terms of itself ("Not-other is not other than Not-other"); and in the absence of Not-other no thing at all is definable. The sky is the sky because it is not other than the sky. The very existence and self-identity of the sky is dependent upon the existence and self-identity of Not-other.

See also *De Visione Dei* 9 (34:10–15); 14 (60:1–10). *De Ludo Globi* 2 (91:10–92:1).

33. *DI* II, 3 (110:4–5). Cf. *DP* 57:21. *NA* 7 (26:1–2); 17 (80:6).

34. Cf. *De Coniecturis* I, 8 (35:12–22), a passage likewise often misunderstood.

35. Vincent Martin, "The Dialectical Process in the Philosophy of Nicholas of Cusa," *Laval théologique et philosophique* 5 (1949), 257.

36. Mark Fuehrer claims, mistakenly, that for Nicholas "everything is, in fact, God himself." But Fuehrer bases this claim on his mistranslation of *DI* I, 22 (69:3–4). See "The Principle of *Contractio* in Nicholas of Cusa's Philosophical View of Man," *Downside Review*, 93 (October 1975), 290.

37. Cf. chap. 34 of St. Anselm's *Monologion*. Also see Augustine, *Confessions* 7.15.21 (*PL* 32:744).

38. *DI* II, 2 (104:5–11).

39. *DI* II, 3 (110:15–21).

40. *DI* I, 24 (77:13–15).

41. And what entitles him to assert?: "The negations which remove the more imperfect things from the most Perfect are truer than the others. For example, it is truer that God is not stone than that He is not life or intelligence. . ." (I, 26). See *PNC*, p. 20.

42. *IL* 24:2–3.

43. *Ap.* 18:26–19:4.

44. *DI* I, 4 (11:7–9); I, 12 (33:4–6); I, 26 (87:1–3). In II, 13 (177:1) Nicholas sets forth a proportionality: "Earth is to fire as the world is to God." But he includes the word "*quasi*": "so to speak," "as it were." And this word must be understood as still applicative when he goes on to write: "Fire, in its relation to earth, has many resemblances to God."

45. See especially the dialogue *DP*.

46. The first of these observations is Werner Schulze's, the second Rudolf Haubst's. Both are cited from W. Schulze, *Zahl, Proportion, Analogie. Eine Untersuchung zur Metaphysik und Wissenschaftshaltung des Nikolaus von Kues* (Münster: Aschendorff, 1978), 35n.

47. Cf. *DI* I, 20 (61:28–31). In discussing God's relation to the universe, Nicholas frequently uses the language of "as if"; see II, 2 (104:3, 6); II, 3 (111:15); II, 4 (114:14, 15).

48. *DI* I, 16 (46:5–6).

49. *DI* II, 11 (156:27–29).

50. Moreover, the universe's shape and motion are said to be ungraspable by us [*DI* II, 11 (161:12–13)]. Or again: "Since it is not possible for the world to be enclosed between a physical center and [a physical] circumference, the world—of which God is the center and the circumference—is not understood" [II, 11 (156:24–27)].

51. Sometimes "absolute" means, for Nicholas, "in every respect" and is contrasted with "in some respect." So God is also *Absolute* Maximum in the sense that He is in no relevant respect not Maximum.

52. See especially *DI* II, 8 (136:9–10); II, 9 (150:9–10); III, 1 (183:10–13). But also note *DI* I, 2 (6:9–10); I, 6 (15:3–4); II, 8 (140:6–8); II, 9 (148:8); III, 1 (182:5–6); III, 2 (192: 4–5).

53. ". . . what is contracted [falls short] of what is absolute—the two being infinitely different." *DI* II, 8 (140:6–8).

54. Fuehrer, "Principle of *Contractio*," *op. cit.*, 290.

55. Martin, 258.

56. Frederick Copleston, *A History of Philosophy*. Vol. III (Westminister, Md.: Newman Press, 1953), p. 239.

57. Martin, 225, 234.

58. Kurt Goldammer, "Nicolaus von Cues und die Überwindung des geozentrischen Weltbildes," in *Alte Probleme-Neue Ansätze. Drei Vorträge von Fritz Krafft, Kurt Goldammer, Annemarie Wettley* (Wiesbaden: Steiner, 1965), p. 37. Cf. Ernst Hoffman, *Cusanus-Studien. I. Das Universum des Nikolaus von Cues. SHAW*, 1930, p. 11: "Der Kosmos [dem Nikolaus nach] ist Erscheinung. . . ."

59. But notice *DI* III, 4 (204:13–17).

60. *DI* II, 2 (100:3–4).

61. *DI* II, 2 (103:3–4; 104:2).

62. *Ap.* 28:18–19. Cf. *DI* II, 2 (103:5–9).

63. *DI* II, 2 (104:9).

64. *DI* II, 2 (99:11–13).

65. *DI* II, 3 (110:11–12).

66. *DI* II, 3 (107:11–12).

67. Cf. *Ap.* 16:21–17:2: "From the fact that all things are in God as things caused are in their cause, it does not follow that the caused *is* the cause—although *in the cause* they are only the cause. . . . For number is not oneness, although every number is enfolded in oneness, even as the caused [is enfolded] in the cause. But that which we understand as number is the unfolding of the power of oneness. Thus, in oneness number is only oneness."

68. *DI* II, 2 (101:10–13). See the Sermon "*Ubi est qui natus est rex Iudaeorum?*" sections 23–25 in Josef Koch, ed. and trans., *Vier Predigten im Geiste Eckharts. SHAW* 1936–37. Also see *De Ludo Globi* 1 (17:4–7); 1 (18:10–14); 2 (87:10–14).

69. Cf. the two kinds of seeing discussed in *NA* 21 (98).

70. *DI* I, 24 (77:5–7).

71. *DI* II, 5 (118:3–8).

72. *DI* II, 2 (103:5–8).

73. Cf. *DI* II, 3 (107:11–12) and II, 3 (111:11–15). Note Anselm, *Monologion* 14.

74. *DI* II, 3 (111:14–15).

75. Note the title and the contents of *DI* II, 4.

76. *DI* II, 4 (116:9–15).

77. Cf. *DI* II, 4 (115:4–7) with I, 17 (48:3).

78. To say that God is the Absolute Quiddity of the sun (or of the moon) is not to say that the sun has an absolute quiddity; rather, it is a manner of speaking which serves

to indicate that God is present in the sun absolutely—i.e., is present without any change in Himself or any restriction or contraction of His own Being or Essence. He is present as if in the way that an object is present in a mirror image: the object, as it is in itself, is not at all affected by the restrictions that apply to the image. Accordingly, Nicholas says (paradoxically) that God is present in all things and in no thing [*DI* I, 17 (50:11–12)]. In a secondary sense, the *modus loquendi* serves to indicate that the sun participates, through its own contracted quiddity, in the Absolute Quiddity of all things, viz., God. But it does not participate in God as He is.

79. *DI* II, 4 (115:1–9 and 13–16).

80. *DI* II, 4 (115).

81. *DI* I, 18 (53:15–16).

82. *DI* II, 3 (111:3–5).

83. *DI* II, 3 (111:13–22).

84. See *PNC*, p. 37.

85. For this reference see n. 35 above.

86. Martin, 234, 258.

87. *Ibid.*, 266–67.

88. Cf. *NA* 21 (98:12–13): "The earth's quiddity is seen by the intellect to be other than the quiddity of water or of fire."

89. Cf. *NA* 10 (36). Cf. *DI* II, 2 (103:1–2). *De Venatione Sapientiae* 7 (16:4–8).

90. *DI* I, 18 (53:1–6).

91. Cf. *Complementum Theologicum*, chap. 11, lines 26–29, Paris edition.

92. In "Nicholas of Cusa's Theory of Science and Its Metaphysical Background," *NCMM*, pp. 317–38, Thomas P. McTighe denies this point. His article—judicious and well-balanced—is probably the best article to read in support of the interpretation that, for Cusa, "because there is but one essence, that of the Absolute, there can be no plural positive essences intrinsic to things. . . . Ontologically speaking, things differ only numerically. Or to put it another way, all differentiation is accidental" (pp. 326–327).

93. *DI* II, 3 (107:11–12).

94. *DI* II, 4 (115:17–19).

95. But though all particulars exist in the universe and the universe exists in all particulars, Nicholas does not teach either that each particular qua particular exists in every other particular or that every species qua species exists in every other species. For when he says "*quodlibet in quolibet,*" he means that each actually existing thing contracts the whole of the universe in such way that in this thing the universe is this thing; yet, in this given thing the universe does not exist as a plurality—i.e., as a composite of particulars. So although humanity exists in Socrates and in Plato, it does not exist in dogs or cats because neither Socrates nor Plato qua Socrates or qua Plato exists in dogs and cats.

The most interesting attempt to make sense out of Nicholas's doctrine of *quodlibet in quolibet* is Heinrich Rombach's, in chap. 2 of his *Substanz, System, Struktur*. Vol. I: *Die Ontologie des Funktionalismus und der philosophische Hintergrund der modernen Wissenschaft* (Freiburg: Karl Alber, 1965). Unfortunately, Rombach's discussion—be it ever so intriguing—is an essential part of a more general interpretation of Cusanus which will not hold up. In the future I shall elsewhere give a critique of this interpretation.

Notes to the Introduction

96. Cf. *DI* III, 1 (189:1), which speaks of individuating principles.
97. *DI* II, 9 (148:17–20).
98. *DI*, II, 9 (149:16–20). Cf. II, 12 (166:15–18). Also see *Idiota de Mente* 13 (104:2–3 and 7–9).
99. In *DI* II, 9 Nicholas uses the word "form" ("*forma*") and the word "essence" ("*ratio*") interchangeably. Forms are said to exist both uncontractedly in the Word as Word and contractedly in contracted things. These contracted things include intellects, where forms exist more independently and abstractly than they exist in material objects.
100. *DI* II, 10 (155:1–4).
101. *DI* II, 11 (last lines).
102. *DI* II, 12 (162:15–17) refers to the world's center as everywhere, though in II, 11 (161:14–15) it was said to be nowhere.
103. *DI* II, 11 (157:17–23).
104. Karsten Harries insightfully works out the implications of Nicholas's perspectivism, even relating it in a clarifying way to some points already made by Meister Eckhart. See "The Infinite Sphere. Comments on the History of a Metaphor," *Journal of the History of Philosophy*, 13 (January 1975), 5–15.
105. It is intended to elucidate the conclusion by helping to give a sense thereto.
106. In *DI* the earth, the moon, the sun, the planets are referred to as stars, though they are distinguished from the so-called fixed stars of the eighth sphere.
107. *DI* II, 12 (162:10–12).
108. *DI* II, 11 (161:12–13).
109. *DI* II, 2 (104:6).
110. *DI* II, 1 (97:5–6).
111. *DI* III, 1 (183:3–8). The infinite exceeds all differentiation, all naming, all comparative relation, all degrees. See *DI* I, 5.
112. *DI* III, 3 (195:12–15).
113. *DI* III, 3 (197:8–12).
114. *DI* III, 3 (199:3–16).
115. See *Anselm of Canterbury: Volume III*, ed. and trans. J. Hopkins and H. Richardson (Toronto: The Edwin Mellen Press, 1976).
116. E.g., in the sermon "*Hoc Facite.*" Sermon 3, Vol. 16, fascicle 1 of the *Opera Omnia* (Hamburg: Felix Meiner, 1970).
117. *DI* III, 4 (204:1–2).
118. See the discussion under arabic numeral 5 a little later in this section of the Introduction.
119. *DI* III, 7 (223:1–7). Also note III, 4 (204:2–6).
120. Rudolf Haubst's *Die Christologie des Nikolaus von Kues* (Freiburg: Herder, 1956) gives numerous examples of statements, in Nicholas's sermons, that tend to mislead us regarding his Christology. (E.g., see pp. 121 and 135). Nicholas simply was incautious.
121. Note especially III, 2 (193:3–9). Cf. Sermon XVII: "*Gloria in excelsis Deo.*" Also, see n. 41 of the notes to *DI*, Book Three.
122. Note the end of *DI* III, 3: "But this order should not be considered temporally—as if God temporally preceded the Firstborn of creation. And [we ought not to believe] that the Firstborn—viz., God and man—preceded the world temporally but

[should believe that He preceded it] in nature and in the order of perfection and above all time.'' But cf. III, 5 (214:1–2).

123. *DI* III, 3 (199:1).

124. Cf. *DI* III, 1 (189:1–3).

125. *DI* III, 2 (191:11–12).

126. *DI* III, 3 (199:7).

127. *DI* III, 3 (199:10–11).

128. *DI* III, 2 (191:7–8).

129. *IL* 39:1–5.

130. *DI* III, 3 (197:8–9).

131. ''Through union with Absolute [Maximality], which is the Absolute Being of all things, He would be the universal contracted being of each creature. Through Him all things would receive the beginning and the end of their contraction, so that through Him who is the contracted maximum [individual] all things would go forth from the Absolute Maximum into contracted being and would return unto the Absolute [Maximum] through this same Medium—[in other words,] through [Him who is] the Beginning of their emanation and the End [i.e., the Goal] of their return, as it were.'' *DI* III, 3 (199:11–17).

132. *Cur Deus Homo* II, 8. In II, 21 Anselm explains why the redemption of fallen angels through a God-angel is impossible. Anselm thinks that God had the power to become incarnate as an angel or an ass but that for Him to accomplish such an incarnation would not serve His purposes.

133. Sermon 3, Vol. 16, fascicle 1, pp. 44–45 of the *Opera Omnia* (Hamburg: Felix Meiner, 1970).

134. *DI* III, 3 (202:8–10).

135. *DI* III, 4 (204:7–9); III, 7 (223:9).

136. *DI* III, 3 (200:4–6).

137. *DI* III, 4 (206:12–18). N.B. *Complementum Theologicum*, chap. 5, lines 6-9, Paris edition.

138. *DI* III, 1 (183:10–13).

139. *DI* III, 7 (223:3–4). See H. Senger's note on pp. 125–26 of Vol. III of *De docta ignorantia. Die belehrte Unwissenheit* (Hamburg: Felix Meiner, 1977).

140. *DI* III, 7 (225:11–17).

141. *DI* III, 4 (204:2–6). Cf. III, 7 (223:8–9).

142. *DI* III, 7 (224:21–23), where the humanity is said to be united to the nature of the divine person.

143. *DI* II, 5 (119:18–19). See also I, 22 (69:3–4).

144. *DI* III, 2 (194:4–7 and 16–17).

145. *DI* III, 7 (224:22).

146. *DI* III, 4 (205:1–5 and 13–17).

147. *DI* III, 4 (207:1–3).

148. *DI* III, 4 (206:11–12).

149. *DI* III, 5 (212:6–8). In Sermon 9, *''Complevitque Deus'' [Opera Omnia*, Vol. 16, fascicle 2 (Hamburg: Felix Meiner, 1973)], Nicholas teaches that Mary was ever free of original and of all personal sin (11:24–27).

150. *DI* III, 6 (219:5–14).

151. *DI* III, 6 (218:15–16).
152. *DI* III, 12 (256:16; 256:2).
153. John 15:5. Rom. 12:4–5.
154. *DI* III, 12 (255:10–12).
155. *DI* III, 8 (228:23–25).
156. *DI* III, 11 (252:11–14).
157. *DI* III, 11 (245:10–23).
158. Ex. 33:18–23.
159. *DI* III, 11 (246:15-16).
160. *DI* III, 11 (246:3).
161. *DI* III, 6 (215:7–8).
162. *Ap.* 15:4–16.
163. *DI* III, 12 (259:1–2).
164. *DI* III, 11 (244:12–13).
165. *DI* III, 12 (260:13–14).
166. *DI* III, 8 (228:24–25).

167. In "Wisdom and Eloquence in Nicholas of Cusa's Idiota de sapientia and de mente," *Vivarium*, 16 (November 1978), 152n. Mark Fuehrer writes: "The epistemological similarities between Kant and Cusa are quite striking. Just as Kant argues that there can be no real unity in the world of appearances unless an order of reality is postulated which provides the unity in the manifold of appearances which by themselves the appearances cannot supply, Cusa argues that the realm of the 'more or the less' when judged by the mind indicates a precision which neither the 'more or the less' nor the mind could provide. Thus something which is identified with neither the world (= the realm of the more or the less) nor the finite mind must be postulated. Without this postulate the finite mind could not think the concepts of 'more' or 'less'." But this comparison misconstrues *Idiota de Sapientia* II. (Moreover, Fuehrer should make use of the critical edition of the Latin texts, published by the Heidelberg Academy, rather than, as he does here, using the Strasburg edition of 1488, reprinted by de Gruyter in 1966–1967.)

NOTES TO *LEARNED IGNORANCE*, BOOK ONE

1. *De Coniecturis* is also addressed to Cardinal Julian Cesarini (1398–1444), whom Nicholas also there refers to as his own venerable teacher. In spite of Josef Koch's caveat (*Nicolai de Cusa Opera Omnia* III, p. 186) there is reason enough to believe that Cesarini, though only a little older than Nicholas, had indeed been one of his instructors at the University of Padua. The two were to meet again at the Council of Basel, over which Julian presided.

2. See Aristotle's *Metaphysics*—both the opening sentence and I, 2 (982^{b}12–14).

3. This sentence and the previous one are alluded to by John Wenck, *IL* 22:18–19.

4. See Gerda von Bredow, "Der Sinn der Formel 'meliori modo quo' . . .," *MFCG* 6 (1967), 21–30. Cf. n. 35 of the notes to Book Three.

5. *DI* I, 11 (31:1–4).

6. Throughout *DI* Nicholas frequently uses the word "*proportio*" (as well as the adjective "*proportionalis*" and the adverb "*proportionabiliter*"). I have usually

adhered to the following English renderings: *proportio*–comparative relation, relation; *comparativa proportio*-comparative relation; *proportionaliter*-proportionally; *proportionalis*-proportional; *improportionaliter*-disproportionally, incomparably; *improportionalis*-disproportional.

7. *DI* I, 3 (9:4–5); II, 2 (102:4–5).
8. Ecclesiastes 1:8.
9. Job 28:20–21.
10. Aristotle, *Metaphysics* II, 1 (993^{b}9–11).
11. *"Maximitas"* means not merely *magnitudo* (greatness) but *maxima magnitudo* (maximal greatness). Nor is *"maximitas"* always a shorthand for *"absoluta maximitas,"* for Nicholas also speaks of the universe as *maximitas*—viz., *maximitas contracta* [II, 8 (139:10–11)].
12. I Tim. 6:16.
13. Wenck pays tribute to Nicholas's Latin style (*IL* 19:5), calling it "sufficiently elegant." But, in fact, Nicholas's style can appear elegant only to someone like Wenck, whose own is so much worse.
14. Literally: " . . . showing at the outset learned ignorance's basis in the inapprehensible precision of the truth."
15. In the chapter title Nicholas uses the word *"incomprehensibilis,"* though in the last line of the preceding chapter he used *"inapprehensibilis."* In fact, throughout *DI* and his other treatises he does not systematically distinguish his use of these two terms and their cognates. For example, he does not differentiate between apprehending and comprehending God. Nor does he regard *comprehendere* as simply *apprehendere intellectu*; for he writes not only *"simplici intellectione apprehendere"* but also *"simplicissima intellectione . . . comprehendere"* [I, 10 (29:13; 29:10–11)]. Following the usage of Scripture (John 1:5), he is even willing to say *"tenebrae eam* [i.e., *lucem*] *comprehendere nequeunt"* [I, 26 (86:15–16)], where *"apprehendere"* would serve equally well. And just as at 11:9–10 he uses the expression *"sensu apprehendere,"* so in *Ap.* 2:18 he understands the expression *"comprehendi nequeat"* to mean *"sensu comprehendi nequeat."* It is difficult to know whether at *Ap.* 2:18 he would likewise be willing to say *"apprehendi nequeat."* As a rule, throughout his writings, both *"incomprehensibilis"* and *"inapprehensibilis"* could acceptably be translated by the one English word "ungraspable."
16. *DI* I, 1 (3:2–3); II, 2 (102:4–5).
17. See II, 1 for examples of this point.
18. *DI* II, 1 (91:14–15).
19. The example of an inscribed polygon is also used in *DI* III, 1 (188:15–19); III, 4 (206:12–18).
20. Cf. *NA* 85:15–20.
21. In *NA* Nicholas elaborates upon the motif that God is not *other* than anything.
In calling God Equality of being and Form of being [*DI* I, 8 (22:8–10)], Nicholas is not suggesting that we can conceive of what it is like for God to be such Equality and such Form [*DI* I, 4 (11:7–9); I:12 (33:4–6)]. Indeed, learned ignorance consists of the joint recognition that God is undifferentiated being itself and that such being is inconceivable by every finite intellect.

Notes *to* Learned Ignorance I

22. Regarding the translation of "*[est] omne id quod esse potest,*" see *PNC* pp. 173–174, n. 12 and p. 165, n. 66.

23. Only the maximum thus freed from quantity—i.e., only the absolutely Maximum— coincides with the (absolutely) Minimum. At the end of the present chapter Nicholas makes clear that insofar as the terms "maximum" and "minimum" refer to God, they refer to what is beyond all contraction to quantity (or anything else). See n. 34 below. Cf. *DI* II, 8 (140:7–8); II, 9 (148:8; 150:9–10); III, 1 (182:5–6; 183:10–13); II; 8 (136:9–10). Especially note *De Visione Dei* 13 (57:11–12). *Complementum Theologicum* 12 (last 7 lines), Paris edition. *DP* 69:6–70:11.

Similarly, only absolutely maximum motion coincides with (absolutely) minimum motion [II, 10 (155:1–3)]—both of which are "motion" only in a metaphorical sense. Cf. *DP* 10–11. Likewise, absolutely maximum faith [III, 11 (249:1–2)] is not faith in any sense of "faith" that we can understand; for it coincides with God's knowledge, and God's knowledge is God, who is inconceivable except to Himself.

24. Nicholas does not here distinguish *intellectus* (intellect, understanding) and *ratio* (reason, reasoning), as he does at *DI* III, 6 (215:5–6). Also note I, 10 (27:14–18); I, 24 (76:4–5); II, 2 (100:9–10); III, 9 (233:6–7); III, 10 (240:1–2). See *PNC*, p. 172, n. 175.

25. *DI* I, 23–24.

26. No matter where you stop on the ascending scale, you stop at a finite number. No matter how far you count, you will have counted only a finite series. [Cf. *DI* II, 1 (96:1–18).] In this sense, the ascending scale is "actually" finite, though potentially infinite.

27. Apparently, Nicholas is arguing, straightforwardly, that if there were no *source* of number, which he has already shown to be finite, then there would not be any number. Note the English clause in parentheses at the close of this chapter.

Nicholas regards fractions not as numbers but as relations between two numbers. And like Aristotle [*Metaphysics* X, 1 (1052^{b}24f.)] he does not regard *one* as a number. [Number, says Aristotle (1053^{a}31), is a plurality of units.] He does, however, place *one* as the first member of the number series.

Also note Boethius, *De Institutione Arithmetica* I, 3 [ed. G. Friedlein (Leipzig: B. G. Teubner, 1867; reprinted, Frankfurt: Minerva GmbH, 1966)]: "*Numerus est unitatum collectio, vel quantitatis acervus ex unitatibus profusus.*" Also see I, 23, where Boethius puts *one* at the beginning of the series of natural numbers ("*Ponatur enim naturalis numerus hoc modo*: I. II. III. . . .")

28. At 13:30 "*unitati*" is a dative of comparison, which Nicholas sometimes uses. Cf. I, 21 (63:8–9).

29. *DI* II, 3 (108:1–15).

30. Deut. 6:4. *DI* I, 24 (75:12–76:13).

31. Matt. 23:8–9.

32. *DI* I, 8.

33. E.g., *DI* I, 4 (12:15–16).

34. God, who is uncontracted, is Maximum *Being* only insofar as being is uncontracted. But uncontracted and undifferentitated "being" is not being in any sense conceivable or nameable by us. Hence Nicholas goes on to state: "Wherefore, although

it is evident through the aforesaid that the name 'being' (or any other name) is not a precise name for the Maximum (which is beyond every name), nevertheless it is necessary that being befit it maximally (but in a way not nameable by the name 'maximum') and above all nameable being.'' In *DI* I, 24–26 Nicholas concedes the necessity—for purposes of worship—of conceiving of God *as if* He were contracted to various perfections which are signified by their names in our language, *as if* His trinity were truly describable as Father, Son, and Holy Spirit, and so on.

35. In the previous paragraph Nicholas affirmed that ''the unqualifiedly Maximum exists.'' Proceeding on this basis, he draws the inference that the unqualifiedly Maximum cannot rightly be thought ([*non*] *intelligi potest*) to be able not to exist, since minimal being (i.e., maximal not–being) is maximal being. Apart from the foregoing basis his inference might seem reversible as follows: since maximal being is minimal being (i.e., maximal not–being), the unqualifiedly Maximum cannot rightly be thought to be able to exist.

36. Phil. 2:9.

37. *DI* I, 5 (14:5–8).

38. Klibansky thinks that Nicholas confused Varro's *Antiquities* either with Josephus's *The Jewish Antiquities* XV, 371–379; XVIII, 18 [Loeb Library Series, Cambridge, Mass.: Harvard University Press), Vol. 8 (1963) trans. Ralph Marcus and Allen Wikgren, Vol. 9 (1965) trans. Louis Feldman] or with reports found in Eusebius Caesariensis's *Praeparationis Evangelicae* IX, III, 7 and 13 [ed. G. Dindorf (Leipzig: B. G. Teubner, 1867)]. Josephus and Eusebius ascribe the saying to the Essenes rather than to the Sissennii. Because the references to Josephus and Eusebius are not quite accurate, Wilpert believes that Nicholas was using one or more secondary sources, from which he borrowed the references.

39. John of Salisbury, *De Septem Septenis* VII (*PL* 199:961C).

40. Cf. Boethius, *De Institutione Arithmetica* II, 1 [ed. G. Friedlein (Leipzig: B. G. Teubner, 1867; reprinted Frankfurt: Minerva GmbH, 1966)].

These are not absolutely simple. [Cf. *De Coniecturis* I, 10 (50) with *Idiota de Mente* 9 (87:14–20)—the latter passage having reference to a continuum.] Likewise, when he implies that two objects can be equal—as he does here and in I, 9 (24:7–10), he does not mean *precisely* equal, for only God is precise Equality. [See *DI* I, 3 (9:13–15); II, 1 (91:9–13).] In general, note *DI* I, 11 (32:19–24); I, 17 (47:67); II, 1 (96:4–8).

Cf. n. 26 of the notes to Book Three.

41. In fact, Nicholas, like Leibniz after him, maintains that no two objects differ in number alone. *DI* I, 3 (9:13–15); I, 4 (11:9–12); II, 1 (91:12–13) as well as the whole of II, 1; III, 1 (188:12–20).

42. Literally: ''But these [two things] will produce a doubleness for one of them.''

43. Both *''conexio''* and *''unio''* are translated throughout by the one English word ''union,'' since Nicholas uses the two words interchangeably. In *DI* I, 10 (28:14,19) he writes *''unio sive conexio.''* Cf. II, 10 (152:1) with II, 12 (173:13); II, 11 (155:8) with III, 12 (262:14); I, 10 (29:6) with I, 10 (29:8).

44. In the corresponding Latin sentence the word *''aliqua''* functions as does the French word *''des''* in *''Il y a des choses que je ne comprends pas.''* Neither *''des''* nor *''aliqua''* need be translated by a separate English word.

45. *DI* I, 24 (80:4–8). Throughout his works—e.g., *De Coniecturis* II, 17

(173:11–13) and *NA* 5 (19:7–8)—Nicholas uses "Oneness," "Equality," and "Union" to refer to the Divine Trinity.

46. Much of the terminology in this chapter stems from Thierry of Chartres and Clarenbald of Arras. For a short discussion of Nicholas's use of Thierry see *PNC*, pp. 6–7 and the literature there referred to.

47. See n. 40 above.

48. In the corresponding line of the Latin text (24:13) I am reading "*unitatis*" in the place of "*unitas*"

49. Cf. *De Pace Fidei* 8 (24:6–7). *NA* 6 (19:13).

50. I. e., to human fathers, sons, and " spirits."

51. *DI* I, 24 (e.g., 79:1–5).

52. Martian Capella, *De Nuptiis Philologiae et Mercurii* II, 138–140 [ed. Adolf Dick (Leipzig: B. G. Teubner, 1925; reprinted with corrections and addenda by Jean Préaux (Stuttgart: B. G. Teubner, 1978)]. Nicholas's secondary source is John of Salisbury, *De Septem Septenis* VII (PL 199:961C), which wrongly indicates that *philosophy* (instead of *philology*) left behind circles and spheres.

53. *DI* I, 4 (11:4–9).

54. See n. 24 above.

55. I.e., understandable (intelligible) to itself but not to any finite intellect.

56. E.g., *DI* I, 5 (14:1–6).

57. I surmise that the Latin text needs to be repunctuated so as to place a colon after the first occurrence of "*maximum*" at 29:6 and a comma (rather than a period) after "*unio*" at 29:8. This way "*quoniam*" and "*hinc*" become coordinated , as they so often are for Nicholas [e.g., I, 12 (33:4,6); I, 18 (54:8–9); II, 1 (95:1,4)]. Nicholas's point seems to be that "one is maximal" indicates a trinity: viz., Minimum (which the One is), Maximum, and their Union. Since it has been not only stated but also "established" that the One is maximal, it has been established that the One is the trinity of Minimum, Maximum, and Union—in other words that Oneness is minimal Oneness, maximal Oneness, and their Union.

Since Nicholas does not express himself with perfect clarity in 29:1–11, my translation is not assuredly correct—nor Wilpert's obviously incorrect.

58. This reference is apparently to 27:15–16.

59. *DI* III, 11 (246:15–16). The seeker will even then see God through a cloud, though it be a more rarefied one; God will remain incomprehensible. Cf. *DI* I, 26 (88:16–20).

60. Rom. 1:20. I Cor. 13:12.

61. *DI* I, 3 (9:10–15). The Maximal Image is the Word of God (Col. 1:15).

62. *DI* I, 1 (2:16–17).

63. *DP* 62:10–63:15.

64. *DP* 44:3–7.

65. *De Institutione Arithmetica, op. cit.*, I, 1 (p. 9, lines 6–8; p. 10, line 10 through p. 11, line 1). See also Joseph E. Hofmann, "Mutmassungen über das früheste mathematische Wissen des Nikolaus von Kues," *MFCG* 5(1965), 98–133.

66. *Ad Orosium contra Priscillianistas et Origenistas* 8 (*PL* 42:674).

67. *De Institutione Arithmetica, op. cit.*, I, 1 (p. 10, lines 10–13); I, 2 (p. 12, lines 14–17).

68. *Metaphysics* VIII, 3 (1044ª10–11).

69. *De Anima* II, 3 (414ᵇ29.1–32).

70. *De Quantitate Animae* 8–12 (*PL* 32:1042–1047).

71. *De Institutione Arithmetica, op. cit.*, I, 1 (p. 9, lines 1–8).

72. Wilpert (as well as Klibansky) regards Nicholas as having learned of the mathematical refutation of Epicurus from Albert the Great's *Metaphysica*. See Book I, tractate 3, chap. 15 through I, 4, 2. [Bernhard Geyer, ed., *Opera Omnia*, Vol. XVI, Part I (Münster, 1960), pp. 47–50].

73. Cf. *De Veritate* 1 and 10. Anselm of Canterbury, trans. J. Hopkins and H. Richardson (New York: The Edwin Mellen Press, 1976), Vol. II, pp. 77 and 91–92. Anselm speaks of *summa veritas* rather than of *infinita veritas*.

74. Heimeric de Campo, *Tractatus de Sigillo Aeternitatis* [Codex Cusanus 106, f. 77 (cited from P. Wilpert)].

75. *Ibid.* See R. Haubst, *Das Bild des Einen und Dreinen Gottes in der Welt nach Nikolaus von Kues* (Trier: Paulinus, 1952), pp. 255–262.

76. Nicholas borrows this comparison from Meister Eckhart. See *PNC*, p. 13.

77. Boethius, *De Institutione Arithmetica, op. cit.*, II, 30 (p. 122, lines 1–3).

78. Since the Maximum is all that which can be, how could there be more than one Maximum? *DI* I, 5 (14:5–8).

79. In *DI* I, 13 Nicholas "proved" that an infinite line is a straight line.

80. At 40:21 "*infinitae*" is a dative of comparison.

81. AB was shown to be the same infinite line as BC, which was shown to be the infinite circumference.

82. In an infinite circle the distance from B to C is the same as the distance from B all the way around to B again. If an infinite circle makes an infinite rotation, it describes an infinite sphere.

83. *The Mystical Theology* 1 [*Dionysiaca* (Paris: Desclée de Brouwer, 2 vols., 1937, 1950), I, 572].

84. *The Divine Names* 5 (*Dionysiaca* I, 355–356).

85. *The Mystical Theology* 5 (*Dionysiaca* I, 601–602).

86. *Letter to Gaius*, Part 1 (*Dionysiaca* I, 607).

87. Rabbi Solomon is Moses Maimonides. Nicholas takes the above quotation and the subsequent one from the *Guide for the Perplexed* (*Dux Neutrorum*), I, 59 and I, 58 respectively [pp. 139 and 137 of *The Guide of the Perplexed*, trans. Shlomo Pines (Chicago: University of Chicago Press, 1969, 2nd printing)]. His secondary source is Meister Eckhart's *Expositio Libri Exodi*, n. 184 and n. 174. He confuses Maimonides with Raschi (Rabbi Solomon bar Isaac).

88. *DI* I, 20 (61:20–21); I, 23 (72:1–3).

89. *DI* I, 3 (9:10–17).

90. *DI* I, 11 (32:19–24). Cf. II, 1 (96:1–9).

91. *Metaphysics* X, 1 (1052ᵇ19.1). Cf. *IL* 33:22–24.

92. *The Divine Names* 4 (*Dionysiaca* I, 274). Cf. *NA* 10 (37:1–23).

93. Calcidius, *In Platonis Timaeus*, 330 [*Timaeus a Calcidio translatus commentarioque instructus*, ed. J. H. Waszink (London: Warburg Institute, 1962), pp. 324–325]. Calcidius attributes the statement to Plato, not to the *Phaedo*.

94. *DI* I, 3 (9:10–15).

95. Prima facie it is strange that Nicholas speaks of the Maximum as able to *participate* in essence (*ratio*). What he appears to mean is that since the Maximum is Infinite Essence, then in participating in essence, it participates in itself. To say that it participates in itself is tantamount to saying that it *is*, perfectly, its own essence. Note *DI* I, 19 (56:8): "The Maximum is actually one trine essence. . . . "

N. B. Of God Nicholas uses indifferently the expressions "*ratio omnium*" and "*essentia omnium*" in *DI* I, 16–17. But of an infinite line he prefers to use only "*ratio omnium [linearum]*." Still, at I, 19 (56:5) we find "*essentia*" used of both God and an infinite line.

96. *DI* I, 16 (46:6–8).

97. *First Letter to Gaius* (*Dionysiaca* I, 607). *The Celestial Hierarchy* II (*Dionysiaca* II, 757).

98. *De Anima* I, 5 (411^{a}5–6).

99. *Metaphysics* V, 7 (1017^{a}8–9).

100. *The Divine Names* 1 (*Dionysiaca* I, 10–11).

101. *DI* I, 26.

102. *DI* I, 13–14.

103. *DI* I, 13 and 15.

104. Augustine makes this point at various places in *De Trinitate* V–VIII, though he does not use these exact words. Cf. *DP* 46:1–6, where Nicholas states that God is three but not numerically three.

105. John 10:38.

106. *DI* I, 7–9 and 19.

107. *DI* I, 4 (11:13–18; 12:4–6).

108. Viz., a line, a triangle, a circle, and a sphere.

109. *DI* I, 15.

110. At 63:9 "*unitati*" is a dative of comparison.

111. Nicholas does not believe that there is an actually existing infinite and eternal circle. Nor does he believe that the infinite circle is a supra Platoniclike Idea or even an Idea in the mind of God. Rather, his point here is purely conceptual and illustrative: the "logic" of infinity is such that an infinite circle would have to be eternal, just as its circumference would have to be its center.

112. *DI* II, 3 (111:8–9). Nicholas seems to have taken this idea from Raymond Lull. For a full study of the intellectual relationship between Cusa and Lull, see Eusebio Colomer, *Nikolaus von Kues und Raimund Llull* = Vol. 2 in the series: *Quellen und Studien zur Geschichte der Philosophie*, ed. Paul Wilpert (Berlin: de Gruyter, 1961).

113. In the corresponding line of the Latin text (viz., 68:15) I am reading "*etsi*" in place of "*si*". Although Nicholas generally uses "*etsi*" with the subjunctive, he also sometimes uses it with the indicative, as in the Latin sentence above. [Also note, e.g., III, 11 (249:3–4) and *De Coniecturis* II, 1 (75:5–6).] Similarly, although he generally uses "*licet*" with the subjunctive, he sometimes also uses it with the indicative, as at 68:9–10 above. In opting for the reading "*etsi*" I am following not only the sense of the passage but also a clue furnished by Codex Latinus Monacensis 14213, which has "*et*" instead of "*si*".

114. Cf. Thierry of Chartres, *Lectiones in Boethii Librum De Trinitate* II, 60 [p. 174, lines 88–89 in Nikolaus Häring, ed., *Commentaries on Boethius by Thierry of*

Chartres and His School (Toronto: Pontifical Institute of Mediaeval Studies, 1971)].

115. *DI* I, 21 (64:3–8). Since an infinite circle is also an infinite sphere [I, 13 (35:6–7)], the same conclusions apply to the latter as to the former.

116. *DI* I, 8 (22:8).

117. Nicholas's secondary source may be Pseudo–Bede, *Commentarius in Librum Boetii De Trinitate* (*PL* 95:397C) or John of Salisbury, *De Septem Septenis* VII (*PL* 199:961B).

118. In the corresponding Latin sentence (71:6) I am following the reading of the Paris edition: "*et in ea. . . .*"

119. *DI* I, 16 (45:9–18); I, 20 (61:20–21).

120. At *DI* I, 17 (49:5) the Maximum is said to be *ratio infinita*, just as at I, 16 (45:17–18) it is called *infinita essentia*.

121. The phrase "from Him, in Him, and through Him" is reminiscent of Rom. 11:36. It also occurs at *DI* I, 21 (65:3).

122. *DI* I, 13 (36:8–18).

123. *Asclepius* 20 [*Corpus Hermeticum*, ed. A. D. Nock [Paris: Société d'Edition "Les Belles Lettres," Vol. 2, 1945), p. 321, especially lines 7–9 of the Latin text].

124. *DI* I, 5 (14:9–10, 13–14).

125. Zachariah 14:9.

126. Deut. 6:4.

127. See n. 24 above.

128. Phil. 2:9.

129. *The Celestial Hierarchy* 2 (*Dionysiaca* II, 759).

130. *DI* I, 9 (26:1–4).

131. Here Nicholas writes "*unitatis sive entitatis aut essendi aequalitas*"; at *DI* I, 8 (22:9–10) he says "*Aequalitas vero unitatis quasi aequalitas entitatis, id est aequalitas essendi sive exsistendi.*"

132. Col. 1:16.

133. *De Trinitate* VI, 10 (*PL* 42:931–932).

134. Viz., Oneness, Equality of Oneness, and Love.

135. *De Genesi ad Litteram* I, 4 (*PL* 34:249).

136. Toward the beginning of this chapter.

137. See n. 87 above.

138. Julius Firmicus Maternus, *Matheseos* II.13.6 [Vol I, p. 56, line 30 to p. 57, line 1 of the edition by W. Kroll, F. Skutsch, and K. Ziegler (Leipzig: B. G. Teubner, 2 vols., 1897, 1913)].

139. *Asclepius* 21 (p. 321, lines 18–21 of *Corpus Hermeticum, op. cit.*).

140. Valerius Soranus. See Augustine, *De Civitate Dei* VII, 9 (*PL* 41:202).

141. I.e., "Tetragrammaton" or "Oneness to which neither otherness nor plurality nor multiplicity is opposed." *DI* I, 24 (75:5–11; 76:9–13).

142. See n. 38 above and *DI* I, 7 (18:5–6).

143. *De Natura Deorum* II, 28; II, 6.

144. *DI* III, 11 (253:14–17).

145. John 4:24.

146. John 1:5.

147. *The Mystical Theology* 5 (*Dionysiaca* I, 598–600).

148. *Guide for the Perplexed* I, 59. See n. 87 above.
149. *De Trinitate* II, 1 (*PL* 10:51A).
150. Rom. 9:5.
151. Nicholas's language is here deliberately paradoxical: God *manifests* His *incomprehensible* self. Nicholas continues his point in the Prologue of Book II: the Absolute Maximum shines forth in a shadow. See n. 59 above.

NOTES TO *LEARNED IGNORANCE*, BOOK TWO

1. I.e., Cardinal Julian Cesarini. See n. 1 of the notes to Book One.
2. *DI* I, 17 (49:13–14); I, 16 (46:10–12).
3. Regarding the phrase "*in sua ratione*" ("in its definition") at 92:4–5, cf. *DP* 63:10–12: "For mathematics does not deal with a circle as it is in a corruptible floor but as it is in its [i.e., the circle's] own definition (*in sua ratione seu diffinitione*)."
4. Viz., the rule that except for God all positable things differ (91:12–13).
5. *De Coniecturis* II, 6 (105:9–15); II, 16 (163:1–9).
6. *Ibid*. I, 10 (44–45). Cf. *ibid*. I, 9 (37:6–16).
7. Nicholas's references to mathematics are to be coordinated as follows: no ascent to the unqualifiedly Maximum is possible, as is evident from the illustration of the ascending scale of numbers; no descent to the unqualifiedly Minimum is possible, as is evident from the illustration of the dividing of a continuum. See *DI* I, 5 (13:13–21) and I, 17 (47:5–7).

   In dividing a continuum, no transition is made to oneness, which Nicholas regards as infinite [cf. *DI* I, 3 (9:7–8) with I, 5 (13:29–31) and I, 5 (14:1–8, 13–14). Also note *De Coniecturis* I, 5 (18:1–2).] Oneness is not subsequent to dividing (or subtracting), because it must be *presupposed* in order for dividing and subtracting to be possible. Thus, oneness precedes all plurality; in its absence, "there would be no distinction of things; nor would any order or any plurality or any degrees of comparatively greater and lesser be found among numbers; indeed, there would not be number," states Nicholas in I, 5 (13:25–28).

8. *DI* I, 6 (15:6–10).
9. *DI* I, 5 (13:17–21).
10. *DI* III, 2. Jesus is this alluded-to Maximum.
11. Cf. *DP* 6:8–15.
12. See the reference in n. 4 of the notes to Book One. Also note *DI* I, 1 (2:4–5); I, 5 (13:10); II, 1 (97:19–20); II, 2 (104:5–9); II, 10 (154:7–9); III, 1 (185:8–9); III, 3 (201:13–15).
13. *DI* I, 6 (15:12–18).
14. *DI* I, 13 (35:9–28).
15. Though Nicholas believes that the more *one* a thing is, the more like unto God it is, he believes at the same time that God's oneness transcends the power of human conception [*DI* I, 4 (11:7–9)]. These joint beliefs leave him with the problem of reconciling his language of resemblance with his assertion that there is no comparative relation between the finite and the infinite [I, 3 (9:4–5)]. See *PNC*, pp. 19–28 and 38.
16. In the corresponding line of the Latin text (99:13) I am reading "*contingenter*" for "*contingenti*".

17. Nowhere in *DI* or in any of his writings does Nicholas identify God with creation or creation with God. Note his response (*Ap.* 22:9–23:14) to John Wenck's charge that he taught that all things coincide with God. In his response he cites the above passage.

18. Pseudo-Hermes Trismegistus, "Book of the Twenty-four Philosophers," Proposition 14 [Clemens Baeumker, ed., "Das pseudo-hermetische 'Buch der vierund-zwanzig Meister' (Liber XXIV philosophorum). Ein Beitrag zur Geschichte des Neupythagoreismus und Neuplatonismus im Mittelalter" in *Beiträge zur Geschichte der Philosophie und Theologie des Mittelalters*, 25 (1928), 194–214].

19. See n. 24 of the notes to Book One.

20. In this chapter Nicholas uses both "*abesse*" and "*adesse*" to indicate dependent being. I have translated "*abesse*" by "derived being" and "*adesse*" by "adventitious being."

21. The word "*in*" is here crucial. The universe as enfolded *in* God ontologically prior to its unfolded, temporal existence *is* God, says Nicholas. Insofar as it is unfolded and temporal, however, it is neither God nor from God (i.e., from God in the sense of God's having caused its temporality and plurality); rather, its temporality and plurality derive from contingency. (See 99:11–13 of the present chapter.) Of course, its being qua being *does* derive from God.

22. Cf. *IL* 26:6–13, where Wenck cites Eckhart's reason for why God did not create the world earlier.

23. *DI* I, 3 (9:4–5); I, 1 (3:2–3).

24. Regarding the view that a woman is a man manqué, see Aristotle, *De Generatione Animalium* II, 3 (737ª28f.) and St. Thomas, *Summa Theologiae* Ia 99, 2, ad 1.

25. *De Coniecturis II, 14 (143:7–8).*

26. See the references in n. 12 above and in n. 4 of the notes to Book One.

27. See n. 15 above.

28. *DI* III, 1 (189:4–21); I, 1 (2:3–5).

29. See n. 78 of the notes to Book One.

30. *DI* I, 4 (12:24–25).

31. *DI* I, 5 (14:9–12).

32. In the corresponding line of the Latin text (107:4), I am reading "*complicata*" for "*explicata*".

33. *DI* I, 7 (18:14–15).

34. *DI* I, 7 (21:2–5).

35. *De Coniecturis* I, 2 (7:3–5).

36. *DI* I, 5 (14:18–21).

37. In the corresponding line of the Latin text (108:14) I am reading "*explicare omnia, scilicet*" in place of "*explicare, omnia scilicet*". Nicholas's point here parallels his point at 107:12.

38. In the preceding paragraph (108:9–10) it was said that "God, in eternity, understood one thing in one way and another thing in another way." If God's understanding is His being, then there seems to be a sense in which He is these things, reasons Nicholas.

39. Nicholas is clearer in *DI* III, 1 (184:5–7): "Genera exist only contractedly in species; and species exist only in individuals, which alone exist actually." Cf. II, 6 (124:13–125:20).

40. *DI* II, 2 (102:12–15).

41. *DI* I, 21 (66:4). See n. 112 of the notes to Book One.

42. Nicholas says not only that all things are in God (see n. 21 above) but also that God is in all things. He here attempts to give a clarifying illustration of the latter thesis. Note *DI* II, 4 (118:3–13); II, 3 (107:12).

43. In the corresponding line of the Latin text (112:13) I am reading "*absoluto absolute*" in place of "*absoluta absoluto*".

44. In the corresponding line of the Latin text (113:6) I am reading "*qua*" in place of "*quo*". At 113:8 Wilpert's punctuation needs to be revised.

45. *DI* I, 16 (42:4–5), where Nicholas alludes to what has been shown in I, 13–15.

46. As a rule, Nicholas uses "world" and "universe" interchangeably. At *DI* II, 12 (170:2), however, "*iste mundus*" means "the earth".

47. *DI* I, 11 (30:11–13).

48. Nicholas calls the world infinite and eternal, but in a qualified sense of "infinite" and of "eternal". It is privatively infinite [*DI* II, 1 (97:5)]; and it is eternal in the sense discussed in II, 2 (101). Also see II, 8 (140:1–3) as well as n. 21 above. Cf. Anselm of Canterbury, *Proslogion* 13.

49. Nicholas's use here of the phrase "improportionally short of" is another testimony to his clear rejection of pantheism. See n. 17 above.

50. In *NA* Nicholas changes his mind and is willing to make such statements as "In the sky God is the sky." See J. Hopkins, *Nicholas of Cusa on God as Not-other: A Translation and an Appraisal of De Li Non Aliud* (Minneapolis: University of Minnesota Press, 1979), p. 168, n. 18.

As for the sense in which God is sun without plurality and difference, see *DP* 11.

51. I.e., is not the absolutely First.

52. Nicholas does not hesitate to use the word "*emanatio*" since his version of emanation does not conflict with the doctrine of creation *ex nihilo*. See *PNC*, p. 166, n. 83.

53. *Metaphysica*, tractate IX, chap. 4 (Venice edition of 1498).

54. See *PNC*, pp. 37 and 171, n. 159 regarding the translation of this sentence and the implications thereof.

55. G. S. Kirk and J. E. Raven. *The Presocratic Philosophers* (Cambridge: Cambridge University Press, 1957), pp. 375–376.

56. *DI* I, 2 (5:9–12); I, 17 (50:9–13).

57. See *PNC*, pp. 169–170, n. 153.

58. *DI* III, 4 (204:10–11).

59. *DI* I, 13–15.

60. *DI* I, 16 (42 :4–5); cf. I, 17 (48:1–2).

61. Cf. *DI* II, 6 (125:9–10). See *De Coniecturis* II, 4 (92:13–16).

62. See n. 24 of the notes to Book One.

63. Nicholas is here drawing a parallel. Just as in God there is Oneness, Equality,

and Union [*DI* I, 7 (21:10–14)], so in the universe there is a oneness, an equality, and a union of things. See the passage (in Book Two) that corresponds to the placing of n. 81 below.

64. *DI* II, 1 (91:12–13); I, 3 (9:10–15).

65. See n. 48 above.

66. *DI* II, 2 (104:7); I, 1 (2:4–5); II, 5 (121:6–7). See n. 4 of the notes to Book One.

67. *DI* III, 1 (189:15–21); II, 2 (104:15–20).

68. In the corresponding line of the Latin text (122:3) I am reading "*a qua*" in place of "*a quo*". Cf. 147:15.

69. *De Coniecturis* I, 4. By the time Nicholas wrote this treatise his views had become modified. The four onenesses are now said to be God, intelligence, soul, and body. See n. 73 below.

70. *Ibid.* I, 3 (e.g., 10:6–8; 11:1–2).

71. *DI* II, 3 (109:13–15); III, 1 (184:5–7).

72. *DI* I, 22 (68:4–10); II, 9 (150:20–25); III, 8 (227:12–14).

73. Nicholas does not discuss this topic in *De Coniecturis*, as he had planned to. Josef Koch claimed that during the intervening time Nicholas switched from a *Seins-metaphysik* to an *Einheitsmetaphysik*. See *Die Ars coniecturalis des Nikolaus von Kues* (Cologne: Westdeutscher Verlag, 1956), e.g., pp. 16 and 23.

74. *DI* I, 20 (59:4–20); I, 7–9; I, 19.

75. *DI* II, 10 (154:7–13).

76. *DI* I, 7 (18:14).

77. *DI* II, 9 (140:3–8).

78. In I, 7 (18:10–11) Nicholas identifies otherness and mutability.

79. In the corresponding passage in the Latin text I have *not* adopted Wilpert's editorial addition.

80. *DI* II, 9. According to Nicholas (in II, 9) the Platonists regarded connecting necessity as the world-soul. Nicholas does not endorse this view either here or in the later passage. He believes that, in a special sense, God is World-soul.

81. Nicholas previously mentioned a different way in which the oneness of the universe is three. See *DI* II, 5 (120:3–4) and n. 63 above.

82. *DI* II, 9. See n. 80 above.

83. In *DI* II, 8 (140:1–2) Nicholas identifies Absolute Possibility with God [N.B. II, 8 (136)]. Absolute Possibility is minimum being; but in God minimum and maximum coincide.

In the passage above, however, Nicholas is not identifying absolute possibility with God. See n. 84 below and n. 48 of my introduction in *Nicholas of Cusa's Debate with John Wenck*.

84. By "the last three modes of being" Nicholas means connecting necessity, actually being this or that, and *possibility*. He does not mean *Absolute* Possibility qua God—as is shown clearly by his subsequent example of the rose and his reiteration of the three modes as "the mode of being of possibility, the mode of being of necessity, and the mode of being of actual determination." Nicholas, in fact, here leaves open the question of whether absolute possibility is or is not God. In chapter 8, where he discusses the

Platonists' view that Absolute Possibility is not God, he puts forth his own diametrically opposed view.

85. It would *precede* because the simple (incomposite) precedes the composite [*DI* I, 7 (21:4); *DP* 46:9].

86. *Asclepius* 14. [p. 313 of *Corpus Hermeticum*, ed. A. D. Nock (Paris: Société d'Edition "Les Belles Lettres," Vol. 2, 1945)].

87. Cf. *Idiota de Mente* 5 (66:13–18).

88. *DI* II, 9 (150:9–10); III, 1 (183:10–13).

89. Nicholas's placing of "*non . . . nisi*' in his Latin sentences does not always accurately reflect what he means. Here what he means is expressible with the help of hyphens: "God is only the cause-of-actuality" (i.e., He is not the cause-of-possibility). This thought is better expressed in English as "God is the cause only of actuality" (i.e., not also of possibility).

90. *DI* I, 16 (42:13–14).

91. See notes 21 and 48 above.

92. *De Coniecturis* II, 9. Several of the topics signaled in *DI*, including this one, are not dealt with in the detail which Nicholas's words herald. Cf. n. 73 above.

93. *DI* I, 6 (15:13–15).

94. Regarding the translation of this sentence (143:16–17), cf. the Latin with the sentence in II, 10 (151:26–29).

95. Nicholas concedes this distinction. He does not claim that the fact that God is the Essence of all things precludes each thing's having its own essence.

96. A major problem for the reader of *DI* II, 9 is to determine when Nicholas is endorsing a statement and when he is not. His own viewpoint throughout this chapter is presented unclearly. In the above passage he is merely representing the Platonists' view.

97. *DI* I, 6 (15:6–10); II, 1 (96:1–4); II, 8 (136:1–8).

98. *DI* I, 6 (15:3–4); II, 8 (136:9–10).

99. This statement is inferrable by piecing together various of Nicholas's assertions. E.g., *DI* I, 5 (14:6–8); I, 7 (21:1–3); I, 23 (70:23); I, 21 (66:7); I, 14 (37:12–13).

100. *DI* I, 16 (42:4–5).

101. Nicholas does not subscribe to the view that intermediate between God and the world there is a world-soul (whether contracted or uncontracted) which harbors the Forms of the objects in the world. (If there were such a soul, however, he believes that it would have to be contracted.) Instead, he teaches that the Word of God is the one infinite Form of forms. He is prepared to call this Word "World-soul" for much the same reason he is prepared to call God "sun". Cf *DI* II, 9 (150:13–16) with *DP* 11. Also note *DP* 12:15–21 and *Idiota de Mente* 13 (104:7–9).

102. Nicholas is not here endorsing the view that there is a world-soul contracted through possibility. (See notes 96 and 101 above.) He is drawing the conclusion that a Platonistic type world-soul would have to be contracted, could not exist apart from other things (and therefore would not be divine), and could not be the repository of a plurality of exemplars.

103. *DI* I, 16 (45:7–18).

104. *DI* II, 2 (103:1–4).

105. Cf. *DI* II, 10 (151:18–29)

106. *DI* II, 4 (115:10–14); II, 5 (118:5–6).

107. Note that the Latin text corresponding to this long English sentence needs to be repunctuated.

108. *DI* I, 6 (15:3–4); II, 8 (136:9–10); II, 9 (148:8); III, 1 (183:10–13).

109. Since in the Word of God these forms *are* the Word of God, they do not retain their plurality but exist absolutely in the Absolute, teaches Nicholas. In the subsequent sentence Nicholas makes clear that contracted forms exist in one way in the finite objects whose forms they are and in another way in the abstracting intellect. [See II, 6 (125)]. Forms, therefore, have three different modes of being: (1) as they are in God, so to speak; (2) as they are in formed objects; (3) as they are in the abstracting intellect.

110. *De Anima* III, 8 (431^{b}28–432^{a}4).

111. See n. 73 above.

112. I am considering "*et subsistere*" as deleted at 152:5 of the corresponding Latin text.

113. Matt. 10:20.

114. I.e., the spirit called "nature".

115. Wisd. 1:7.

116. *DI* I, 1 (2:4–5); II, 2 (104:5–9); II, 5 (120:14); II, 1 (91:12–13); etc.

117. *DI* II, 7 (128:6–11).

118. Col. 1:16–17. *DI* II, 5 (118:3–8). See n. 21 above.

119. *De Coniecturis* II, 9–10.

120. *DI* II, 7 (130:10–12).

121. Combine *DI* II, 7 (130:3–4,10–12) and II, 10 (154:4–7).

122. *DI* II, 8 (137:9–14); II, 10 (154:7–9).

123. *DI* II, 10 (155:1–3); II, 8 (136:10–14); III, 1 (183:3–10). *DP* 10:19–21.

124. Cf. *DI* I, 23 (70:7–8). Nicholas's reasoning seems to be the following: The center-of-the-world, an unqualifiedly minimum, cannot be a fixed, physical center, because with regard to motions and other things that can be comparatively greater and lesser, we do not come to an unqualifiedly minimum, with which the unqualifiedly maximum coincides [*DI* I, 3 (9:4–7); II, 1 (96:1–9); II, 10 (155:1–3); II, 12 (164:2–4); III, 1 (183:3–10). See *DP* 10:19–21]. Hence, only God, who is the unqualifiedly Maximum and Minimum, can be the center of the world. In the next chapter Nicholas states that the world has "its center everywhere and its circumference nowhere, so to speak; for God, who is everywhere and nowhere, is its circumference and center."

125. *DI* II, 11 (159:1–2); II, 12 (162:15–17). See n. 131 below.

126. The poles of the spheres are not fixed, physical poles because if they were there would also have to be a fixed, physical center—something whose existence Nicholas has argued to be impossible. Rather, since God is the center of the spheres and since there could not be a center without there also being poles, God is also the poles. He is pole in such way that pole is center; and He is center in such way that center is pole. See n. 124 above.

127. I.e., it would appear to the one at the pole that the center is where he is. (He is, by hypothesis, at the zenith.) That is, it would appear to him that he is at the center.

128. Nicholas is not saying that the north pole of the heavens and the point on the earth are identical. Indeed, the distances are real distances. Rather, he is observing that

no *absolute* physical center exists. God is the absolute center of the world in that—qua infinite, conscious Spirit—He is equally close to, and equally distant from, all things. For this reason Nicholas calls Him Infinite Equality and regards Him not only as the center and circumference of the world but also as the center and circumference of each thing within the world.

129. Rather than saying (1) that the world (i.e., the universe) has no motion and no shape or (2) that it makes no sense to ascribe to it motion and shape, Nicholas regards it as having a motion and a shape which are unknowable by finite minds.

130. *DI* II, 11 (157–159).

131. *DI* II, 11 (157:23–26; 159:1–2). *De Ludo Globi* II (84). *PNC*, p. 13. See Karsten Harries' insightful discussion in "The Infinite Sphere. Comments on the History of a Metaphor," *Journal of the History of Philosophy*, 13 (January 1975), 5–15.

132. *DI* II, 11 (160:5–6).

133. *DI* II, 12 (170:7–11).

134. *Timaeus* 30B; 38E. *DI* II, 13 (176:14–17).

135. *DI* II, 12 (166:1–2).

136. *DI* II, 12 (164:11–13).

137. In the corresponding line of the Latin text (171:6) I regard "*non*" as deleted.

138. According to Nicholas there are an *indefinite* number of stars—from the point of view of the human mind. He does not, however, believe that there is an *actual infinity* of stars (or of anything else). Note II, 1 (97:15–16); II, 11 (156:27).

139. Wisd. 11:21.

140. I.e., destructible.

141. *Georgica* 4.226.

142. DI III, 9.

143. These courses constitute the medieval *quadrivium*.

144. Wisd. 11:21.

145. See n. 134 above.

146. I.e., God is not at all contracted.

147. I John 1:5.

148. Deut. 4:24. Heb. 12:29.

149. Ps. 144:3 (145:3).

150. In the corresponding line of the Latin text (179:14) I am reading "*quem vult*" for "*qui vult*". In indirect discourse Nicholas sometimes uses the nominative case for the subject of a passive infinitive; but he does so erroneously. Cf. *DI* I, 1 (4:15).

151. I Tim. 6:16.

152. Matt. 7:7–8.

153. Ps. 16:15 (17:15).

NOTES TO *LEARNED IGNORANCE*, BOOK THREE

1. Cardinal Julian Cesarini. See n. 1 of the notes to Book One.

2. John 14:6.

3. Wisd. 11:21. Nicholas, like Leibniz after him, teaches that no two things differ in number alone. *DI* I, 3 (9:13–15); I, 4 (11:9–12); I, 11 (30:16–17); II, 1 (91:12–13; 96:4–8).

4. *DI* I, 6 (15:6–9).

5. *DI* I, 5 (13:7–9). Since the infinite cannot be compared to anything finite, it cannot be named by words which have a meaning imposed in relation to finite things. Hence, the infinite could not be said to be *degree*, could not rightly be thought to exist as *degree*. Cf. I, 5 (13:13–16).

6. *DI* II, 8 (136:9–10); II, 9 (148:8; 150:9–10); III, 1 (182:5–6).

7. *DI* II, 3 (109:12–15); II, 6 (124:16–19).

8. See n. 4 of the notes to Book One.

9. *DI* II, 13 (179:7–10); II, 12 (174:1–9).

10. *De Coniecturis* II, 10 and 13. See notes 73 and 92 of the notes to Book Two above.

11. *DI* I, 5 (13:11–16).

12. Cf. *DI* I, 5 (13).

13. See n. 3 above.

14. *De Coniecturis* II, 3.

15. *DI* II, 12 (170:1–171:2).

16. *DI* II, 12 (169:8–13).

17. *DI* II, 2 (104:13–20); II, 5 (121:1–3).

18. Phil. 4:7.

19. *DI* II, 11 (156:11–18). *DP* 10–11. Cf. *DI* III, 6 (220:14–18). With one exception Nicholas does not believe that there is an actually existing contracted maximum which reaches the limit of contraction [*DI* III, 1 (184:1–3)]. The one exception is Jesus's humanity, which is so maximum that it is in some sense also minimum [III, 2–4 (especially 190:15–191:14)]. Encompassed in the exception are also Jesus's faith, love, and humiliation [III, 11 (249:1–2); III, 12 (254: 16–17); III, 6 (220:14–16)]. See n. 23 of the notes to Book One. N. B. *The title of* DI *III, 1 alludes to a maximum contracted to a species; it does not allude to the universe.*

20. *DI* I, 16 (42:4–5; 45:13–18); I, 21 (64:6–10).

21. In the corresponding passage of the Latin text (191:9–10) the words "*contractionis illius*" should be taken with "*omnem naturam.*" Cf. 190:14–15. By "individual" Nicholas means *particular* (in contrast to *universal, genus,* or *species*). In the species *human being*, a particular will be a human nature, a man. Cf. n. 36 below.

22. *DI* I, 16 (45:13–15).

23. See n. 6 above.

24. I.e., able to exist as contracted maximum only if . . . .

25. See n. 78 of the notes to Book One.

26. Nicholas does not believe that there is *actually* an infinite line. See *Ap.* 32:10–11; *DI* II, 1 (97:15–17), and I, 5. He sometimes, as here, uses the future tense to express a counterfactual sense.

27. Heb. 2:7–8. Ps. 8:6–8 (8:5–6).

28. See 197:9–10 above. Also see n. 36 and n. 77 below. Some of Nicholas's statements—e.g., the one above—sound Nestorian. However, they must all be interpreted in the light of his clear rejection of Nestorianism in III, 7 (223:1–12). The following additional texts are noteworthy: III, 4 (204:1–4); III, 7 (225:11–21); III, 12 (260:1–4).

Jesus is not *first* a human nature which subsequently ascends (i.e., is subsequently united to) the Divine Word. See III, 5 (211:10–18), cited in n. 40 below.

29. Rev. 21:17.

30. Col. 1:16.

31. *DI* I, 24 (80:11).

32. *DI* III, 4.

33. In the corresponding line of the Latin text (201:6) I agree with the reading "*non possent*" in spite of Klibansky's later having opted to delete "*non.*" See the list of *corrigenda* (on p. 159 above) for Klibansky's text as found in Book III of *De docta ignorantia. Die belehrte Unwissenheit* (Hamburg: Felix Meiner, 1977).

34. *DI* II, 5 (121:1–2); II, 12 (166:9–12).

35. *DI* II, 1 (96:19–21). See also I, 5 (13:10); II, 2 (104:5–9); II, 5 (120:13–14); II, 10 (154:7–9); III, 1 (184: 12–15; 188:1–4); III, 3 (202:16–17). Infinite Power cannot create a thing to be better than it is (i.e., better than it has already been created); but Infinite Power can create something still better than that thing.

36. Cf. 198:5–6 with 199:2–3. Nicholas speaks both of *human nature's* being elevated to union with Maximality and of *one man's* being so elevated (viz., Jesus). In both cases he uses the word "*homo*". In the above passage "*homo*" may be translated either as "a human nature" or as "a man". But the sense of the passage is to be understood in accordance with the considerations and references presented in n. 28 above and n. 40 below.

Cf. the various nuances of *DI* III, 3 (202:12); III, 4 (204:2–3, 9, 21–22). Note that the phrase "*maximus homo*" has a different connotation in 204:22 from its connotation in 208:10–11. Other medieval writers use "*homo*" in the same fluctuating way. E.g., see Anselm of Canterbury, *De Conceptu Virginali et de Originali Peccato*, opening paragraph of chapter 1 (Schmitt, ed., Vol. 2, p. 140, lines 3–7). Anselm, unlike Nicholas, attempts some clarification in *De Incarnatione Verbi* 11.

37. "*Operatio*," as used by Nicholas, sometimes means *activity* and sometimes the *product of an activity*. Here (202:4)"*operatio*" is best translated by "work," even though at III, 5 (211:16) and elsewhere it is better translated by "operation" or "activity." Nicholas uses "*opus*" and "*operatio*" interchangeably at III, 3 (201:9–10).

38. In the corresponding line of the Latin text (202:9) I am reading "*ut sunt, ab ipso*" in place of "*ut sunt ab ipso*".

39. I.e., is personally united with the Son of God, who is Equality of Being. Cf. I, 8 (22:10) with I, 9 (26:13).

40. In the corresponding line of the Latin text (202:14) I follow *p* in reading "*ut sic*" instead of "*ut sit*".

41. Col. 1:15 refers to the Son of God as "the Firstborn of all creation." Nicholas, as the next sentence testifies, uses this epithet with regard to Jesus, who is God and man. (See also the opening sentences of III, 4.) Though the Son of God preceded ontologically His own created and assumed humanity, He did not precede it temporally—any more than He preceded the world temporally. Jesus enters into time through the virgin birth, Nicholas teaches (III, 5); but He existed "with God above time and prior to all [other] things"—prior in the order of perfection. By way of further explication Nicholas writes,

in III, 5 (211:10–18): "As a sound [is formed] from forced air, so, as it were, this Spirit [viz., the Holy Spirit], through an outbreathing, formed from the fertile purity of the virginal blood the animal body. He added reason so that it would be a human nature. [To it] He so inwardly united the Word of God the Father that the Word would be human nature's center of existence. And all these things were done not serially (as a concept is temporally expressed by us) but by an instantaneous operation—*beyond all time* and in accordance with a willing that befits Infinite Power." Nicholas is motivated by Col. 1:17, which states that the Firstborn of all creation is prior to all things. (See the lengthy citation, in III, 4, of Col. 1:14–20.) He apparently believes that a created, maximal humanity exists in God the Son in such way that (1) it takes precedence over all other created things and that (2) they may be said to go forth into contracted being by its mediation. In III, 7 he teaches that Jesus's humanity "was corruptible according to temporality, to which it was contracted; but in accordance with the fact that it was free from time, beyond time, and united with the divinity, it was incorruptible" (225:18–21).

42. Gal. 4:4.

43. Eph. 4:10.

44. Rom. 3:31; 7:22.

45. II Cor. 12:2–4.

46. Col. 1:14–20. This is not an exact quotation. N. B. In Col. 1:20 the phrase "*per eum*" (cf. 203:33 above) suggests a switch of reference. The Douay version has: "Because in him, it hath well pleased *the Father* that all fulness should dwell: And through him to reconcile all things unto himself. . ." (italics added). The Douay version also prefers, for Col. 1:17, the translation ". . . by him all things consist."

47. *DI* III, 12 (260:2–4).

48. *DI* II, 5 (118:8–10). Cf. II, 5 (121:9–13).

49. *DI* II, 5 (118:3–8). See *PNC*, pp. 169–170, n. 153.

50. I.e., since the maximum human nature is present in God without degree and God is present in it without degree, there is a maximal union—in the person of God the Son—of the human nature and the divine nature.

51. *DI* III, 1 (183:3–6; 186:1–2; 188:1–9).

52. Cf. *DI* I, 3 (10:9–13).

53. Col. 2:3.

54. *DI* II, 7 (130:1–9).

55. Literally, an inbreathing, i.e., a breathing into (*inspiratio*).

56. "Reason" here means *rational soul*. In Sermon 17, "*Gloria in Excelsis Deo*," (Heidelberg Academy *Opera Omnia*, Vol. 16, fascicle 3) section 4 Nicholas indicates explicitly that Jesus was made from a rational soul and human flesh. He thus follows the *Symbolum Quicumque*.

57. In maintaining that Jesus's rational soul was formed even from the moment of conception, Nicholas distinguishes the birth of Jesus from the birth of all other infants, who were usually thought to receive their souls at some unspecifiable point between conception and birth. For example, Anselm of Canterbury states in *De Conceptu Virginali et de Originali Peccato* 7: "But no human intellect accepts the view that an infant has a rational soul from the moment of his conception. For [from this view] it

would follow that whenever—even at the very moment of reception—the human seed
which was received perished before attaining a human form, the [alleged] human soul in
this seed would be condemned, since it would not be reconciled through Christ—a
consequence which is utterly absurd.''

58. Wisd. 18:14-15.

59. See n. 24 of the notes to Book One.

60. I Cor. 2:14.

61. According to John 4:24 God is spirit. But Nicholas here adheres to the *via
supereminentiae*, as propounded by Pseudo-Dionysius (and by John Scotus Erigena).
See *DI* I, 18 (54:6–13).

62. In the corresponding line of the Latin text (216:9) I follow *p* in reading
"*passionum*" instead of "*passionibus*".

63. Nicholas here formulates this rule negatively rather than positively. He thereby
tacitly implies that the New Testament formulation surpasses the natural law.

64. Ps. 50:7 (51:5).

65. Formed faith is faith formed by love. See *DI* III, 6 (219:13–14), III, 11
(250:13–14), and Gal. 5:6.

66. John 1:13.

67. This is one of the passages which most upsets John Wenck. He cites it at *IL*
38:28–31.

68. Matt. 25:40.

69. Col. 2:11–12. Rom. 8:30.

70. *DI* III, 11.

71. I Cor. 15:53-54.

72. Luke 24:25.

73. *DI* III, 6 (218:13–15).

74. John 12:24–25.

75. John 12:32.

76. "Corruptible," used throughout as the translation for "*corruptibilis*," has the
sense of *destructible*.

77. Though Nicholas's language sometimes sounds Nestorian [e.g., *DI* III, 3
(199:2–3); III, 12 (260:2–3)], he here clearly rejects Nestorianism.

78. See n. 74 above.

79. Luke 24:46.

80. I Cor. 15:20, 23.

81. Col. 1:18. The phrase "the Firstborn from the dead" has a different meaning
from the phrase "the Firstborn of all creation"; but it has the same referent, viz., Jesus.
See n. 40 above.

82. John 10:18.

83. I Cor. 15:20, 23.

84. *DI* III, 6 (219:5–8): "For the maximality of human nature brings it about that in
the case of each man who cleaves to Christ through formed faith Christ is this very man
by means of a most perfect union—each's numerical distinctness being preserved." See
also III, 12 (260). Such passages disturb John Wenck.

85. See n. 84 above.

86. I Tim. 2:5. Luke 2:11. John 1:1,14. John 14:6.

87. Nicholas of Cusa, *Cribratio Alkoran* II, 18 (149). [Strasburg edition, reprinted Berlin: W. de Gruyter, 1967, Vol. II].

88. Cf. *DI* III, 1 (185:1–3); II, 11 (157:23–26).

89. Eph. 4:10.

90. Ps. 35:10 (36:9).

91. Luke 17:21.

92. *DI* III, 6 (215:4–11). See n. 24 of the notes to Book One.

93. I John 1:5.

94. Heb. 12:29.

95. I Cor. 3:13.

96. I Cor. 15:28.

97. Col. 3:3.

98. Col. 3:4.

99. In the corresponding line of the Latin text (238:11) "*satiantur*" takes the "*de*" construction, as also at III, 12 (258:4–5). The verse of Scripture alluded to above is John 1:16.

100. *DI* III, 12.

101. Col. 1:16. Cf. *DI* III, 4 (203:29).

102. Ps. 32:9 (33:9).

103. *DI* III, 6 (215:7–8).

104. *DI* I, 11 (32:9–11). *DP* 62:10–63:15. *Idiota de Mente*, last chapter.

105. I Cor. 13:12.

106. *DI* III, 7–8.

107. Nicholas, following Pseudo-Dionysius, often speaks paradoxically. Regarding the statement that God is comprehensible above all understanding, see *DI* I, 4; III, 11 (245:13–23); *NA* 8 (30:5–7); and *PNC*, p. 24.

108. *DI* I, 1 (2:16–17); I, 11 (31:3–4).

109. Isa. 7:9 in the Old Latin Bible.

110. Just as Jesus is called Truth, so Nicholas calls Him Faith.

111. Eph. 2:8.

112. John 1:12.

113. John 20:31.

114. Matt 11:25.

115. Col. 2:3.

116. John 15:5.

117. Nicholas also teaches that God is not cognitively apprehensible by us even in the life to come. The redeemed will be acquainted with Him by "seeing," not by conceiving and comprehending; and it will be primarily the seeing of God in Christ. Note *DI* I, 26 (88:16–20). *DP* 15 and 75.

118. II Cor. 12:2–4. In the present chapter Nicholas is discussing the ascent-by-faith of the pilgrim in *this* life and the possibility, in *this* life, of a mystical vision.

119. Heb. 12:18–22.

120. Rom. 9:5.

121. Rom 15:4.

122. Ps. 32:6 (33:6).

123. *DP* 38:11–12.

124. John 1:14.

125. Not only *is* Jesus faith (244:15–16) but He *has* maximum faith, which is knowledge (254:16–21; 248:19–20).

126. *DI* III, 12 (254:5–6).

127. Matt. 17:19.

128. Rom. 8:18.

129. "*Potestatem*" and "*supra*" are to be taken together here (252:9–10). Cf. 218:1; 253:24.

130. This kind of foolish ignorance stands in contrast to learned ignorance.

131. *DI* III, 11 (249:3–4).

132. In the corresponding line of the Latin text (254:9) I am following *p* in reading "*quae*" instead of "*qua*".

133. See n. 125 and n. 110 above.

134. *DI* II, 5.

135. John 15:1–5.

136. Matt. 25:40.

137. *DI* III, 12 (260:14–16).

138. John 15:5.

139. Ps. 16:15 (17:15). The Douay and the King James versions here differ considerably.

140. *DI* III, 6 (215:4–6). See n. 24 of the notes to Book One.

141. The church of the triumphant ["a congregation of many in one" (256:1–2)] is the assembly of unfallen angels and of resurrected believers, united in and through the deity of Christ (261:8–9). In the present passage Nicholas mentions the union of the two natures in Christ as propaedeutic to considering, *deinde*, the union of the blessed with Christ, i.e., the union of the church of the triumphant.

142. *DI* III, 11 (252:10–11).

143. In the corresponding line of the Latin text (262:8) I am reading "*illa. Quae*" in place of "*illa quae*".

144. John 17:22–23.

145. See n. 1 of the notes to Book One.

146. Nicholas had been sent to Constantinople to propose a future council which would discuss the possibility of reuniting the Greek and the Roman churches. His voyage began during August, 1437; he was enroute back from Nov. 27, 1437 to Feb. 8, 1438.

147. James 1:17.

148. *DI* I, 12 (33:7–18).

149. See note 24 of the notes to Book One.

150. The *explicit* reads: I finished [this work] in Kues on February 12, 1440.

INDEX OF PROPER NAMES

Absalom, 128
Adam, 138, 174
Anaxagoras, 98
Anselm, of Canterbury, 6, 32, 34, 35, 63, 183n132, 200n36, 201n57
Aquinas, Thomas, 16, 26
Aristotle, 22, 25, 26, 50, 62, 68, 71, 110, 111, 186n27
Augustine, Aurelius, 19, 20, 33, 62, 73, 82, 190n104
Avicenna, 97
Bartholomew (St.), 67
Boethius, Anicius, 1, 61, 62, 186n27
Calcidius, 69, 189n93
Capella, Martian, 59
Cassirer, Ernst, 2
Cesarini, Julian, 1, 2, 43, 49, 158, 184n1
Cicero, Marcus, 83, 172n2
Clarenbald, of Arras, 188n46
Clarke, Samuel, 29
Dionysius, Pseudo-, 1, 11, 15, 67, 69-71, 81, 84, 177n2, 202n61, 203n107
Eckhart, Meister, 1, 10, 41, 182n104
Epicurus, 62, 106
Erigena, John, 202n61
Eusebius, of Caesarea, 187n38
Firmicus, Julius, 82
Fuehrer, Mark, 179n36, 184n167
Gerson, Jean, 1
Harries, Karsten, 182n104, 198n131
Haubst, Rudolf, 179n46, 182n120
Heimeric, de Campo, 15
Hermes, see 'Trismegistus'
Hilary, of Poitiers, 84
Isaiah, 149
Jerome (St.), 82
Jesus, *passim*
John, the Apostle, 131, 149
John Andrea, see 'Vigevius, John'
John, of Salisbury, 188n52
Josephus, Flavius, 187n38

Kant, Immanuel, 43, 184n167
Klibansky, Raymond, 187n38, 189n72
Koch, Josef, 195n73
Leibniz, Gottfried, 29, 187n41
Maimonides, Moses, 189n87, see 'Solomon (Rabbi)'
Martian, see 'Capella'
Martin, Vincent, 23
Mary, the Virgin, 40, 135, 137, 176
McTighe, Thomas, 181n92
Meuthen, Erich, 2
Mohammed, 144
Moses, 41
Nicholas, of Cusa, *passim*
Parmenides, 78
Paul, the Apostle, 14, 133, 150
Plato, 9, 26, 69, 92, 97, 102, 110, 118, 122, 154, 181n95
Proclus, 9
Pythagoras, 50, 56, 58, 62
Rombach, Heinrich, 181n95
Sampson, 128
Schulze, Werner, 179n46
Senger, Hans, 172n2
Socrates, 3, 26, 50, 92, 97, 181n95
Solomon, the King, 50, 128
Solomon (Rabbi), 67, 82, 84, 189n87
Soranus, Valerius, 82
Spinoza, Baruch, 20
Thierry, of Chartres, 188n46
Thomas (St.), see 'Aquinas'
Traversari, Ambrose, 15, 177n2
Trismegistus, Hermes, 80, 82, 105
Valerius, see 'Soranus'
Varro, Marcus, 56
Vigevius, John, 177n12
Virgil, Publius, 120
Wenck, John 6, 10, 11, 13, 14, 18, 29, 34, 40, 41, 43, 177n9, 178n28, 184n3, 185n13
Wilpert, Paul, 2, 3, 172n2, 189n72

205